HOUDINI

His Legend and His Magic

OINI

gend

Magic

HENNING

S REYNOLDS

WARNER BOOKS

A Warner Communications Company

HOUDINI
His Legend
and His Magic

WARNER BOOKS EDITION

Copyright © 1977 by Doug Henning

Designed by Thomas Nozkowski

Library of Congress Catalog Card Number: 76-52817

ISBN 0-446-87328-4

Warner Books, Inc., 75 Rockefeller Plaza, New York, N.Y. 10019

 A Warner Communications Company

Printed in the United States of America

Not associated with Warner Press, Inc.
of Anderson, Indiana

First Printing: October, 1978

10 9 8 7 6 5 4 3 2 1

This book is dedicated to my mother,
Mrs. Shirley Henning,
for her continued love and support,
and for fishing my Chinese Wands out of the garbage
so that I could master them
and go on to perform greater mysteries;
and in memory of my father,
Clarke Henning,
for instilling in me a sense of wonder,
and for forgetting each time
his eleven-year old son showed him a trick,
so that he could be shown again.

The authors would like to gratefully acknowledge the following people who contributed in various ways to the making of this book:

Barbara De Angelis for her wonderful rewriting and editing.

Regina Reynolds for her inspiration and editorial help.

Slydini who, along with Vernon, has been instrumental in shaping my personal philosophy of magic.

Collectors Jay Marshall, Sidney Radner, Pat Culliton, Manny Weltman for sharing their knowledge of Houdini with us, and for the use of material from their private collections, and to Stanley Palm, who both supplied material from his collection and aided us in invaluable research work.

Dai Vernon for his comments and for the silhouettes which appear on the title page of this book.

Arthur LeRoy and Arnold Furst, who knew Bess, and the late Al Flosso, a close friend of Houdini's, who shared their reminiscences with us. Walter B. Gibson, magic's most prolific author, for his generosity with his memories of the great magician and his various excellent books on Houdini.

Jack Rennert of Darian House Inc., publishers of 100 Years of Magic Posters, who supplied many of the color photographs of posters reproduced in this book.

Twilla Duncan, who helped in ways too numerous to list.

No contemporary book on Houdini could be written without leaning heavily on the writings of Milbourne Christopher who has written the definitive biography of the great escape artist. Our thanks to him.

Special thanks to the surviving members of the Houdini family, Bess Houdini's sister, Mrs. Marie Hinson and Bess' niece, Ruth Kavanaugh, who supplied us with the bulk of the visual material in this book and many personal reminiscences.

Doug Henning would like to express thanks and unbounded love to Maharishi Mahesh Yogi, for teaching him to see the real magic in life.

TABLE OF CONT

TS

Introduction

I first became fascinated with magic as a young child through seeing a magician on television. The performer made a beautiful lady float in the air and passed a solid hoop over her levitated body. It was easily the most wonderful thing I had seen in my short lifetime. From that time on I couldn't learn about magic fast enough, and the first magician I actually heard about by name was, of course, Houdini. This is hardly surprising. Houdini was a name equated with magic, wonder and almost supernatural triumph over impossible odds. To be a "Houdini" was to be a great magician, and even though my study of magic has revealed that there were many magicians of greater skill and technical accomplishment, most of these performers have been forgotten, whereas the name of Harry Houdini endures.

It's fascinating to realize that each of the network television magic specials I've done was seen by more people than saw Houdini on stage in his entire lifetime; yet today, if one were to ask the man on the street to name a magician, he would be much more likely to name Houdini than Doug Henning. Houdini died fifty years ago, and though relatively few of the people who saw him perform are still with us, Houdini is a magician who persists in popular legend as the symbolic hero of the miraculous.

What is the force behind this legend? It is obvious that much of Houdini's reputation derives from his ability to escape from impossible restraints, to walk through walls, to make elephants disappear. Many other magicians have performed similar feats, and yet Houdini remains preeminent. What was it that has made him outstanding among magicians? What was the real magic that Houdini possessed?

As a professional magician, I have been fascinated with these questions, and over the past few years my spare time has been spent studying the elusive image of Houdini. I have read every available book written about him as well as the books that he wrote in collaboration with professional writers. I have spoken with many of the people who knew Houdini well and who were able to offer valuable insights into his personality and his art. On my first

NBC television special, I presented my own version of his greatest escape, "The Chinese Water Torture Cell," as a way of paying homage to the great escape artist. Finally, through the kindness of the surviving members of his family, I have been fortunate to acquire pieces of his magical apparatus and a wealth of personal material that, until this time, has never been released to the public.

Most of this material—photographs, letters, clippings, publicity information and other memorabilia which the great magician and his devoted wife, Bess, kept as family souvenirs—offers no insight into the secrets of how he did his magic. Instead, some of the real secrets of this twentieth-century mythological hero are brought to light therein. They give us hints of what kind of man he really was and offer some interesting clues as to how he became a legend. They also, very appropriately, pose a few new mysteries about the great mystifier.

There were many Houdinis: Houdini the simple, honorable man with strong roots to his Middle-European heritage, devoted husband and son with a love of family and a puritanical sense of behavior that could not be violated; Houdini, supreme egoist and ruthless self-promoter, beer hall, dime museum and circus showman, master publicist and vaudeville headliner; Houdini, scholar, collector and tireless researcher into the roots of his chosen profession of legitimate deception; Houdini, crusader against fraud and charletanism, and tireless seeker for the answer to the riddle that was implicit in all of his performances—that of death and resurrection. All of these are part of the real Houdini and of the legend that remains a half-century after his demise.

It is that legend and the man behind it with which this book is concerned. It is not intended as a detailed biography of Houdini, as several excellent ones already exist; and it is certainly not an "exposé" of his methods, for I believe that revealing the methods of magic only robs it of its essential mystery and wonder. Instead, this book is my tribute to Houdini, the tribute of a young magician dedicated to his art, a tribute to the man whose name is still synonymous with enchantment, illusion and wonder.

THE ART

OF MAGIC

This book is written by a magician about a magician. I'm writing this as a professional magician of today about a professional magician of half a century ago. Times have changed since Houdini stood on stage, and in order to understand the life and times of Houdini, I can only read old newspaper clippings, diaries, letters, and try to get a feeling for what Houdini's world must have been like, what *he* must have been like.

But one thing has not changed—the meaning of magic. Magic, that art which has uplifted the minds and hearts of people down through history, creating wonder. Wonder is a very subtle, precious emotion, often lost in the gross hustle and bustle of modern life. When we feel wonder, we are immediately reminded of the purity and innocence of our childhood. Then everything was magical, everything was mysterious. Einstein has said, "The fairest thing we can ever experience is the mysterious. It is the fundamental emotion which lies at the cradle of true art and true science, and he who knows it not and can no longer experience amazement is as good as dead, a snuffed-out candle." That is what Houdini was trying to do, and I am still trying to do: to keep all the candles of wonder from snuffing out.

So it is not so difficult, so bold for me to try and present my insights into Houdini's world and legend. For the breath of his world is the breath of my world—magic. And so to talk about the magic of Houdini, I must start by talking about magic itself.

The performance of magic is a metaphor. When we witness the performance of a magician and are mystified, we realize that there must be more to the illusions he performs than what we can perceive with our senses or grasp with our minds, just as there is more to life than our narrow knowledge and perception of it. This is the central metaphor of the magician. The magician creates a world of wonder and asks us, for the period of his performance, to believe in that world. If he is a good magician he convinces us, through his personality, showmanship and technique, that we should accept this world not as a puzzle to be solved but as a mystery to be experienced. Through his magic he creates in us "a willing suspension of disbelief" (to borrow a term from Coleridge) and makes us live with wonder in this special world of illusion, just as we should live with wonder in the everyday world of reality. This is what I believe magic is really about, and it is what I always try to achieve in my own performances. In his own very special way, I think Houdini did the same.

If we accept the idea that magic is symbolic of the mystery that is all around us in the real world, then it becomes apparent that particular illusions performed by a magician are symbolic expressions of various aspects of that mystery. This is also true of other types of fantasy that have evolved from folk consciousness through constant repetition and refinement over thousands of years, just as the classic tricks of the magician have evolved. The most obvious examples of this are the myths and legends of cultures the world over, all of which, in different forms, tell the same stories. Another good example, with many interesting parallels to magic, is the fairy tale.

If magic is the creation of a metaphorical world of wonder, then there is another important thing that magic is *not* (or, at least, should not be). That is a series of perplexing puzzles presented by the performer as a challenge to the audience. Even when a magician is skilled, the spectators may feel that they have been made fools of if he presents his magic as puzzles to be figured out. To say that magic is a puzzle is like saying that ballet is exercise. Both statements are true, but neither really expresses what the arts are about. One might just as well go to a play and, instead of becoming immersed in the events on stage, spend his time concerned with the way the scenery is painted, or go to a film and concentrate on the camera angles. These are, of course legitimate and important concerns for those involved in the craft of the stage or of film, but are hardly the concern, and would spoil the enjoyment, of a member of the general audience.

People rarely become irritated because the wall of a room on stage is not made from real bricks and plaster, but is only an artfully painted piece of canvas. Such misplaced anger would be just as destructive to the theatrical experience as is going to a magic show to figure out how the tricks are done. I don't mean to say that a good magician should ask his audiences to be gullible. Quite the contrary; his job is to mystify them as cleverly and charmingly as possible. But once mystified, he asks them to be entertained *instead* of irritated, and to accept the deception as the same kind of unquestioned theatrical artifice as stage lighting or make-up. A magician is successful at his art to the degree that he can transcend the puzzle and get down to his real business of creating a metaphorical world of wonder. I firmly believe that a large degree of Houdini's success as an entertainer was based on the fact that his audiences exalted in his triumphs. They were uplifted by the fact that he escaped rather than irritated by the puzzle of *how* he escaped.

There's one final thing that I think magic is *not*, and it is central in examining the magic of Houdini: Magic is not primarily children's entertainment. It is difficult to change the notion that a magic show is exclusively for the "kiddies," but I believe that one of the reasons that Houdini's fame as a magician was so great is that he was not thought of as a children's entertainer.

J.R.R. Tolkien, author of *The Lord of the Rings*, delivered a lecture at the University of Saint Andrew in Scotland in 1938. The subject was fairy stories. In this fascinating lecture he effectively demolished the commonly held idea that children are the natural, or the specially appropriate, audience for fairy stories. Tolkien says, "The common opinion seems to be that there is a natural connexion between the minds of children and fairy stories, of the same order as the connexion between children's bodies and milk. I think this is an error; at best an error of false sentiment, and one that is most often made by those who, for whatever private reason (such as childlessness), tend to think of children as a special kind of creature, almost a different race, rather than as normal, if immature, members of a particular family, and of the human family at large."

Tolkien further comments that "all children's books are, on a strict judgement, poor books. Books written entirely for children are poor even as children's books."

There are striking parallels between magic and fairy tales. Both are very old and have evolved over endless repetitions. Both fulfill needs on a symbolic level and manipulate reality to create illusion. Both have also, to their considerable detriment, been classed as exclusively children's entertainment. Tolkien comments, "If a fairy story as a kind is worth reading at all it is worthy to be written for and read by adults." I feel very much the same about magic. To play magic down to children is demeaning both to magic and to childhood. Children respond to good magic just as they do to other things of quality. One of the things that I learned early in my career as a performer was not to aim my magic exclusively at children. I like to think that the "appetite for marvels" (to again quote Tolkien) is present in all audience members no matter what their age, and that if the oldest member of the audience responds to my magic then the youngest will too.

There is another concept (borrowed in somewhat modified form from Tolkien) that, I believe, goes a long way in explaining the magic of Houdini and how it differed from that of many other magicians, myself included. In my magic performances I try to invite my audiences (not in words but through the style of the presentation) to enter a secondary world of enchantment and wonder. This world has its own Secondary Reality every bit as consistent as, but very different from, the Primary Reality of the real world.

In every age there are certain Primary Reality magicians who do not ask their audiences to willingly enter a world of wonder in which their disbelief is suspended, but instead ask them to believe that their magic is real in the everyday world. The fraudulent spirit medium is a good example of this. Houdini's arch foe "Margery" asked her believing followers to accept her "psychic powers" as real and not as legitimate deception as a professional magician does. At the present time, a psychic such as Uri Geller does the same thing. He asks us to accept his bending of spoons and keys as a real demonstration of psychic power rather than as a clever magic trick. Without entering into a discussion of the questionable ethics of such Primary Reality magicians, it must be said that their followers have been many and that they have been willing to simply believe rather than willing to suspend their disbelief.

There are two members of the mystery profession who make a more legitimate appeal to Primary Reality. These are the "mentalists", or mind readers, and the escape artist.

A professional mind reader does not (if he is ethical) say to his audience, "I am really possessed of psychic powers," but he also does not (if he is to be successful) say, "I am a fake." The power of his performance lies in the *possibility* of what he presents, and the audience is left to make up its own mind about the reality of his "extrasensory powers." While the performance of the mentalist depends just as much on misdirection and other principles of deception as does that of the professional magician, he addresses it to Primary Reality rather than trying to create a Secondary Reality.

A mentalist friend of mine once analyzed his performing task in the following way. He saw his audience as divided into three groups. The first of these groups came to his show already convinced. They believed totally in the reality of mind reading and nothing, short of an outright bungling of his performance, could shake them in that belief. The second group was as totally unconvinced of the reality of mind reading as the first was convinced. Nothing he could do, no matter how baffling, would be accepted by them as anything more than clever trickery. The third group was unsure. If, indeed, they harbored some disbelief about the performer's ability to read minds, and if he was good enough, that disbelief could be suspended. It was this third group that the mentalist, using all of his powers of showmanship, tried to win over. If he could convince them that what he did was "real," he had succeeded in giving an effective performance.

Classical magic makes no such attempt to convince an audience of the reality of the miracles it is witnessing. The lady floating in the air or the lady sawed in half and restored again are the stuff of fantasy (Secondary Reality) and are powerful precisely because they are part of a world of enchantment and not of the real world.

Like the fraudulent psychic, the mentalist, and the classical magician, the escape artist is a mystery worker, in the sense that it is a mystery how his miraculous escapes are done. However, he addresses himself to Primary Reality in that he asks us to believe that his escapes are real (which, indeed, they are). His appeal is not, as in the case of a classical magician, to a world of "once upon a time," but to a world of "here and now." He does not even appeal, as does the mentalist, to the idea that his miracles *might* be possible. He does exactly what he says he is going to do—he escapes. In some ways, then, he is closer to such nonmystery performers as the high-wire walker in a circus or the matador in a bull fight, both of whom are acting out just as symbolic and ritualistic roles as is the escape artist.

I talked to many people who saw Houdini perform, and the universal opinion was that he was a much better escape artist than he was a magician. It was in the role of challenger rather than enchanter that his powerful showmanship was able to spellbind audiences. A number of people have commented that the contemporary mystery performer closest in style of showmanship to Houdini was the late Joseph Dunninger, the master mentalist of radio and television fame. It is interesting that Dunninger's appeal was also to Primary Reality. As we shall see, even Houdini's most effective magic was presented as a challenge to reality and, like his escapes, had more the impact of real life than of theater.

The great French magician, Robert-Houdin, defined a conjuror as "an actor playing the part of a magician." I believe that this is true and that every good magician plays a particular role over and above the particular mysteries he performs. That role may be of a high priest presiding over miracles, of a benevolent confidence man, of a befuddled gentleman to whom strange things happen or any other character, but it is important that it be there. The

character that a magician plans is one of the devices he uses to make his art "transcend the puzzle." To a greater or lesser degree with all actors, the part played is the person himself, and with Houdini one senses that the character on stage and the real man off stage were almost identical.

One of those who detected this nontheatrical aspect of Houdini's personality was Edmund Wilson, the great American literary critic (who had a lifetime interest in magic and wrote several interesting essays on the subject). Wilson found it significant that Houdini was drawn to escapes which he described (correctly, I believe) as "that branch of magic furthest from the theatre," and describing his style of performance, said, "When he performs tricks, it is with the directness and simplicity of an expert giving a demonstration and he talks to his audience not in the character of a conjuror, but quite straightforwardly and without patter. His professional formulas—such as 'Will wonders never cease!', with which he signals the end of a trick—have a quaint conventional sound as if they had been acquired as a concession to the theatre."

In a later essay (written after Houdini's death) Wilson writes: "He saw himself as a romantic figure. He lived his own drama and had otherwise little of the actor about him—so little that... one has the feeling that in his role of public entertainer, he was a little out of his orbit."

I feel that Wilson, who greatly admired Houdini and saw in him more an embodiment of the spirit of scientific curiosity than "an actor playing the part of a magician," is giving us, more than any other critic of the time that I have been able to find, a real clue to Houdini's performing style. If Wilson, who was one of the most perceptive critics of his day, is correct in his insights, he tells us a lot about why Houdini was more effective when dealing with the Primary Reality of escapes or exposing mediums than he was at creating the Secondary Reality so necessary for the successful presentation of classical magic.

Houdini never asked for the *willing* suspension of disbelief in his audience and was not the kind of actor to evoke this suspension. Instead, Houdini asked for disbelief that he could escape from *real* handcuffs or walk through a real brick wall, and then he challenged that disbelief and triumphed (he really *could* do these things). It was in the spectators' exaltation over his triumphs, as they would exalt over any brave man who pits himself against difficult obstacles and bests them, that Houdini's powerful impact lay. So we can see that Houdini's result was wonder, the same result as a good theatrical magician's, but that his method of achieving this wonder was quite different.

Let us now look at Houdini's life and see how he lived the magic he performed.

The Houdinis toured with the Welsh Brothers Circus during the season of 1898-1899 and young Harry kept a diary of their adventures. In addition to performing in the side-show Houdini also worked to perfect other circus skills. These selected pages from the diary, published here for the first time, give a fascinating insight into the life of the two young performers before they hit the big time.

THE WORLD

OF HOUDINI

Ehrich Weiss: King of the Backyard Circus

In the year 1920, Harry Houdini, then at the peak of his career, was justly proud that his name had become an accepted part of the English language. That year's edition of *Funk and Wagnall's New Standard Dictionary* carried the following entry:

Hou'di-ni, 1. hu'di-ni; 2. hu'di-ni, Harry (4/6 1874-) American mystericist, wizard and expert in extrication and self release,—hou'di-nize, vb. To release or extricate oneself from (confinement, bonds, or the like), as by wriggling out.

The verb to "houdinize" has hardly found its way into standard usage, but the name of Houdini has become part of the vocabulary not only of American culture, but of cultures throughout the world. If we say a person is a "Houdini," what we mean is immediately understood. That Houdini escaped from handcuffs, packing boxes and strait-jackets; that he made an elephant disappear on the stage of the world's largest theater; that he could swallow needles and thread, and bring the needles up threaded; that at one point in his career he performed the astonishing feat of walking through a brick wall—these are all parts of the legend. And today, fifty years after his death, to be a Houdini is to be able to do the seemingly impossible.

The time in which Houdini lived spanned roughly the last quarter of the nineteenth century and the first quarter of the twentieth century. This was a time of profound change in America, and, in his own way, the charismatic Houdini was both a product of this change and a folk hero who, in symbolic terms, helped to explain to a mass audience the nature of the cultural upheaval that was taking place.

Like all mythological figures, Houdini's origins have, until very recently, been shrouded in mystery. Dr. Bernard Meyer, author of a fascinating psychiatric study of Houdini, points out that not only did Houdini help to obscure the facts about his family origins, often providing inaccurate autobiographical material, but other members of his family aided him in this purpose. One example of this is the original of a letter written from Houdini's sister Gladys to his widow Bess after his death, discussing events that investigators have since proved to be almost certainly sheer fabrication. I have included this as an illustration of how Houdini's family tried to hide his identity.

The young Ehrich Weiss posed as a messenger in this early tintype, c 1885.

Ehrich about age thirteen, tintype, c 1887.

In cummerbund and with straw hat, the later conservative Houdini posed as a dapper young man, tintype, c 1891.

Throughout his lifetime, Houdini always claimed to have been born and bred American. Perhaps this was important to him and to his carefully constructed image as an American archetype, a sort of theatrical Horatio Alger whose basic appeal was his ability, through perseverance, to triumph over great odds. In literally hundreds of interviews with the press, Houdini always gave his birthdate as April 6, 1874, and his birthplace as Appleton, Wisconsin. It's likely that, at least in the early years of his life, he believed this to be true, and that is the day on which he always celebrated his birthday. The first Houdini biography to offer evidence to the contrary was written by William Lindsay Gresham in 1959. Gresham reveals that Houdini's true place and date of birth was March 24, 1874, in Budapest, Hungary. This information was based on research by a Hungarian magic enthusiast prior to World War II. Subsequent research by American magical historians has substantiated that Houdini was indeed born in Budapest, and not in America.

My feeling about this discrepancy is that the actual place and date of Houdini's birth are not important. What is important is that Houdini was proud to be an American, and wanted to be remembered as an American. Naturally, his family would support him in his desire to be known as the great American magician.

Houdini's real name was Ehrich Weiss, and he was alleged to be the son of a Hungarian rabbi, Meyer Samuel Weiss, and his wife, Cecilia Steiner Weiss. Legend has it that Rabbi Weiss was forced to leave Budapest because of a duel he had fought with a nobleman in which his opponent was killed. Some old-time magicians who knew Houdini have said that Rabbi Weiss was actually Houdini's stepfather, Cecilia Weiss having married a second time after her first husband (Houdini's real father) had killed a man in Austria and been imprisoned for the deed.

When Houdini was still an infant, he came with his family to the United States, and from then on the events of his life become somewhat clearer. For a

The private side of Houdini—good-humored and a prankster—was prominent in early years. Tintype, c 1891.

Houdini at twenty. Tintype, 1894.

while, Rabbi Weiss headed a congregation in Appleton, Wisconsin, at an annual salary of $750. In Houdini's own account of his father in these times:

Some of the leading factors in the congregation, thinking he had grown too old to hold his position, supplanted him for a younger man, and one morning my father awoke to find himself thrown upon the world, his long locks of hair having silvered in service, with seven children to feed, without a position, and without any visible means of support.

Times were hard for the Weiss family. Neither parent was successful in mastering the English language, and employment opportunities for a German-speaking, Old-World rabbi were slight. The family moved to Milwaukee, where they moved from address to address, probably just a jump ahead of the rent collector. Houdini comments on those years in Milwaukee as a time when "such hardships and hunger became our lot—the less said on the subject the better."

During the years in Milwaukee, the young Houdini made his "show business" debut in a neighborhood circus (tickets, five cents) staged by a friend in a nearby lot. Billed as "Ehrich, the Prince of the Air," Houdini presumably did some sort of trapeze act. In later accounts, this account has been somewhat embellished: The neighborhood circus has become a traveling circus that came to town, and young Ehrich persuades the manager to let him display the miraculous feat of hanging head downward from a rope and picking up pins with his eyelids! This amazing stunt, like the later much-reported one of Houdini conversing with friends while idly tying and untying knots in a rope with his toes, is probably more fiction than fact, but it is certainly the stuff from which legends are made.

It was during the years in Milwaukee that Ehrich was first exposed to magic. Most professional magicians, including myself, first became fascinated with magic by seeing and being astonished by another magician, and Houdini was no exception. The performer could have been in a traveling circus, an event recounted in the legendary version of Hou-

PRESIDENT.
HARRY McMILLAN.
A. C. S. N.

VICE-PRESIDENT.
FRANK W. EDDY.
D. A. C.

AMATEUR ATHLETIC UNION
OF THE UNITED STATES.

SECRETARY.
JAMES E. SULLIVAN.
P. A. C.

TREASURER.
HOWARD PERRY.
C. A. C.

Member of Board of Directors, FRED'K WM. JANSSEN, S. I. A. C.
241 & 243 BROADWAY, N. Y. CITY.

New York City, Sep 19 1890.

*Mr. Ehrich Weiss.
227 East 75 St. City-
dear sir,-
At a meeting of the Board of Managers of the A.A.U. held on Sept 13- 1890 the penalty for having competed in unapproved games held Aug 16-90 was remitted.
Be very particular about this in future and please consider this an official notice
Yours truly
F.W. Janssen
Chairman
A.A.U.*

From in the mile race, won a Prize & was disqualified - but was reinstated. being born in 1874 I was only sixteen years of age at this time. H Houdini Sept 26-1914.

Houdini was athletic from his early years. At sixteen he was disqualified from accepting a prize in track but was later reinstated as noted in his comment at the bottom of this letter from the Amateur Athletic Union.

dini's life. More likely, this happened when Rabbi Weiss took the young Houdini to a stage performance of a traveling magician named Dr. Lynn. Dr. Lynn's magic act featured an illusion called "Palegenisia." In this illusion, he pretended to administer chloroform to a man, and then, after tying him in place inside a cabinet, Dr. Lynn proceeded to dismember the man with a huge butcher knife, cutting off legs and arms, and finally (discreetly covered with a black cloth), the man's head. The pieces were then thrown into the cabinet and the curtain was pulled. Moments later, the victim appeared from the cabinet restored to one living piece, and seemingly none the worse for the ordeal. Many years later Houdini purchased this illusion (reportedly for $75) from Dr. Lynn's son and presented it during the last two years of his show without the chloroform, playing more for laughs than for shocks. It is significant that, at an early age, Houdini had been fascinated by this particular illusion literally embodying the theme of death and resurrection, for this was a motif that reoccurred in all of Houdini's performances throughout his career.

By 1888, Rabbi Weiss moved his family to New York, believing that the city's large Jewish population could support a religious teacher of his background. Ehrich had run away from home on his twelfth birthday in an attempt to find work and help support the family, but he joined them at their new house on East Sixty-ninth Street. At that time, Ehrich worked as a messenger and later as a cutter in a necktie factory.

During this early period in New York, fourteen-year-old Ehrich became seriously interested in the art of magic. Here again we can do some sorting of the legend from the reality. Houdini's publicity, and a biography by Harold Kellock published in 1928 (based on the memoirs and recollections of Houdini's wife, Bess) have the young Houdini learning the rudiments of magic from a sideshow conjuror in a circus that played Appleton, Wisconsin. The Gresham biography conjectures that Houdini was introduced to magic at the age of sixteen by his friend, Jacob Hyman, who worked next to him in the necktie factory. Another historian of magic, Milbourne Christopher, says that in the time before Ehrich entered the necktie factory, during which he worked as newsboy, messenger, electric driller and photographers' helper, his younger brother, Theo, showed him a simple coin trick. Young Ehrich became proficient at the trick and the startled reaction he elicited with it prompted him to begin reading books

It is likely that Houdini first became interested in magic when taken by his father to see a traveling magician named Dr. Lynn. Lynn featured an illusion called "Palegenisia" in which he appeared to dismember and restore a chloroformed man. Many years later Houdini purchased this illusion from Dr. Lynn's son and presented it during the last two years of his show.

family portrait, c 1891. Cecilia Weiss,
oudini's mother, sits in the center with
oudini's sister, Gladys, on the left. Behind
and the Weiss brothers, from left to right,
athan, Erich, Theo, and Leopold. (Girl on right
unidentified). Tintype, c 1891.

on conjuring. At this time he met Joe Rinn, a fellow member of the Pastime Athletic Club where Ehrich was a star member of the track team. Rinn, who was four years older than Ehrich and already had a knowledge of magic, was to remain Houdini's close friend throughout his life, and later became a noted psychic researcher. Houdini's other friend, Jacob Hyman, assisted the young magician, who was playing shows wherever he could under the name of "Eric the Great" or "Cardo," doing an act with cards and silk handkerchiefs.

2nd—For such other purposes as two-thirds (⅔) of the members at a meeting may decide providing that there are not less than twenty-five (25) members present from ten (10) shops.

SEC. 2.—If at any time the liabilities of the association exceed the receipts thereof, the deficiency shall be raised in such a manner as two-thirds (⅔) of the members present at any regular meeting may agree upon.

ARTICLE X.

DUTIES OF MEMBERS.

SEC. 1.—It shall be the duty of every member of this association to bring in all persons belonging to our craft, as members of the same, whom shall be known for honesty and ability.

SEC. 2.—Knowing how detrimental it is to our welfare to instruct others concerning the workings of our craft, we hereby pledge ourselves from doing the same, except it be a member of the association.

SEC. 3.—This association may adopt a scale of prices for the government of the trade in its particular branches, and such scale of prices shall not be altered or amended except by a two-thirds (⅔) vote of the members present at a general meeting of the association, when not less than 25 members from at least 10 houses shall constitute a quorum, and not then unless notice of such alteration or amendment shall have been made two (2) weeks previous.

SEC. 4.—It will be the duty of every member of this association to report all members who may violate any of the rules of this association, especially appertaining to Art. X, Sec. 2 and 4.

When the Houdini family moved to New York from Wisconsin, young Ehrich worked for a time as a necktie cutter. It is interesting to note that he took special interest in the union's promotion of secrecy—an attitude that later affected his outlook on magic.

Harry and his brother Theo played beer halls, dime museums and small-time vaudeville in the years 1892 & 1893 and tried their luck at the Columbian Exposition in Chicago. They were not a success and Theo returned to New York while Harry remained to perform alone at Kohl & Middleton's dime museum.

One of the books Ehrich was reading at the time was *The Memoirs of Robert-Houdin*, the life story of the great French conjuror who is generally conceded to be the "father of modern magic." (I personally feel that it is Robert-Houdin who, of all the magicians down through history, achieved the highest artistic magical performance.) Ehrich told his friend Hyman of his desire someday to be as great as Robert-Houdin, and Hyman suggested that if Ehrich added the letter "i" to Houdin's name, it would mean "like Houdin" (sic), and he could call himself "Houdini." This, with the Americanization of his nickname, "Ehrie" into Harry, produced the name that was, forever after, to mean "magic," Harry Houdini.

The Birth of the Great Escapes

For awhile, Houdini and his friend Jacob Hyman played small-time dates as "The Brothers Houdini." Later Hyman was replaced by Houdini's younger brother Theo.

Along with the small magic in the act, Houdini included one larger stage illusion. It was a high-speed switch of Houdini and Hyman from within a locked box, and it was billed as "The Metamorphosis." (This illusion, which was perhaps the single most important magic feat in Houdini's career, is discussed in detail in the section on Houdini's magic).

April 3, 1891, was an important turning point in the life of Houdini. He left his job at the necktie factory, and, at the age of seventeen, made the plunge into a career as a professional magician. One year later, the already impoverished Weiss family suffered the death of his father, and the support of his mother and sister became the responsibility of the brothers. Through the years 1892–1893, Houdini and his brother barely scraped along playing dime museums, beer halls and very small-time vaudeville. The act consisted mostly of small stock magic of the day: a flower that appeared in Houdini's buttonhole; a silk handkerchief was pulled from a candle flame; water was changed to wine and back again; a large die passed magically through the crown of a top hat; a glass of bran changed to water and goldfish; a borrowed watch was fired from a big, old-fashioned gun at a hanging target where it magically appeared; an egg mysteriously appeared and vanished in a small cloth bag; silk handkerchiefs passed through a paper tube and changed color; knots appeared and disappeared; selected cards mysteriously appeared on the points of a wooden star; and of course, the act ended with the spectacular "Metamorphosis."

By the summer of 1893, Harry and Theo had scraped together enough money from club dates in the New York area to purchase train tickets to the Columbian Exposition in Chicago and to try their luck there. Bookings did not turn out to be as plentiful as they had expected, and Theo ended up returning to New York, while Harry remained to perform alone at Kohl and Middleton's dime museum, doing as many as twenty shows a day at a salary of $12 per week. Since it was no longer possible to do

Jacob Hyman was the original partner in the "Brothers Houdini" but sold his share in the act in 1894. Harry's brother Theo replaced Hyman.

NEWMAN YEAST COMPANY,

INCORPORATED 1893.

MANUFACTURERS OF

FRENCH WHITE WINE, CIDER AND MALT VINEGAR,

and COMPRESSED YEAST.

38, 40 & 42 John Street.

Brooklyn, N. Y. April 10th 189.4

To all Whom it may Concern:

Know ye, that I Jacob Hyman known as J. H. Houdini of the Bros Houdini for value recieved do hereby agree to dissolve said firm

J. H. Houdini

the trunk exchange without Theo's assistance, Harry used the cabinet for escapes from ropes and handcuffs.

This was probably the official beginning of Harry Houdini's career as an escape artist, but exactly how he got started in the specialized field of escapes is perhaps more obscured in legend than any other aspect of his life.

There is first, of course, the "official" version concocted by Houdini for publicity purposes. Here is the story as it is told in the Houdini souvenir program:

> It is often asked how did he ever go into the business as a lock-opener. It happened in a curious way and while it may be unbelievable, it is nevertheless true—it was simply his healthy appetite and love for his mother's apple pies.
>
> One day Houdini's boyish appetite began to gnaw at his vitals. He sniffed the freshly baked apple pies, the delicious odor issuing from the recess of the old-fashioned cupboard. His mother was absent, the door of the cupboard was not locked, and Houdini ambled up to the closet and, when he left, the pie left with him. His mother, the dear old soul, thought she would remedy this; a locksmith was called in and a new lock was put on the cupboard. Next pie-baking day, the same old Houdini, the same delicious odor, the same sniffing; of course, according to Einstein's theory, it was an entirely different place, but when our hungry hero was confronted with a locked door—the key being hidden—he resorted to a method of opening the lock which had never been explained in a textbook and which has been his secret ever since.
>
> Houdini does not believe in reincarnation, but he does admit that something within him told him how the lock could be opened. It might have been an inspiration, it might have been an inborn talent for mechanics.
>
> Be that as it may, when he left, the cupboard resembled "old Mother Hubbard's." His mother, surprised, the locksmith was called in, a conference was held, a new lock applied. Again the pies were locked up, again Houdini conquered the lock as well as the pies. They never questioned him as to how he opened the door. They took it for granted that there was something unusual about the boy.
>
> Like an inspiration, it dawned upon Houdini that he possessed unusual powers. After that no door could bar him. He amazed the neighbors by the ease with which he could go in or out through any locked door. As he grew up he mastered other feats along this line, freeing himself from ropes and so on; then came his perfection in the art of ocular illusion.

The Metamorphosis was the one successful illusion in the Brothers Houdini act, advertised in this early program. In later years, Houdini

PROGRAMME

Subject to Change.

Jos. MAGGIE LOU F.
CAMPBELL, EVANS and SHAW
Original 3 Tourists, in a Melange.

Harp Virtuoso,
INEZ CARUSI
In Selections.

QUAKER CITY QUARTETTE,
PIERI, ERNEST, HANSON and GRAHAM
Introducing Vocal and Instrumental Selections. Kind permission Manager Sam Devere.

GEORGE MURPHY
German Dialect Comedian.

MUSICAL DALE
Presenting an Act without an Equal.

MARION and HASTINGS
" The Road to Ruin."

FULGORA
The World's Greatest Transfigurator.

EDWARD LESLIE
Dialect Imitations.

THE SOHMER GRAND PIANO USED ON THIS OCCASION.

Kellock also recounts an interesting follow-up anecdote. On Houdini's last Sunday at home in New York before leaving on the tour on which his death occurred, Bess, his wife, had made two strawberry pies (a Houdini favorite) for dinner. She, like Mother Weiss, also locked her pie closet, "not to keep out Houdini, for no lock was too complicated for him, but for other domestic reasons." The Houdinis went for a walk in Central Park, during which Harry seemed particularly self-satisfied. On their return, Bess discovered one of the pies missing and Houdini's visiting card on the empty plate.

While there seems to be little historical evidence of it, another official Houdini story is that he was once apprenticed to a locksmith. Houdini tells this story in the British *Magicians Annual* (1909–1910):

noted on the program which performers had died, perhaps part of his life-long obsession with death.

thought struck me to attempt to pick the lock. I succeeded in doing it, and the very manner in which I then picked the lock of the handcuff contained the basic principle which I employed in opening handcuffs all over the world. Not with a duplicate key, which seems to have been the only way others had of duplicating my performance.

In the Houdini souvenir program, yet an-other colorful explanation is given for the origin of the handcuff escape act. In this version, Houdini is traveling through Kansas and the Indian Territory with Dr. Thomas B. Hill's California Concert Company. (Actually, Houdini did tour the Midwest with a medicine show of this name, but it was in 1897, some four years after he had introduced handcuff escapes into his act.) The account is as follows:

> One night when Houdini was issuing his challenge to be bound with rope, one of the Jesse James Gang walked into the ring and said good-naturedly, "I'll tie the boy." He was a reformed outlaw and sheriff of the town. When Houdini escaped from the ropes the sheriff took out a pair of handcuffs and said, "If I put these on you, you will never get out." The crowd yelled, "Put them on, son, try 'em," and Houdini was game.
>
> That was the turning point of his life. Remembering how he had picked the locks of the cupboard in the dear, old days when he wanted to become better acquainted with his mother's pies, he accepted the sheriff's challenge. The handcuffs were snapped on his wrists, forced down to the bone so he could not slip them off his hands, and in six and one-half minutes they were taken from his wrists, open, to the astonishment of the sheriff and the huzzahs of the audience.
>
> This created so much talk that it was made a regular feature of the performance. Houdini gradually developed the stunt until he got out of jails and prison cells, and the escape act was born.

All of these stories, like the picking up of the pins with the eyelids and the untying of the knots with the toes, clearly seem to be more fairy tale than fact. The impoverished Mrs. Weiss repeatedly calling in a locksmith to protect her pies; the repeating of the childhood prank on Houdini's last Sunday in New York before his death; the police officer going off to dinner with the locksmith leaving his prisoner with young Harry; the outlaw turned sheriff—all seem elements of fantasy, small but significant building blocks of the great Houdini myth.

Well, one characteristic of all myths is that they grow in the telling. The Kellock biography, published

One day whilst working as an apprentice in a locksmith's close by the police station, one of the young bloods of the town was arrested for some trivial offense. He tried to open the handcuffs with some keys he had on his person, and, in the attempt, broke off one of the keys in the lock of the handcuff. He was brought to the shop to have the cuff opened or cut off his wrist and this incident, trivial as it may seem, in after years changed my entire career.

While the master locksmith was trying to open the handcuff the whistle blew for the dinner hour. Being a loyal union man, and incidentally, perhaps, having a sharpened appetite, he called me to his side and said, "Harry, get a hacksaw and cut off this handcuff," and then went out with the police officer to dine.

I tried to cut off the cuff, but the steel was too hard, and after breaking half-a-dozen saw blades, the nineteen years after Houdini's version of his introduction to the handcuff act, also has him escaping from ropes at the backyard circus where he did his trapeze act, has his brothers and friends tying him up at an early age and him escaping, has him haunting circus lots as a young child to pick up "a variety of ingenious rope ties from the goodnatured canvasmen," and, during the year he ran away from home, has him touring with several circuses doing his escape act.

These are just a few of the stories contributing to the fable of how this remarkable man became the world's greatest escape artist. But if most of these stories are fiction, what are the facts? How did Houdini become fascinated with the art of escape?

Several sources indicate that Houdini's interest in escape was stimulated by a rare book that he acquired when he was still a struggling young magician. The book was entitled *Revelations of a Spirit Medium, or Spiritualistic Mysteries Exposed—a Detailed Explanation of the Methods Used by Fraudulent Mediums*, by A. Medium. The book had a profound effect on Houdini, not because it exposed fraudulent spiritualists, a subject that was to become an obsession with him in later life, but because it revealed the "real work" of how mediums, under cover of darkness or within their "spirit cabinets," could release themselves from rope ties, metal "spirit" collars, and knotted and sealed bags. Houdini used the escape from tied wrists and a knotted bag in the course of "Metamorphosis," the only effect in his early magic act that concerned itself in any way with escapes.

The idea of escaping from handcuffs was not a new one. Many magic dealers' catalogues listed trick cuffs from which one could easily get out. It was Houdini's brilliant idea to do the cuff escapes as a challenge, allowing people to bring real cuffs to restrain him. It is likely that Houdini saw some carnival or circus performer escaping from cuffs with little effect and was genius enough to grasp the potential of the idea. It can be truly said that Houdini was the first magician to really learn to "sell," for maximum impact, the handcuff escapes.

In the early days of his career, Houdini's act consisted of small stock magic—silk handkerchiefs pulled from candle flames, water changing to wine and back, disappearing eggs, and a variety of card tricks. For a time he advertised himself as the "King of Cards".

"Houdini
King of cards

3 The Houdinis: Vaudeville Headliners

After his solo engagement in Chicago, Harry returned to New York and joined up once again with his brother Theo to present the "Brothers Houdini" act complete with the "Metamorphosis" trunk substitution as a climax. Their engagements were mostly in dime museums in New York City and Coney Island, but a new escape feature was added to the act. Harry was padlocked in an empty beer barrel from which he escaped in twenty seconds.

In the spring of 1894, Houdini met Wilhelmina Beatrice Rahner, a petite Brooklyn-born brunette from a German Catholic family. Houdini was twenty, Bess was eighteen. It was love at first sight and within two weeks they were married. Exactly how they met is typically obscured in the swirling mists of the Houdini legend. Even Bess' and Houdini's stories do not agree in all the details. In Bess' version, she had been taken by her mother to see Houdini perform at a high school and was sitting enthralled in the front row when Houdini accidentally upset some acid on a table which stained her dress. Houdini offered to replace the dress and did so. They met again, love blossomed, and soon they were married.

In Harry's version, he was on his way to give a five-dollar show at a birthday party. While riding on a streetcar to this engagement, he dropped his wand and some of his magic equipment and a pretty girl helped him pick them up. To his delight she was part of the audience at the party, and similar to Bess' version, he spilled one of the chemicals from his "wine and water" trick on her dress. From that point on, the two accounts coincide.

In a later interview in the June 1920 issue of *Photoplay Magazine*, Houdini simplified the tale considerably:

> *One day I was hired to give an exhibition at a children's party in Brooklyn. At the close a little girl about sixteen said to me, very bashfully, "I think you are awfully clever," and then, with a blush, "I like you." "How much do you like me?" I said. "Enough to marry me?" We had never seen each other before. She nodded. And so, after talking the matter over, we were married.*

Other biographies of Houdini subscribe to quite a different story: Bess was already in show business when she met the young escape artist. She was half of a song-and-dance act called "The Floral

In 1894, Harry Houdini married Wilhelmina Beatrice Rahner. He was twenty and "Bess" was eighteen. Their marriage lasted thirty-two years.

Bess was half of a song & dance act called the "Floral Sisters" when Houdini met her and she became a partner in the "Houdinis." Though in later years, Houdini worked a single act, Bess continued to perform the trunk illusion with him, even in his final tour. Here is Bess as she appeared in 1901.

When Houdini married Beatrice Rahner, she replaced Theo in the act, renamed simply the "Houdinis."

Sisters" and used the stage name of Beatrice Raymond. She had previously dated Houdini's brother Theo ("Dash"), who introduced her to his older brother, and the whirlwind courtship followed. Those who knew Dash in later years said that he would occasionally comment that he "saw her first." At any rate, Houdini's marriage to Bess was apparently a happy and thoroughly devoted one, and lasted for thirty-two years until the great magician's death. The marriage marked the end of the act "The Brothers Houdini" and the beginning of "the Houdinis"—and Bess was a decorative addition to Houdini's great trunk exchange, "Metamorphosis."

Five years of hardship and struggle followed. Harry and Bess played any spots that would pay them even the most meager salaries. During this period they briefly played the famous Tony Pastor's Music Hall on New York's Fourteenth Street and were a moderate success, but after that it was back to the saloons and dime museums. In the seasons of 1895 and 1898 they toured with the Welsh Brothers Circus where, by Houdini's admission, the pay was low but the food was good. In 1896 Houdini unsuccessfully managed a burlesque company known as "The American Gaiety Girls," then joined a medicine show, and then toured with another magician named Marco whose show folded in New Brunswick. (It was here that Houdini visited an insane asylum and got the idea for the straitjacket escape.) These were years of deprivation for the young Houdinis. On occasion their props were impounded for baggage bills due, and they were often without food. When things were at a particularly low ebb, Houdini successfully posed as a spirit medium, bilking the gullible public of its money by apparently delivering messages and physical manifestations from their departed loved ones. This experience was to serve Houdini well when in later years he was to launch his crusade against spirit mediums. It might also have produced some feelings of guilt that helped motivate that crusade.

I think that the most important thing about these difficult years was that they gave the Houdinis a chance to give thousands of shows in front of the toughest and most demanding kinds of audiences. An important thing for any young performer is to be given a chance to be bad, and then many more chances to correct it. Only in this way can he find what plays well for an audience in terms of his own personality. Houdini used these years of struggle to polish and perfect the escape act that only a few years later would make him a headliner at fabulous salaries in the most prestigious theaters in the world.

Bess was an attractive addition to Houdini's act and proved to be a good performer.

In 1896, Houdini managed a touring burlesque company known as the "American Gaiety Girls." It was a failure.

A Show ...
Up-to-Date.

The American Gaiety Girls.

HARRY HOUDINI, Proprietor and Manager.
FRED HARVEY, Business Manager.

Presenting the Leading Artists of —— Burlesque and Vaudeville.

Special Paper, Stand and Window Work..

Bess & Harry (number 6 in the photograph) toured with the Welsh Brothers Circus in 1895 and 1898 where "the pay was low but the food was good."

During their lean years, the Houdinis sometimes posed as spirit mediums, bilking the gullible public of their money by delivering messages from the dead. Houdini gained the experience to back his later investigations of fraudulent mediums and the experience perhaps induced a guilt that motivated that crusade.

It might be said that Houdini's luck changed with the close of the nineteenth century, but the sudden upturn his career took in 1899 was not just a stroke of good fortune. It was, of course, fortunate that Houdini's act was seen by vaudeville impresario Martin Beck, but when that break came, Houdini was ready for it. All of the tough years in beer halls, dime museums and circuses had paid off. Beck sensed the act's potential and felt that Houdini's concept, with some minor changes, could be a hit with his audiences. Beck's first suggestion was that Houdini drop the magic from his act and concentrate on the challenge escapes, closing with "Metamorphosis." Houdini took the advice and his star began to rise.

At this same time, a new form of entertainment was also on the rise in America—vaudeville. The major vaudeville circuits under the directorships of a number of canny showmen-impresarios, were to mass-produce variety shows that would play in theaters (often opulent entertainment "palaces" built by the circuits themselves) in major American cities. In the eastern United States there was the gigantic B. F. Keith circuit with more than thirty theaters in the heavily populated cities, and its "flagship" house, the spectacular Bijou Theatre in Boston. In strong competition to Keith was B. F. Proctor, based in New York City. Other circuits were headed by such showmen as Marcus Loew, S. Z. Poli, and Klaw and Erlanger. The major west coast vaudeville circuit was the Orpheum, created by Martin Beck. All of these were to become multimillon-dollar enterprises in the first years of the twentieth century. Vaudeville was in the ascendancy, to become the biggest mass-produced entertainment business that America had yet seen, and Houdini was moving right along with it.

Vaudeville was an urban phenomenon, drawing its audiences from the melting pot of the rapidly growing American cities. As might be expected, the vaudeville of the western United States, a part of the country that had not yet completely lost its frontier and agrarian roots, was more rough and ready and less sophisticated than that of the more established and urbanized eastern states. It was these western Orpheum circuit audiences that first undersood the beer hall- and carnival-spawned showmanship of a Houdini. His act was to take considerably more polishing before it was a big hit with eastern audiences.

Martin Beck's professional intuition about Houdini was right. His act was a smash on the vaudeville circuit. Both the press and the theater managers gave him glowing reports. In a matter of weeks Houdini's salary was raised from $60 to $90 per week, and a short time later Houdini wired Beck asking for a raise to $125 per week and got it. As Houdini toured on the Orpheum circuit, his knowledge of locks and handcuffs increased in quantum leaps. His challenges at that time specified that he would escape from "regulation" cuffs and locks, and he assiduously collected every standard make and devised new and more efficient methods to escape from them. It was during this period, and not as a young boy, as his publicity would have us believe, that Houdini studied with locksmiths and read every available book on locks and how they worked.

In addition to increasing his technical knowledge with each engagement he played, Houdini developed another skill at which he was an undisputed genius—the technique of handling the press and gaining publicity. There was scarcely a day when

Houdini played a town that he was not on the front pages of the newspaper. Such press coverage was almost a full-time job. With the possible exception of P. T. Barnum, Houdini might be said to have been the greatest natural publicist of all time. The great magician Dai Vernon (who was my teacher in magic and who, in 1925, hand-cut the silhouette of Houdini on the title page of this book), knew Houdini well. Bess Houdini was the godmother of Vernon's eldest son, Edward. Vernon remembers Houdini not as a particularly skilled magician but as "without a doubt the world's greatest handcuff king and also a great showman."

Vernon says of Houdini: "He was a supreme egotist, true, but we must be honest and say it was this egotism, plus his ability to live up to his claims, that made Houdini the famous person he was and still is today! Houdini was determined to succeed—

When Martin Beck, one of vaudeville's great impresarios, saw Houdini's act and hired him Houdini was ready for his big break. He kept this wire, noting below it that it "changed my whole life's journey."

43

Houdini in His Weirdest Trick of Chewing Needles.

HERE is a trick that will outrival the most fantastic illusion ever created by the wonderful jugglers of mystical India.

Put a handful of needles in your mouth, masticate them thoroughly, swallow them carefully; then take a long piece of sewing thread, swallow it judiciously until only a tiny bit of one end remains in the mouth; wait a few minutes and look wise—then catch the end of the thread with the thumb and finger and, drawing it slowly forth, find all the needles unbroken and neatly threaded. That seems easy, doesn't it? Of course you mustn't mind a needle going astray in your system once in a while and floating gradually around to play Cupid's arrow in your heart.

Houdini, the wonder, who has been setting the police agog by his remarkable handcuff escape and a few other hair-raisers, has performed this trick for a private committee of seekers into the mysterious. The whole illusion was accomplished with his audience close around him and in the face of a camera as well as an instrument not subject to hypnotic influence.

The materials were simple and furnished entirely by the audience, and the trick was done with the hands well on a level with the shoulders and away

Houdini's Needle Trick, Which Surpasses Anything He Did at the Orpheum.

from the body—thus precluding any palming or getting rid of the needles in the clothes.

Houdini takes from the audience any number of needles they may see fit; places them in his mouth and proceeds to crunch them. You can hear the steel crush and snap under his iron teeth. A light is held close to his face in order that no detail of the trick may escape the committee. He opens his mouth and the needles have disappeared.

He is then given a long piece of white linen thread, peculiarly knotted by some one of the committee for future identification; one end of this he places in his mouth and begins swallowing. This operation is continued until only the smallest particle of an end is visible in his throat. Then with open mouth and in the glare of a bright light, he catches the end of the thread and slowly draws forth, not only the same knotted thread, but on this thread are strung the identical number and kind of needles given him by his judges.

Of course it is a ... ere trick—so says Houdini—but how does he do it?

It is claimed by some who profess to know, that by filling the stomach with breadstuffs, needles may be actually and safely eaten, and after the trick is over a little drink of ipecac does the rest. But if Houdini does really swallow the needles, how does he manage to palm a reserve supply—to say nothing of duplicating a marked string and further bringing up the string with the needles all neatly threaded.

Houdini has a remarkable anatomy anyway, besides his skill as a magician. Just as a bit of pastime he showed the committee a vanishing pencil trick that would beat the proverbial small boy with a bean up his nose. He takes a pencil two inches long, places it in his mouth and presto! the pencil has disappeared. This trick he kindly explained. The pencil really goes up the nose passage at the back of the throat and upon close examination the end can be seen hanging over the throat. The act is a reverse sword swallow. Possibly he uses this extra receptacle as a storage during the needle trick?

Los Angeles Daily Time

The Playhouses.

ORPHEUM. A lively array of features and an audience in keeping both as to numbers and quality ushered in the week at this theater last night. The mystery of mysteries, Houdini, made his first appearance and scored a big success. This wizard of the handcuffs presents a performance that is entirely unique, and one that is likely to keep the guessers guessing for some time to come. A man who can have four pairs of regulation policeman's handcuffs locked on his wrists by officers of the police department, who retires to a cabinet and reappears after a lapse of time no longer than it took to fasten the "darbys" on him, freed thereof and with the gyves locked into each other, showing that his hands have not been slipped out, is too much of a mystery for the novice's unraveling. But clever as is this feat, Houdini's trunk trick is even more baffling to one who doesn't know how it is done. The performer's hands are closely tied behind him with a length of broad tape. His first feat in this condition is to remove his coat almost instantly upon retiring to the cabinet. One of the police officers on the stage then hands Houdini the coat bearing the officer's star; the performer retires momentarily to the cabinet and, although his hands are still bound, he appears wearing the garment of the officer. Then there is wheeled from the cabinet a large trunk, which rolls on casters. Houdini, with his hands still bound and wearing the officer's coat, is enveloped in a large sack; the sack is tied over his head and sealed with wax. The trunk is closed with Houdini inside it, double locked, bound with rope and wheeled into the cabinet. Mme. Houdini announces that she will enter the cabinet, clap her hands three times, and asks the audience to note the result. The little woman enters the cabinet swiftly, closes the curtain, claps her hands three times as quickly as one can fire a self-cocking pistol. The curtain is slipped aside, whereupon Houdini is disclosed standing in the enclosure in his shirt sleeves, the trunk is in the same condition as when it was locked and bound with the performer inside it. When the packing case is unlocked and unbound, Mme. Houdini is found inside it and the wax-sealed sack, wearing the officer's coat, her hands tied behind her with the tape—in other words, she has changed places with Houdini, and that almost instantaneously. It is left for the guessers to do the rest. Houdini also presents a number of clever card tricks, and altogether his work is a record-breaker as a mystery to the understanding of the uninitiated.

McAvoy and May, who were here some years ago, made their reappearance last night and captured everything in sight with their swift turn at horse play, which, strong, bright and clever as it is, would be still more so if some of the syphoning and other coarseness was eliminated. This is an immensely hard-working team and there is a contagious dash and breeziness in everything they do. The house rose at them last evening with wild enthusiasm, and that they "made good" was so strongly in evidence that even ...ceptious individual could not pro-

Antonio Vargas, a baritone of considerable ability, presents three numbers. Johnstone Bennett holds firmly her place in popular favor; Henri French is doing his great bicycle, or rather unicycle, feats; Caswell and Arnold continue their flip-flops, etc., and a team of new-comers, the Wartenberg brothers, offers some unique feats of foot juggling, vaulting, equilibrium, etc. The bill throughout is an especially strong one and one that is bound to "hold 'em for awhile." It goes all the week.

To Tie Houdini

Houdini, the king of handcuffs, will submit to be tied up in a coil of rope today at the police station by Officer Hill, who is a sailor man and knows all about donkey hitches, hawser knots, carrick bands and diamond hitches, not to speak of a hangman's knot and Nelson crown. Houdini is satisfied that he cana stand the test, though he knows that a failure will ruin him as a performer who has never been manacled or tied in a manner from which he cannot loose himself in a minute or two. The show will occur at the First street station at 11 oclock today. Yesterday Houdini submitted to an elaborate examination.

HOUDINI SAYS IT IS EASY IF YOU ONLY KNOW HOW

The "Handcuff King" Talks Concerning His Remarkable Feats---The More Rope Used the Easier it is to Get Away.

As a slight concession to the curiosity excited by his strange escapes from handcuffs, ropes and manacles of different sorts, Harry Houdini is willing to give an anxious public a tip on how to fool a man who wants to nail you down with a rope.

Those who say the youth emerge from a closet last Thursday in the police station, after Officer Davis had wound him round about with coils of rope, will no doubt be interested, with the many who have heard and read of Houdini's performances at the Orpheum, in the following explanation of how he escapes from the ropes when bound. To a newspaper man Houdini recently gave the following signed statement:

"I do not believe it possible for any man or committee to tie me to a chair so securely that I cannot get away, and without untying a single knot. Years ago, when I was making that my line of work, I frequently found smart people who thought that they had a new kink and could tie me good and fast, but I never in all my experience found myself tied so securely that I could not get away. For years I had a standing offer of $100 to any one who could so tie me that I could not get away in less time than it took to tie me.

"Any one can do the escape act if they only know how, and this being aided by spirits in a dark cabinet is all bosh. Of course one must do the act out of sight of the audience, just as I do the escape from the handcuffs at the Orpheum, or after people had seen how simnple it is, they would not pay to see it again.

"The whole secret is in getting the first hand free; after that it is all plain sailing. The quickness with which one gets out depends upon how soon one can get a little slack in the rope. When I am about to be tied I always sit a little forward from the back of the chair; the people tying me do not notice this. If my feet and legs are to be tied to the chair, then I sit so that my knees are at least one-quarters of an inch from the chair leg. My feet may be close against the chair.

"After I have been tied and carried into the cabinet I settle back into the chair and begin to squirm about so as to bring the slack of the rope to a point over the hand that I wish to free. One cannot be tied so that they cannot get some slack in the rope when they want it; if by no other means they can secure it by expending the chest while being tied. I have been tied to tight that the blood almost stopped and I have turned blue in the fact.

"Try it once and see how easy it is to twist about in the chair, no matter how securely they have tied you. With a little experience one soon learns to twist and squirm so as to bring all the slack of the rope to one point. As soon as one hand is free it is then plain sailing, for the release of the hand not only gives it freedom to assist in removing the rope, but the slack gained is enough to make the ropes loose at all points.

"As soon as both hands are free I then start in to remove the roper from around my neck, as they are usually yrather uncomfortable at this point. Next the feet are freed; then the rest is easy, for all one has to do is to squirm out of the ropes around the body, and that is an easy matter, for they are very loose by this time.

One mistake that committee make in trying to tie a person to a chair is to use so much rope. They think that the more rope is used, and the more knots that they put in it the harder it is to get free. After the explanation that I have given the reader will see that the more rope the more there is to work with in stretching it to gain slack. When I was doing the 'escape' from the ropes I was always meeting people who have thought out a sure way of tying me so that I could not get away, but they never succeeded in doing it. On the same prnicíple, everybody who sees me 'escape' from the handcuffs at the Orphheum has a theory as to how I do it, but I never argue the matter with them. If I told them how it was done they would not believe me, it is so simple. However, my offer of $50 for a pair of regulation handcuffs that I cannot escape from is still open to the doubting Thomases.

"HARRY HOUDINI."

HONDINI, "KING OF HAND-CUFFS

Orpheum.--Hondini, styled the "King of Handcuffs," an illusionist and prestidigitateur of remarkable abilities, is the star card of the Orpheum's new bill next week. He has appeared before the police of all the big cities and completely mystified them by the ease with which he releases himself from the links. Chief Glass yesterday morning joined the list of the officers puzzled by Hordini's remarkable skill. Hondini's stage exhibition will, it is promised, discount anything in the illusionist line ever produced at the Orpheum.

McAvoy and May are knockabout artists with a good reputation as fun-makers.

The Wartenberg brothers, jugglers and acrobats; Antonio Vargas, a baritone opera singer; Johnstone Bennett and company, and Henri French, the trick cyclist, complete the bill.

THE CAPITAL

☆ ☆

This page is prepared too early to include a description of the Jonathan's Club's night at the Orpheum, but there is no possibility of the affair being anything but a howling success. The house will be jammed to the roof with masculine and feminine loveliness, the decorations I am assured could not be more swell, and altogether those present will have one of the times of their lives.

☆ ☆

A small section of the club, with a lot of newspaper men, saw Houdini perform last week a number of the smoothest card tricks that ancient or modern history mentions. To try and describe such tricks is worse than relating the flavor of a perfect fruit. They cannot be adequately described. They must be seen to be believed. And even then believing does not always follow sight. One finds it not easy to accept the apparently miraculous, in this age. And Houdini does the miraculous, to all seeming. His seances with the police first stimulated interest in the man's work, and his stage performances have but added fuel to the flame. He is the most profitable card the Orpheum has sheltered in many a long day.

☆ ☆

The difference between Houdini's and Johnstone Bennett's engagements—one a huge success, the other not so huge—illustrates very nicely how expectation affects an artist's reputation. Too much was expected of Johnstone Bennett. She is so well known and well advertised that people came with their ideas keyed way up—Johnstone Bennett was to take everything by storm. She was to be Ada Rehan, Lillian Russell, Maude Adams, Anna Held and several other persons rolled into one— thus went a host of people's ideas. She didn't happen to be an eighth wonder of the world, a prodigy of stage cleverness, the apotheosis of comedy art, and hence—disappointment, in certain circles.

☆ ☆

Now Houdini comes heralded not as an illusionist who has set the Chicago or other rivers afire, but merely as a talented prestidigatateur. He proves to be better than was suspected he could or would be, and it seems impossible for the public to say too many kind things of his work. There's a moral in this thing for players, and people who are not players. For players—be sure that your advance notices are not too lurid to prevent your making good with them, and for the public, don't let sensational advertising blind you to genuine merit, even if all the feats done on the billboards are not done on the stage boards.

☆ ☆

By 1899, Houdini had become an expert at self-promotion. In each city he played he provided the press with articles and material for interviews.

Expose of Houdini's T

By Professor Be

And How You Can Disconcert This Clever P Kind When They Blandly Ask for Them at Their Tric

IF you want to have a little amusement at the expense of Houdini, all you have to do is to take a pair of handcuffs to the theatre with you when you attend a performance given by that professor of the art of trickery.

Not the common, every-day style of handcuffs such as are clapped on the wrists of prisoners here and there the world over, but a pair with a newfangled lock and key.

Then you can sit back in your seat and wait for developments.

These developments will be the utter inability of Professor Houdini to execute his usual gymnastics in a cabinet for the mystification of an easily-fooled audience.

It is because an audience is so accommodating and altogether obliging in the matter of allowing itself to be deceived that the professor finds his favorite handcuff trick the safest in his stock. Indeed, it is his stock in trade, for upon its invariable success has depended his reputation for inexplicable cleverness.

When the handcuff trick is about to be performed for the dazzlement of onlookers, Professor Houdini advances to the footlights and blandly requests the loan of a pair of handcuffs.

Now, who in the name of all that is unexpected and unarrested goes about to places of theatrical amusement with jail jewelry up his sleeve? Nobody, of course. The professor is wise in banking upon the scarcity of handcuffs.

So he produces a pair and invites some one in the house to put them on his wrists and clasp the iron bands until they click sharply together, after which the manacled entertainer retires to his cabinet to reappear shortly minus his coat, but still handcuffed. Another temporary eclipse of the professor and he returns with the handcuffs removed, securely locked.

And the accommodating audience loudly applauds the consequences of its own ingenuousness.

In reality, this trick is absurdly simple. Handcuffs not being an article in extensive demand, there are but few kinds made. Professor Houdini is supplied with these, and with the keys that unlock them. He keeps conveniently about him all keys known to the handcuff trade. Should a pair like those in the illustration be used, he unlocks them with his fingers. If by chance a pair be produced so made that it is impossible to get the fingers to the keyhole, the professor is equal to the emergency, for he has previously slipped the key into a crack in the chair or cabinet, and, holding it in his teeth, he quickly unlocks his bracelets.

Less simple but hardly more mysterious to be uninitiated than the handcuff trick is the trunk trick.

This trick is not by any means a new one, having been performed in London and Paris as far back as 1897. The original idea was to have a trunk brought upon the stage, a portion of the audience was invited to examine it, and those who wished could help tie it. After that a cloth was put around it, it was retied and sealed, and in a few minutes a Hindoo had managed to get into the interior without breaking the ropes and seals, the trunk being still closed.

To perform this trick it is of course necessary to have a trained assistant. A trunk to all appearances an ordinary one must be used. Half the bottom of the trunk constitutes a trap door which may be opened by inserting a round key in what appears to be one of the ventilating apertures. Members of the audience are permitted to tie and seal the trunk, and it is then placed under a canopy, the curtains of which are let down so as to hide the trunk from the spectators. As soon as the curtains are drawn the assistant, who is also invisible to the spectators, turns the trunk over on its side, unbuckles the cover, slides it down, unlocks the trap-door, gets into the trunk, puts the cover in place, buckles it, and then closes the trap-door.

Now, before the curtains are raised the trunk must be returned to the position in which it was before the curtains were let down. To do this the man in the trunk takes a long screw, something like a gimlet, from a pocket, which snugly fits one of the ventilating apertures, through which he screws it until the end touches the floor. Then he has only to turn the screw, which operates on the principle of a "jackscrew," and gradually raises the trunk from its position on its side. As it rises slowly and reaches the point of its equilibrium it suddenly overbalances and falls back to its original position on its bottom, making a slight noise just loud enough

a signal to the operator, who the curtains once more, finds b that there is something in the slowly undoes the straps, unloc and presents the mysterious tr mystified audience.

Sometimes an Indian appear in a bag in the trunk. This of the trick—a trick within a bag trick, like that of the trunk perhaps more generally unders

HANDCUFF

x and Handcuff Trick.

and Others of His
to Help

San Francisco
Examiner
July 9th, 1899

THE SECRET OF THE UNLOCKING

DE FAST.

HANDS FREE

SECRETS OF MY HANDCUFF TRICKS

By Harry Houdini.

COMPLETELY HANDCUFFED.

ONE FOOT FREE.

I STILL call myself king of hand-cuffs. I earned the title through my knowledge of a trick and retain it through my ability to keep a secret. My ability to free myself from steel, leather and hempen cords is considered enough of a rarity to give me a place as a public entertainer, and almost every exhibition has been followed by alleged exposures, which so far have all turned out to be wild or ingenious guesses at the secret of my methods.

I am not going to throw away my bread and butter by explaining how I open handcuffs and defy straitjackets. I do it by a trick, and any one in possession of my secret could laugh at locks just as heartily as I do. The path of a handcuff king is not all roses, and some of my adventures with the army of doubting Thomases would hardly be credited.

When I escape from a dozen pairs of handcuffs up comes somebody with a smile of superior wisdom and a hand grip that would make a vise envious. "I know how that's done. You have a very flexible hand and can compress it into a smaller space than your wrist occupies." I hold out my hand for examination, and the man with the grip soon has the bones of my fingers crackling and aching in his effort to make my anatomy conform with his theory.

I call his attention to the fact that I have not only freed myself from the cuffs, but have brought them all out interlocked. He mutters something about concealed keys, magnets, wires or other appliances and walks off still unconvinced, while I go to the arnica bottle for relief for my mangled hand.

One of these tests I went through a few nights ago for the edification of the Sherlock Holmes brigade in the "upper office" of the San Francisco Police Department.

They squeezed my hands and advanced all kinds of theories, and when they told me how they proposed to test me I thought for a while that I was very much "up against it."

I was taken into the detectives' apartments and told to strip until entirely nude. This done, I was conducted into another room, where Police Surgeon Roland E. Hartley searched me for concealed keys. I was then loaded down with handcuffs.

They used ten pairs. My hands and arms were shackled up to the elbows. My ankles were then imprisoned and my hands shackled to my feet. Then Dr. Hartley sealed up my mouth with adhesive plaster and I was shown a closet where I could retire and free myself if I could.

FEET FREE.

ss than ten minutes and
cuffs all interlocked. I
d satisfy them, but they
one more test in store.
d the plaster, testified to
been moved or tampered

sfied those present that
ll my own, of rendering
aps useless as means of
gentlemen present were
mit this, and when I left
t a statement giving the
est, signed by everybody

ONE HAND FREE

who had been present.

I have been doing this handcuff trick for
nearly fourteen years. I have during that
time made a close and constant study of the
many different kinds of cuffs and believe
that, to-day, I know more about locks and
how to work them than any man living.

HARRY HOUDINI.

Photos by Bushnell

"THERE YOU ARE."

CAN HOLD MAGICIAN HUDINI.

Handcuffed and legs locked.　　Legs freed.　　All freed and handcuffs interlocked.

He Performed for the St. Louis Police in a Costume So Brief He had No Place to Conceal Keys or Wires.

HARRY HOUDINI claims unique distinction. He says no one can handcuff or tie him so tightly that he cannot release himself.

Houdini is at one of the suburban gardens and his feat attracts much attention. "King of Handcuffs" is the peculiar title to which he lays claim and there is appropriateness in it.

Houdini's delight is to perplex the detectives and shrewd ones around police headquarters in the large cities. Recently, Chief of Detectives Desmond and aides experienced like chagrin of their fellow officers elsewhere.

They loaded him down with handcuffs and chains. Then they placed sticking plaster over his mouth so that he could not have resort to his teeth. In little more than a twinkle Houdini handed the officers their irons. He had slipped through them like an eel, figuratively speaking, but just how he untied the knots is an eye-opening mystery the St. Louis Police Department cannot explain.

Thursday night Chief Campbell handcuffed Houdini's hands to his neck and locked the neckcuff at the back. Yet the magician released himself.

Houdini's feat is largely a trick, aided by wonderful hands. He has been working at it 14 years and makes it more mystifying each year.

He will not let anyone see him work. However, in private tests, he permits himself to be stripped and placed in a room in which he has never been. This is his way of showing that he has no aides, neither men nor material. He declares that if anyone knew his trick he could work it as easily as he, and would laugh at locksmiths just as merrily.

The St. Louis official test referred to was witnessed by all the important men at headquarters. It was more severe than that seen nightly, but seemingly it was no harder work for the magician.

Two pairs of the latest improved handcuffs were placed around his wrists. They were double locked. A pair of shackles were placed around his ankles. These, too, were double locked. Then another pair of cuffs was produced and his hands and feet were shackled together. Chief Pickel retained the keys. In just 2 minutes and 40 seconds every handcuff was off and they were all interlocked.

The magician archly says the secret lies in knowing how to release the first band. After that it is dead easy. With equal frankness he says one must know how to sit or stand when being shackled. This is important, you doubtless will agree, but when you attempt the trick you cannot help thinking Houdini has left much unsaid in explanation of it.

When completely shackled and handcuffed, Houdini is stooping. His feet are 10 or 14 inches apart. He appears perfectly helpless. With a laugh that is catching he bids the attendants pile on more chains. Then he disappears and in a jiffy is back again with the irons in his hands.

Heretofore, and even now when exhibiting in small towns, Houdini lets the doubters tie him with ropes. He finds they do not bind him more tightly than iron, nor are the knots harder to untie than locks are to loosen.

The man has wonderfully developed hands. They are supple to a degree seldom seen. The body is also developed along the lines most helpful in the performance of his tricks. His ability to squirm is evident.

The "handcuff" trick is not the only one which he does well. Cards are manipulated in a manner that is fairly dazing. One of his best card tricks is to have a spectator pick a card from the pack, then replace it without letting him see it. The cards are shuffled while Houdini is blindfolded. Then he asks the one who has drawn the card to take him by the wrist and think intently. At a signal from the man Houdini lays his hand on the card.

Another trick he does is full of mystery. He places twenty needles in his mouth, three or four at a time. Then he swallows them. After washing them down with a drink of water he breaks off a piece of silk thread and swallows that. Then he draws forth the thread and all of the needles, with the thread running through the eyes.

Houdini said: "My ability to free myself from steel, leather or rope has caused many to explain how I do it. Nearly all say I have keys, electric wires or knives concealed. Even some have said I have confederates.

"I am not going to explain how I do it, because that would be throwing away my livelihood. Anyone could do the trick if he only knew how.

"My experiences have been varied and not always pleasant. Policemen have used the Oregon boot, a straight jacket and all kinds of cuffs, but I have been able to come out of them all right. My hands have been nearly crushed by big-muscled fellows who thought I had a flexible hand and grasped mine to prove the assertion. Others have given weird explanations of how easy it is for me to release myself, yet none have come forward with a scheme by which I can be held.

"As I said, it is all a trick, but it is my own."

DOWN THE LINE

○ ○ ○

Harry Houdini Could Beat Poker Davis

A very polite, unassuming fellow is Harry Houdini, who came to town yesterday to fill an engagement at the Orpheum. He is the man who cannot be handcuffed or shackled so that he cannot free himself in a few moments. He has done this in almost every city in the country, and has an engagement with Chief Glass this morning at 11 oclock. The chief, it seems, thinks that he can fasten Mr. Houdini with an Oregon boot, and the test will take place at the police station. Mr. Houdini stated last evening that he expected this would be the hardest ordeal he had ever had, for the chief proposes to load him down with handcuffs and shackles, as well as two Oregon boots. "You can say for me if you will," he said last night, "that I do not agree with Johnstone Bennett at all in her expression of opinion that San Francisco is a jay town, and the coast not appreciative. I have been treated splendidly and have nothing but good opinions to offer about the people. I am quite confident that I will be able to free myself tomorrow in four or five minutes, though it may take me a little longer if the chief can fix up a hard program for me." There is nothing that Mr. Houdini cannot do with the cards; he would like to have a little game with Poker Davis while he is here. He says his money is worth 90 per cent to him in a game; the ordinary gambler's cash is worth 80 per cent, while the average poker player's is worth only 40 per cent. If "Papa Poker" would like to try conclusions with Mr. Houdini for his "roll" he can be accommodated, and from what I saw of the performer's cleverness yesterday, I will promise "Poker" that he will see bigger hands and more of them than he ever dreamed could come together in one vening. Mr. Houdini is certainly the greatest juggler and mystifier ever seen in the city. He does not rely so much on paraphernalia as in sleight of hand and general cleverness. Mrs. Houdini is a very important part of his act, as will be believed when her bonny face is seen. The couple had the pleasure of celebrating the sixth anniversary of their wedding yesterday.

THE GOSSIPER.

LOS ANGELES

SATURDAY, JUNE 24, 1899.

THE HERALD

CAN'T HANDCUFF HIM

Police Force Mystified by the Marvelous Houdini

The entire police force of the city failed to shackle a young man yesterday so that he could not escape his bonds. The momentary prisoner was Harry Houdini, the "king of handcuffs" and the prince of cards. He was simply passing a pleasant hour in his kind of amusement. He informed Chief Glass that he would be pleased to show him and his staff how uncertain life and the bracelets are and he did. In the first test of his powers the officers placed him in an Oregon boot. Then anklecuffs were locked above this. Not satisfied with this two pair of handcuffs were fastened about Houdini's wrists and he was thrust in a room by himself and trussed like a turkey at a Thanksgiving shoot. In four minutes the prisoner walked jauntily from the room and handed back all the paraphernalia to the officers. This did not satisfy the officers and pair after pair of cuffs were locked tightly on Houdini's wrists, causing them to swell from the pressure. Each time he was fastened alone in a room and each time he skipped forth free from his fetters. There was not an instrument in police headquarters that could hold him for two minutes. Mr. Houdini appears at the Orpheum next week and is keeping up practice by little tricks as above.

FRIDAY, JUNE 23, 1899.

HE JESTS AT HANDCUFFS

Houdini, a Vaudeville Magician, Give a Unique Exhibition Before Chief Glass, the Detectives and Many Officers

Officer Hill has been for years the butt of the Los Angeles police force, because of his belief in spiritualism.

Today he is exultant, triumphant, jubilant, and his voice trembles with the thrill of joy as he faces his brethren of the club and hisses through clenched teeth:

"I told you so."

He spoke thus after Houdini, the "king of handcuffs," had, in the police station assembly room, freed himself from five pairs of handcuffs, an Oregon boot and a pair of leg shackles.

"Only the spirits could enable a man to do that," cried the big Hibernian, who dallies with mediums and believes in the subtle spook, the shadowy specter, and the lucre-loving shade of commerce.

Houdini, an Orpheum artist, calls himself the "king of handcuffs," and this morning submitted to a severe test of his claims before Chief Glass, the entire detective force, and a score or more of officers. Houdini made a short preliminary speech, and then, as a "teaser," performed the "needle and thread" trick. A committee of newspaper men examined his mouth and found it empty. The magician swallowed fifteen needles and remarked that this was called "taking iron for the blood." A couple of yards of common thread followed the needles. In a minute the needles were drawn from the mouth, all threaded.

The crowd gasped.

"Now bring on your handcuffs, leg shackles, Oregon boots, etc.," said Houdini.

The detectives were loaded. They had an Oregon boot and handcuffs ready, all supposed to be impregnable. The irons were attached to Houdini's hands and feet by Detectives Flammer and Hawley, and Houdini was carried, thus heavily manacled, to an empty room, near by.

It was conceded by the waiting officers that if the man could free himself from the irons, he would be the record breaker in that line of business, and a "handcuff king" indeed.

It had taken six minutes to shackle Houdini. He appeared with nothing binding him, in four and one-half minutes. He was timed by Chief Glass.

A cheer and a round of hand-clapping bespoke the crowd's admiration for the achievement.

Houdini then produced a pair of handcuffs, his own. The detectives examined them, and pronounced the irons even more complicated than their own. Houdini was locked with them, and stepped from the room, to return, hands free, in thirty seconds. A second cheer went up.

There were thirty puzzled men in the room, and pretty nearly as many opinions of how the trick was done. There were no two opinions of its cleverness.

"Gentlemen," cried Chief Glass, "you observe what I have often told you—that an officer's eye on a person is better than irons."

To Houdini, the chief expressed praise of the performance, and declared it to be unique.

Officer Hill, whose hour of triumph had come, improved the occasion to preach a batch of spiritualistic truths. Strangely enough, his erstwhile cynical audience was apparently impressed.

Officer Hill challenged Houdini to a rope-tying contest. Hill is an old sea captain. He claims to be able to tie Houdini so that the magician cannot escape. Houdini laughed at the challenge. Rope-tying seances are his strong suit.

"I will submit to any test, rope-tying or handcuff shackling you wish me to endure on the Orpheum stage next week, during my engagement."

As every policeman is at least as good as a "three-sheet," Houdini's performance before the officer's today is doubtless a superb advertisement for him and the Orpheum people.

TUESDAY, JUNE 27, 1899.

EVENING EXPRESS

LOS ANGELES, CAL.

Orpheum.

"Houdini," the wizard of the handcuffs, presented last night one of the most novel acts ever put on at the Orpheum. Houdini by the aid of his press agent and a dull day at the police station stirred up interest in his act ahead of time and a large audience was on hand last night eager to see him do his tricks.

Last night officers of the regulation handcuffs department. Houdini retired to his cabinet for two minutes and ten seconds and came out with his wrists free. The trick which followed was bewildering...

He entered the cabinet in his shirt sleeves with his hands securely bound and a the officer handed him a coat, bearing the officer's star. In a moment he reappeared with his hand still bound, but wearing the officer's sack, which was locked with wax.

A trunk was then rolled into the cabinet. Houdini with his hands still bound and enveloped in a large sack, was tied over his head and double locked. The trunk was closed and sealed with wax.

Mme. Houdini entered the cabinet, and was heard to clap her hands three times in quick succession. The curtain being drawn aside disclosed Houdini standing in the enclosure. The trunk was unlocked and when discovered in the officer's coat, while Mme. Houdini was in the shirt sleeves, and when the trunk was opened Houdini was found therein, the sack tied and sealed about her head.

McAvoy and May, a comedy sketch team who were out here some years ago, caught on tremendously again last night. Their act is fast and furious but it takes all kinds of people to make up a vaudeville show, and it is feared some of the refined, but none too refined, folks will vote the pair to be the best they ever saw. Some of it is very clever, Antonio Vargas, a baritone singer of considerable ability, gave three selections, and the Warren brothers do some clever foot juggling and tumbling this week. Johnstone Bennett, a comedienne of consider...able... and Arnold repeat their last week...Powell and Arnold repeat their last week...Henri French and...

DISPATCH---WEDNESDAY

HE PUZZLED THE POLICE.

Houdini Removed the Irons Placed on Him by Captain Angle.

Houdini, in an exhibition given in the City Hall yesterday before Chief Howard, Captain Angle, and many other of the police force, puzzled these officers and some thirty or forty other gentlemen who were present. Houdini seems to have fairly won his title, the King of Handcuffs. He stripped himself of all clothing yesterday, that it could not be charged that he had keys or springs concealed about his person, and with his mouth sealed with plaster, and bound with a handkerchief, he removed four pairs of irons that had been placed upon him by Captain Angle.

Houdini explained that many people believed he carried duplicate keys either in his clothing or his mouth, and for this reason he stripped himself and allowed his mouth to be sealed and bound. Dr. C. W. P. Brock attended to thoroughly closing the "King's" mouth, and then Captain Angle placed the shackles upon the performer. Irons were put not only upon Houdini's wrists, but also upon his feet, and then his hands were shackled to his legs. Houdini did not remove the irons in the presence of the spectators, but got behind a chair, over which a rug was thrown. However, he was almost entirely within the sight of those in the room, and many even saw the performer as he worked upon his shackles. In 2 minutes he stepped from behind the chair holding the four pairs of irons in his hands. It was simply a wonderful exhibition, and every one in the room admitted that the King of Handcuffs was one too many for them.

Even more startling than this was another feat performed by Houdini. With Dr. Brock standing just in front of him, he swallowed some half a dozen needles, and then followed these with a long piece of silk thread. After allowing a few seconds to pass, in order to aid his digestion, he placed his fingers in his mouth, secured the silk, and pulled it out, with the thread through the eye of every needle that had been swallowed. While waiting for the handcuffs, which were those used by the police force of Richmond, Houdini performed several card tricks that were way ahead of those of the majority of magicians.

APRIL 24 – 1900

THE RICHMOND DISPATCH.

BY THE DISPATCH COMPANY.

THE KING OF HANDCUFFS.

He Puzzles His Audience at the Bijou—Others on the Bill.

Every inch of standing room was occupied at the Bijou last night, when the week was opened with an excellent performance. There are six acts on the bill, and all of them are good. Houdini, who has earned the title of "King of Handcuffs," accomplished feats that thoroughly puzzled his audience. A member of the police force of this city went upon the stage, and, assisted by another gentleman, placed upon Houdini's wrists a pair of handcuffs that had been brought from the office of the Chief. Houdini stepped behind his curtained cabinet, and in a few second emerged therefrom, holding the irons in one hand. A second pair of handcuffs were placed upon him, and these he removed in view of the audience, though the spectators could not see his hands, which were locked behind him. Houdini next allowed himself to be tied in a sack and placed in a trunk, which was securely locked and fastened. Before doing this he put on a coat belonging to one of the gentlemen who had stepped from the audience. The trunk was tied in the cabinet. Then Houdini's assistant went behind the curtain, immediately the "King of Handcuffs" made his appearance; the trunk was drawn out and opened, and the Houdini was found tied up in the sack, wearing the coat.

T. Thorne and Grace Carleton did the most laughable acts that has been here in vaudeville this season. There was a decided freshness about it. man, Holcombe, and Curtis, a singer that made such a hit here earlier season, repeated their success in the act. Raymond and Clarke were good in a comedy acrobatic act, and Bush, and Lelliot pleased in their turn. The Barom Brothers, who eat contortionists and acrobats, the performance.

will be a matinee to-day, and performances continue through the

HARRY HOUDINI'S HAND.

The "Handcuff King's" Palm Read by Professor Johnstone

Harry Houdini calls himself the "handcuff king." The soubriquet has been well earned. His marvelous feats have made police officers and handcuff experts quit guessing.

Last night after having finished his "turn" at the Orpheum, Houdini walked over to 517 West Tenth street, where Prof. Paul Alexander Johnstone's business rooms are, and had his hand examined.

"I feel nervous. This constant fear of exposure is almost unbearable. I fully realize it is only a question of time until I am caught, and it is this suspense that causes my nerves to keep stirring."

Houdini was sitting in a large leather chair, and kept talking while he watched Prof. Johnstone prepared the plaster of Paris.

"To be stripped of all clothing and then locked in the strongest steel cage the jail can afford, and this, too, with a hundred pounds of iron on your forearms and ankles; to hear the bolts of the cell door scrape and crash as they pass into their sockets, and then to walk out into the

HOUDINI'S PALM

corridor and hand the officers their handcuffs and shackles unlocked! It makes me nervous."

"You have been caught once or twice, have you not?"

Houdini measured the palmist very deliberately from top to toe.

"Yes; twice. Once in Denver, and the man died the day after. Three months later Nero, the great medium, detected how I performed these feats, and three days afterward he died. Rather a singular coincidence, don't you think?

Houdini's hand was in plaster to the wrist, and the flexor and extensor muscles of his forearm stood out like chiselled alabaster.

"Unless you are exceedingly careful during your thirty-seventh year a violent death is written in this Line of Life," said the palmist. "Your money making period began, I should judge, last year. Provided you save, you will attain great wealth."

"How about my work?" Houdini asked.

"Your brains will protect you," said the palmist, assuredly. "I will trust to you getting out of anything put on you. You need not worry, Mr. Houdini. The safest way to keep you is to turn you loose on the prairie." After this jest a great many personal matters were talked about by the palmist.

Prof. Johnstone was very conservative in expressing himself as to how these marvelous feats are performed, although he admitted having a very distinct conception of Houdini's methods.

Prof. Johnstone's fee for an oral reading of the hand is $1. It is said that more than 20,000 people have patronized him in Kansas City within the past two years. He tries to close his rooms at 7 o'clock at night.

Mr. and Mrs. Houdini were guests of honor at a delightful entertainment Wednesday evening at the conclusion of their performance. The hosts were Mr. and Mrs. Goldsmith of 1919 Dodge street. After a short musical program by Prof. Sutorius, Mr. and Mrs. W. H. Wilbur and others, the clever magician and his pretty little wife presented some extraordinary feats in magic, including the famous thread and needle trick. In this Mr. Houdini sfallowed, apparently, several papers of needles and half a spool of thread. In an incredibly short time he drew out of his mouth the needles, neatly threaded with the cotton. The evening closed with a dainty luncheon.

Sidney Drew is the most exclusive man on the vaudeville stage today. He spends as little time as possible about the theater, and never mingles with the other performers. The only thing which has interested him this week has been Houdini's turn. He has watched that at every performance. On Wednesday night he professed a desire to enter the mysterious trunk. Houdini was most obliging. Mr. Drew took the same position in the trunk that is assumed by Houdini, but he could not get e was no

Harry & Bess spent all they could afford on promotion. This was an ad they circulated to theatre managers in 1898.

and he did. He told me many times, 'Vernon, keep your name in front of the public—that's all you have to do. But it must be constant and be sure your name is spelled correctly Get them to talk and write about you. It makes no difference what they say as long as they talk about you.' Harry certainly practiced what he preached!"

Yes, Houdini practiced what he preached, all except the part about not caring "what they say." On the contrary, any publicity that in any way violated the constructed legend of HOUDINI (whom he often thought of as a person separate from himself) was very painful to him, and on many occasions was known to throw him into deep despair, or, more often, a towering rage.

In the years before his big break, Houdini had become increasingly adept at garnering publicity, as many clippings from the period attest, but during his first Orpheum tour, which lasted from the early summer of 1899 into the fall, almost every engagement found him on the front pages. It was during this tour that Houdini developed a sure-fire publicity stunt that he'd begun to use almost a year earlier. In each town, it was his policy to challenge the local police department to put him in irons from which he would escape. He added the additional features of being locked and fully manacled in the jail's most escape-proof cell from which, of course, he escaped. To make sure that he had no keys or lock picks concealed on his person, he was stripped and

IMPORTANT.

Very Rare

NOTICE.

I OFFER $100.00 to any human being living that can escape from all the cuffs I carry, and from which I release myself.

I escape from the celebrated Bean Giant Cuff with them locked behind my back, a feat no one else has ever accomplished. My hands can be fastened back or front. It makes no difference how many pair of cuffs are locked on me (**at the same time**), and I will allow the **keyholes to be stamped and sealed,** and as I bring out all the cuffs interlocked, it proves conclusively that **I do not slip my hands.**

I have escaped out of more handcuffs, manacles and leg shackles than any other human being living. As I carry a very rare, curious and costly collection of torture, antique and modern Handcuffs (of every style and make), I give a scientific and historic lecture on them; in fact, I have the ONLY complete act of this description in existence.

Harry Houdini

Of the Team

Harry and Bessie Houdini

The Expert Handcuff Manipulator.

NOTE.—There is a **$50.00 REWARD** offered to any one that can escape from the Bean Giant, but that offer is for the cuffs to be fastened behind the back.

Did you ever see any handcuff worker have his hands locked in back to escape from the Bean cuff?

In his scrapbook, Houdini noted that this early
publicity poster was "very rare." Today these
charming handbills are impossible to find.

searched by the police physician and locked up stark
naked except for the manacles. Gresham points out
that, during this process, Bess modestly left the
room. In that age of Victorian prudery, the story of a
handcuffed *naked* man added no small amount to the
exotic aura of the young escape artist. Houdini was to
use the "naked test" jailbreak as a top publicity
puller for many years to come, at times embellishing
it with such newsworthy pranks as opening all the
other cells in the jail and exchanging the prisoners
into different cells, or opening the cell in which his
clothes were locked and appearing in front of his
would-be captors not only free but fully dressed.

On one occasion in San Francisco, a newspaper
published a story by a local escape artist purporting
to expose the methods of Houdini, who had just
finished an engagement at the Orpheum theater.
Houdini, with his typical skill as a publicist, parlayed
this into a return engagement by challenging not

only the challenger (who said Houdini had keys and
lock picks on his person) but the San Francisco Police
Department to the "naked test," which he performed
at their jail with great resulting publicity. By the end
of the Orpheum tour, Martin Beck was able to book
Houdini as a headline act into a short tour on the
Keith circuit, playing some of the top vaudeville
theaters on the east coast.

Despite his west coast success, Houdini's drawing power and impact on more sophisticated eastern
audiences was still not as great as it had been on his
western tour and he felt the need to establish himself
elsewhere as the star act he knew himself to be. The
obvious choice was Great Britain and the Continent,
for European acts were enjoying tremendous prestige
in American vaudeville. And so for the first time
since he was an infant in Hungary, Houdini returned
to Europe.

Houdini led the bill and a minor comedian
named Jack Benny appeared on this
Orpheum Circuit program.

HOW ⬦ SLEEVES ⬥ ARE ◉ STUFFED ❖ WITH ✦ CARDS.

Fresno Chronicle June 14-99

An Ingenious Piece of Mechanism Which Is Employed by Shrewd but Unscrupulous Gamblers to Aid Them in Robbing Their Dupes.

HOUDINI, an Austrian, is exhibiting as a sleight-of-hand performer at the Orpheum, and aside from his handcuff tricks, which have puzzled the Police Department, he is betraying some of the tricks of the gambling fraternity. One of the methods employed by gamblers to fleece their dupes is shown in the above illustration. A mechanical device is employed to carry cards up the sleeve of the operator. Houdini says there are only twenty of these devices in existence, and they cost $175 each. It consists of an extension frame with a spring grip at the end of it into which a card, or a number of cards, can be slipped at pleasure whenever it is extended within reach of the palm. It is operated by an appliance strapped to the chest of the operator and worked by respiration. Drawing in the breath extends and contracts the card-clip attachment, which is strapped to the bare arm under the coat sleeve, at the will of the operator. The first figure shows the machine contracted; the second shows it extended, with the card which is to be sleeved in the palm; the third shows the card inserted in the clip ready to be drawn under the sleeve; the fourth shows the clip closed, with the card safely under cover. When the desired number of cards have been manipulated in this way to suit the gambler's wishes the set is thrown back into his hand, with, of course, disastrous consequences to his opponent, and perfect security apparently against discovery of the cheat. The exhibition is, at least, a good object lesson, if nothing more, and ought to cure the spectator of the gambling habit, if possessed of it.

WINFRED GOFF — GRAND OPERA HOUSE
MLLE. BEATRICE HOUDINI AT THE ORPHEUM
MISS FLORENCE ROBERT

The Orpheum's New Bill.

"Houdini," a slippery young gentleman who can disentangle himself from anything except fame and free advertising, is to be the star of stars at the Orpheum this week. His act is an unusual one and has been attracting much attention. Besides mysteriously freeing himself from ropes and handcuffs he has various mystifying tricks of illusion, in which his wife takes part.

McAvoy and May, a couple of rapid-fire comedians who met with success here on a previous visit several years ago, will be back again this week. Wartenberg Bros., an European importation, who do some remarkable good jugglery, and Antonio Vargas, a baritone singer, who sings the Toredor song, will be of the bill.

Johnstone Bennett will repeat her sketch, "A Quiet Evening at Home," and Henri French will have a better place on the bill for his unique tricks of wheel riding and jugglery. Caswell and Arnold, acrobats, will open the show.

Orpheum Dashes

The best advertised actress in the country to-day, barring none, is Johnstone Bennett. Every man, woman and child in the land who has ever been to a theatre, and many that have never seen the inside of a playhouse, have all heard of this versatile comedienne. She is the originator of the "mannish" style of dressing affected by the fin de siecle girl, and is constantly evolving new ideas of attire and deportment, some of which, to say the least, are radical changes from the customs of by-gone days. She certainly is an independent woman, who has the courage of her convictions, and column upon column have been written by the press throughout the country about her sayings and doings. Miss Bennett has been induced by the Orpheum management to temporarily desert the legitimate stage for a short season on the vaudeville boards, and she will appear here next week, accompanied by Antonio Williams, in the delightful comedietta, "A Quiet Evening at Home," by Lew Rosen and Kenneth Lee, which gives her ample scope to display her well-known talents. A specially organized company of vaudeville celebrities open with her, in conjunction with the Orpheum's company of stars.

Houdini, known as the "King of Handcuffs," also opens next week. He is a magician with decidedly up-to-date methods. His "Metamorphosis" is the greatest and best trunk trick ever seen anywhere. He is assisted by Mlle. Beatrice Houdini.

McAvoy and May, the "cylonic" comedians, open here next week. They present a performance that is replete with laugh-producing sayings and actions, and as a provoker of boisterous merriment their act has no peer.

A novelty act is that of Maude Caswell and Arthur Arnold, who come to the Orpheum next week. Their performance consists of a series of acrobatic feats combined with pantomimic comedy.

LOS ANGELES, CAL, FRIDAY, JUNE 23, 1899.

"KING OF HANDCUFFS" AT THE POLICE STATION

Houdini Mystifies the Police by Freeing Himself From the Strongest Shackles.

Should a young Austrian named H. Houdini, temporarily sojourning in this city, ever have the misfortune to fall into the hands of the Los Angeles police, it is safe to say that they will not trust to shackles and ropes in controlling him, but will keep him well in hand. Even then it is not certain that he would not escape, if he wished to, judging from his performance at the central station today.

Houdini, who, by the way, commences an engagement at the Orpheum next week, modestly calls himself the "king of handcuffs," and he demonstrated his right to the title in an unmistakable manner today. Shortly after 11 o'clock, Houdini, with his press agent and one or two newspaper men, put in an appearance at Chief Glass's office, and announced that he was ready for the test. He brought with him several shackles of his own, but these were dispensed with, and, after getting an "Oregon boot" from the station stock, the Chief and the visitors made their way to the assembly room on the third floor.

The noon watch was just getting ready to go out, but the appearance of the visitors temporarily suspended operations, and the men crowded around the man for whom handcuffs had no terrors, and who is making a fortune showing people how easy it is to escape shackles—if you only know how.

Houdini wasted no time in preliminaries, but removing his long-tailed coat and rolling up his shirt sleeves, announced that he was ready to proceed. But before doing so he told the men that he would show them a little trick just to put them in a good humor. He then produced a paper of needles, which he opened, and, after asking every one to look into his somewhat capacious mouth to see that he had nothing concealed therein, he calmly swallowed the needles—at least it looked as though he did. He then produced a spool of thread, and breaking off a length, rolled it up and swallowed that. After a few seconds he threw his head back, and fishing about for the end of the thread in his mouth, drew it forth with all the needles threaded upon it, while the policemen crowded around in open-eyed wonder.

Apparently refreshed by his novel diet, Houdini announced himself ready for the great test. He removed his own shoe, and the "Oregon boot" was securely locked upon his right leg. Four separate pairs of handcuffs were then locked on his arms, which were then handcuffed to an extra pair of irons, which had been placed on his legs. Captain Bradish superintended this work and expressed himself as satisfied that the man was as securely shackled as it was possible to do it.

Six and a half minutes were consumed in putting on the irons, and then a couple of stalwart policemen picked Houdini up bodily and carried him into an adjoining room and shut the door.

The men crowded around the door listening for any sound from the inside. At the end of three minutes a thump was heard, and the remark was made, "There goes the boot," and about a minute later Houdini opened the door and walked out with the boot and the handcuffs in his arms, all the cuffs being interlocked, showing that they had been unlocked and then relocked. The trick was done in just four minutes and ten seconds from the time Houdini entered the room, and the test was regarded as conclusive.

Houdini then amused the men by getting out of any pair of handcuffs they put on him in from ten to twenty seconds, and, after thanking them for their attention, left the building.

Of course, Houdini did not tell how the trick was done, and all sorts of guesses were made as to how the feat was accomplished. But only one man was thoroughly satisfied, and that was "Commodore" Hill. He did not guess anything about it. "I tell you, boys, it is the spirits," said the Commodore. "I have seen the same thing dozens of times at spiritual meetings, and there can't nobody do these things but spirits, I tell you."

Houdini declined to either deny or affirm the Commodore's declaration, and told the boys they could figure it out for themselves.

In the early days of his career, Houdini apparently claimed to be an Austrian as noted in these articles from 1899 & 1900.

The Call

SATURDAY..............JUNE 3, 1899.

SAN FRANCISCO

KING OF HANDCUFFS MYSTIFIES POLICE

HARRY HOUDINI is a performer known throughout the profession as "King of Handcuffs." That he is entitled to the appellation was demonstrated yesterday afternoon in the assembly room of the Central police station, when he did some marvelous tricks with the darbies and shackles locked on his dapper person by several of the 400 policemen surrounding him.

Houdini has been performing similar feats for years in the large cities of America, and carries with him letters attesting his prowess from the Chiefs of Police of Chicago, St. Paul and Omaha. He claims that there is no handcuff extant from which he cannot release himself, and his performance yesterday went far to establish the truth of the assertion. By invitation of Houdini and the management of the Orpheum, at which theater he makes his first appearance to-morrow afternoon, and with the consent of Chief Lees, Captains Wittman and Spillane invited the men under them to witness the performance of the "King of the Handcuffs," which was timed to coincide with the change of watches at 5 o'clock. At that hour the assembly room was crowded, except a small space in the center occupied by a table, to which Houdini was conducted.

The young man, who claims Austria as the land of his nativity, began by telling the assembled bluecoats that they had nothing in the way of irons that would hold him. Next he produced a deck of cards, and, claiming to be "some punkins" with the pasteboards, he proved his boast by doing some extraordinary cutting, shuffling and palming of the pack. At last he came to the handcuffs. Baring his arms and rolling up his trousers, he invited manacles from any policeman in the crowd—the more the merrier. Four pairs of cuffs as many different makes were fastened on his wrists, while two pairs of legirons, brought by Detective Harry Reynolds from the "upper office," were fastened to his legs.

It took six minutes to secure him in this fashion, and he was so trussed up that he could not walk. He asked that he be carried into a vacant room and left to his own devices to rid himself of the fetters. This apartment, just off the assembly room, had been provided by Captain Wittman, and into it Houdini was carried by Patrolmen Bakulich, Wilson and Phillips. Wittman stood guard at the door.

At the end of seven minutes by the watch Houdini emerged, free of irons, and was loudly applauded.

"How do you do it?" asked a big policeman.

"Oh, I just sneak out of them," was the reply, although it is doubtful if Houdini does, as his wrists and ankles are small and his hands and feet undeniably large. There are only two methods, he claims, of getting rid of shackles, with keys or with springs. Which of the methods does he use? Or is there another?

15 Cents. Automobilism in America. Admiral Dewey's Home.
Miss Ellen Terry.
15 Cents.

METROPOLITAN

NEW YORK. JANUARY, 1900.

HOW GAMBLERS FLEECE VICTIMS.

One of the methods employed by gamblers to fleece their dupes is shown in the accompanying illustrations. A mechanical device is employed to carry cards up the sleeve of the operator. Houdini, an Austrian, who has met with much success in the United States as a "card manipulator," states that there are only twenty of these devices in existence, and they cost £35 each. It consists of an extension frame with a spring grip at the end of it, into

ODD ACTU

with the card which is to be "sleeved" in the palm; the third shows the card inserted in the clip ready to be drawn under the sleeve; the fourth shows the clip closed, with the card safely under cover. When the desired number of

FIG. 1.

FIG. 3.

FIG. 4.

which a card, or a number of cards, can be slipped at pleasure whenever it is extended within reach of the palm. It is operated by an appliance strapped to the chest of the operator and worked by respiration. Drawing in the breath and expelling it extends and contracts the card clip attachment, which is strapped to the bare arm under the coat sleeve, at the will of the operator. The first figure shows the machine contracted; the second shows it extended,

cards have been manipulated in this way to suit the gambler's wishes, the set is thrown back into the hand, with, of course, disastrous consequences to his opponent, and perfect security apparently against discovery of the cheat.

FIG. 2.

This is Photo of my arm article copied from Frisco Chronicle. June 11 – 1899 original in front of Book.

THE RECORD

Nos. 917 and 919 Chestnut Street.

WILLIAM M. SINGERLY

EDITOR AND PUBLISHER FROM 1877 to 1898.

Philadelphia, February 6, 1900.

Minnie Seligman, Parisian Farce and Houdini—Keith's.

Concerning Houdini, the King of the Handcuffs, his preliminary seance at the City Hall is elsewhere reported. He is certainly a wonderful manipulator of the wristlets, and is a master trickster as well. His lightning exchange of places with Mlle. Houdini, at Keith's yesterday, involving the displacement and rearrangement of wrist-shackles, tie and sealed bag, and locked trunk, was as mystifying a cabinet trick as we have ever witnessed.

HE LAUGHS AT HANDCUFFS.

Houdini Easily Frees Himself From Intricate "Irons."

Henry Houdini, known as the "Handcuff King," gave an exhibition at the Detective Bureau in the City Hall yesterday afternoon. Chief of Detectives Miller fastened a pair of leg-irons of the latest make about Houdini's ankles and a pair of handcuffs about his wrists, the hands being held behind the operator's back. Houdini had stripped off his clothing and was examined by a physician to show that he had nothing concealed by which he might unfasten the manacles. As an extra precaution a piece of court plaster was put over his mouth.

Houdini withdrew behind a screen, and in one minute and a half he was free from the handcuffs and leg-irons. The other tests were equally successful, Houdini unlocking the manacles in each case. Chief Miller said the tests were unusually severe, owing to the intricate construction of the "irons," which were of the very latest manufacture. He further declared that he didn't believe there was a handcuff made that would not yield to Houdini's cleverness. Hou-

4 The European Sensation

The Houdinis sailed for England with no bookings, but with the strong conviction that they would be a smash hit. They proved to be correct. An early publicity break in which Houdini escaped from the handcuffs of London's Scotland Yard made his name a household word and launched the most triumphant period of his career. Houdini was not to perform again in America for over five years.

During these years in Europe, Houdini played the largest and best theaters in England, Germany, France and Russia, sometimes making over $2000 for a single weeks' work in days when a good meal cost less than a dollar and there were virtually no income taxes.

While playing in Germany, Houdini developed a publicity stunt that would serve him well for the rest of his career. This was the famous bridge jump in which the escape artist, handcuffed and chained, leapt from a bridge into the local harbor or river, only to escape from his restraints while under water. There is some evidence that Houdini had long had the idea for this sensational publicity stunt in mind, and was simply waiting for an opportunity to pull it off successfully. Gresham reports that as far back as September 14, 1899, there was an announcement that Houdini, then performing in St. Louis, was to jump from the Eads Bridge while locked in irons. Presumably, the local police interfered with the stunt, as there are no follow-up clippings in Houdini's scrapbooks, clippings he certainly would have saved if the bridge jump had garnered the expected publicity.

According to reports, Houdini was also refused permission to do the dive in Germany but he eluded the police and did the stunt anyway. This anecdote, told in several Houdini biographies, has the ring of much of the deliberately constructed legend, but nevertheless, the bridge jump became one of the most popular standard challenges and was repeated hundreds of times in the course of his career.

Houdini showed his usual genius for devising unusual publicity challenges in each city he played. For example, while playing in Holland with the famous Corty-Althoff circus, Houdini had himself tied to the blade of a Dutch windmill with the idea that he was to free himself while the arms turned in

Houdini played the best theatres in Europe at a star's salary. Here he rides in a motor car (front seat, right) in front of the Circus Busch in Germany where he was a sensation.

An old herald, used about ten years ago by the English Music Hall. BARRASFORD'S

NOTE: Telephone 4110 4111

Hippodrome, Sheffield

Resident Manager Mr. P. R. ELBOURNE

NOTE: Telephone 4110 4111

HOUDINI

IS COMING ON JULY 26th

July 26th

July 26th

July 26th

Book your Seats now for the most Sensational and Marvellous Act of the Century

THE WORLD'S HANDCUFF KING AND AMAZING PRISON BREAKER.

BOLTS, BARS, LOCKS, CHAINS AND PRISONS DEFIED

HOW DOES HE DO IT?

MYSTERY! MYSTERY! MYSTERY! MYSTERY!

Has performed before Royalty in every country of the world

A handbill from the days of Houdini's early success in Europe.

the air. Windmills were not so strongly constructed as Houdini had assumed, and the blade snapped off, with the daredevil fortunately sustaining only minor bruises. While it didn't turn out exactly the way Houdini had planned, the incident resulted in favorable news coverage and helped to pack theaters in which Houdini played.

One of Houdini's most widely reported challenge escapes was from the Siberian Prison Van during his Russian tour in 1903. The portable steel cells, lined with zinc and mounted on a wagon body, were pulled by teams of horses and used to transport prisoners to Siberia. The story of the escape has been told many times both in Houdini's own publicity and in the biographies. It remains one of his escapes about which the real method is pure conjecture. The explanation subscribed to by several biographers seems to be impossible to me. It can be traced to an English book published in the 1930s that claims to explain the methods of Houdini's escapes. The author contends that Houdini cut his way out of the Siberian van through a portion of the zinc floor with a small can opener and then sawed through the wooden floorboards beneath with a tiny hacksaw. The method that the author proposes for the way Houdini obtained these instruments is even more absurd. Houdini had been thoroughly stripped and given an even more rigorous examination than usual by the Russian police. This author says that Bess had the tools secreted in her mouth and passed them to the naked Houdini as she gave him a farewell kiss through the bars of the locked van! It must be allowed that a can opener and a hacksaw make quite a mouthful, no matter how miniaturized. Even if they had been somehow passed to Houdini, however, a later examination of the van would almost surely have revealed the method of escape, and this was something Houdini was always especially careful to conceal in order to avoid unfavorable followup publicity.

A more plausible explanation of this feat is offered by Milbourne Christopher, who conjectures that Houdini probably reached through the small barred window of the van and picked the lock. How he could have obtained the pick is not known; perhaps *that* was in Bess' mouth during the farewell kiss. (The "key in the mouth" story is a favorite

Another Houdini feature was the straitjacket escape in which the police trussed him in regulation jacket from which, after great struggle, he would escape.

A still photograph from a film showing a Houdini prison escape. This film was shown in advance of a Houdini appearance in European theatres. It was particularly useful as advance publicity in cities where local authorities would not cooperate with Houdini in his spectacular stunts.

element in the Houdini legend, popping up here and there in different circumstances.) Christopher also astutely observed that in the lithograph made to publicize the feat in other countries, the window of the van is shown smaller than it really was, and higher above the lock. Very possibly it is a clever example of Houdini covering his traces!

Houdini also added new challenges to his regular stage act during his European tour. One of these was the escape from a sealed packing box supplied by a merchant in each city where he played. The challenge was always widely advertised in hand-bills and by the local press, and the box, both before and after the escape, was placed on display in front of the theater. Another Houdini feature was the strait-jacket escape in which the police or officers of a local mental institution trussed Houdini in a regulation straitjacket from which, in full view and after great struggle, he managed to escape.

The tour was a triumph, with theaters fighting for Houdini's services. Booked to appear at a certain date in one city, Houdini was often creating such a sensation in another city that the theater managers there wanted to hold him over for additional weeks of sell-out business. Telegrams were exchanged, holdover clauses in the contract were written up, and Houdini, only a few years out of the dime museums, reveled in the fact that the top European theaters were clamoring for him. Of course, he made capital of this situation. In order to fill all the engagements he was offered, Houdini summoned Theo to come to Europe and outfitted him with a similar escape act under the name of "Hardeen." Theo successfully played in England and Europe for over seven years. Audiences never knew that the two escape artists, often playing in competition to one another, were really brothers.

Houdini's challenge escapes from the police handcuffs, the prison vans and other official re-straints on his European tour were more than the mysterious tricks of a music hall illusionist. They were a symbolic challenge to authority and to the government officials that Europeans, at that time, had good reason to fear. When Houdini triumphed over the minions of the czar or the kaiser, figures of which many of his audiences lived in terror, he was doing something that they, in their secret dreams, wished to do. At no time did Houdini more embody this dream than when, in 1902, he sued the imperial police of Cologne, Germany and won.

A German police officer had accused Houdini of fraud in a newspaper article, saying that he could not live up to his advertised claims and escape from any restraint. When the case came to court, Houdini escaped from chains in full view of the courtroom. The case was appealed, and an inventor brought in a special lock that he claimed could never be opened once it was closed. Houdini opened it in four and a half minutes. He sued for an apology—and he got it. The policeman was ordered to pay a fine or serve a jail sentence and to pay the costs of the trials. Furthermore, the results of the verdict were to be published in the Cologne newspapers at the officer's expense.

The triumphant Houdini had a new poster made that proclaimed an "Apology in the name of King Wilhelm II, Kaiser of Germany." Houdini had

The police of America join the gendarmerie of Europe in declaring

NOTHING ON EARTH :: :: CAN :: :: HOLD HIM A PRISONER

"Nothing on earth can hold him a prisoner." All the strongest cells and prisons in the United States have succumbed to the mysteriously potent force he exerts. Perhaps his most historic feat was his escape last January, 1906, from Cell 2, Condemned Murderer's Row in the United States Jail at Washington, D. C., the very cell in which Guiteau, the assassin of President Garfield was confined until he was led forth to be hanged. Another great work was his escape from double confinements in the Boston Tombs at Boston, Mass., March 20th, 1906.

SOME of the GREAT FEATS ACCOMPLISHED by HOUDINI

Broke out of the Siberian Prison Van, in Moscow, Russia, in May, 1903.

Leaped, heavily handcuffed, in zero weather, from Belle Island Bridge, in Detroit, Mich.; on December 2nd, 1906, and released himself under the icy water.

Leaped into San Francisco Bay, San Francisco, Calif., on August 26th, 1907, handcuffed with hands behind his back, with more than seventy-five pounds of ball and chain locked to his body.

Had he been unable to release himself it would have caused his death.

Escaped from a plate glass box made by the Pittsburg Plate Glass Company, and did not even scratch the glass. Boston, Mass., January 20th, 1907.

After being riveted into a large hot water boiler by the employees of the Marine Boiler Works, of Toledo, Ohio, on March 15th, 1907, Houdini escaped without leaving any traces of his exit. It required over an hour for him to effect his release.

Escaped from paper bags, zinc lined piano boxes, packing cases, padded cells, straight-jackets, insane cribs, willow hampers, iron cages, a U. S. mail pouch furnished with a rotary lock belonging to the U. S. Government, a large football, made by Reach Company of Philadelphia, a large Derby desk with secret locks, etc., etc.

Since his return from Europe Houdini has escaped from cells in almost every city in America, the most notable ones being from the Murderer's Cell, in the U. S. Jail at Washington, D. C., which confined Guiteau, the murderer of President Garfield.

Laughs at . . . . .

Jeers at . . . . .

Sneers at efforts to

Chief of the Secret Police LEBEDOEFF has HOUDINI stripped stark and searched then locked the Siberian Transport Carette, May 10/1903 in and in 28 minutes HOUDI made his escape to t speakable astonishment Russian Police . . . .

HOUDINI

The Magician

HOUDINI

The Marvel of

The Wizard of

The Demon of t

The Mystic of

NOTHING CAN HOLD

triumphed over one German policeman who was foolish enough to libel him. In his posters and in the stories told ever after that event, Houdini had triumphed over the Imperial Police and, by implication, the kaiser himself. In fact, in a later embellishment of the tale, he claimed that a third test was added: Houdini was challenged to open an iron safe. Approaching the massive door with trepidation, Houdini pulled and it swung open. The officials had forgotten to lock it! There is no evidence that this actually happened, but it adds an amusing "kicker"

to an already good story. To the audiences of Germany Houdini was a hero. He had challenged the fearsome police, symbols of oppressive officialdom and representatives of the kaiser himself, and he had won. No wonder they flocked to the theater to see him and applaud him.

When Houdini returned to America with his scrapbooks full of sensational publicity and with box-office records as proof that the publicity paid off, he was ready to make his place as a vaudeville headliner.

incarcerate

ains and ba

m in priso

IOUDINI

The

Magician

IOUDINI

· · ·

ains

s

rld

OTHING !

<table>
<tr><td>You must
see
HOUDINI</td><td>An
astounding
and
bewildering
sensation
❖
The
greatest act
in existence</td><td>You
may never
get another
chance</td></tr>
</table>

BOOK NOW! BOOK NOW!
or you will regret it

:: :: THE ORIGINAL :: ::

HANDCUFF KING AND JAIL BREAKER

The only living being who ever escaped from the **Siberian Transport Van** in Russia, and who has also **escaped** from the **strongest prisons** in all parts of the World. Introducing his latest invention, that of escaping out of an **air-tight galvanised iron can** filled to the brim with water, and **locked** with **six padlocks!** Houdini's remarkable ability to **remain under water a long time** is one of the resources which enable him to accomplish this **extraordinary** trick.

Everybody invited to bring their own Padlocks.

We urge upon you the necessity for Booking your Seats. During his tour round the world thousands have been disappointed through their failure to do so

BOOK NOW! BOOK NOW! BOOK NOW!

Once his reputation was made in Europe, Houdini returned triumphal to America where theater managers were now begging for his services.

The Spectacular Challenges

The years 1905 to 1907 found Houdini as a star in the top vaudeville theaters of America doing the same acts (the straitjacket, the challenge handcuff escapes and Metamorphosis) for $1,200 a week that he and Bess had performed for $12 a week only a few years before. To keep his name constantly in the headlines, he regularly performed the challenges that had worked so well for him in Europe—the "naked test" jail breaks during the cold months of the year and the bridge jumps during the warm months. It was during one of these standard challenges, which had become routine procedures for Houdini in each town that he played, that one of the most popular stories in the Houdini myth had its inception, that of the famous Belle Isle bridge jump. It is illuminating to see how the master showman turned an unforeseen circumstance into the most widely quoted publicity story of his career.

The week of November 26, 1906, Houdini was playing the Temple Theatre in Detroit, Michigan. The weather was cold, and it was the time of year when Houdini arranged jail breaks in each city, not bridge jumps. According to Milbourne Christopher, Houdini's original plan was to escape from the Wayne County jail. On the first day of the run, Houdini made a preliminary casing of the jail, something he always did before agreeing to an escape so that he could formulate, in advance, an absolutely sure method of release. To his chagrin, he discovered that it would be impossible for him to escape without outside help. All the cells in the block were locked with one sliding bar, and the lock on the bars was at the end of a corridor far from the cell where Houdini was to be confined. There was no way he could reach the lock and open it. On the spur of the moment he decided not to do a jail escape but to do a bridge jump. He apparently didn't tell Bess about this decision, for she would have strenuously objected to his performing such a stunt in winter weather.

The next day at lunch hour, a large crowd of Detroiters had gathered to see Houdini make the jump. The stunt made the front page of the *Detroit News* that evening. Houdini had been handcuffed with "two of the best and latest model handcuffs of the Detroit Police Department" when he made the jump, and a 113-foot lifeline was tied around his waist and to the bridge, to safeguard against accident. The story reports that Houdini, "nerved by the confidence of a lion in his own powers," released himself from the handcuffs while under water, swam to a waiting boat, handed over the cuffs and climbed

aboard. Except for the cold weather it was no more remarkable than any of the other jumps that Houdini had routinely performed in cities all over the world. When a shivering but otherwise unscathed Houdini arrived back at his hotel room, Bess was furious that he should do such a stunt in the middle of winter, but at the theater, the result was packed houses.

By the time the story had been told and retold by Houdini to countless newspaper reporters, it had become a legend. Houdini usually gave December 2 as the date, not November 27, when it actually took place. He said the temperature was zero, when actually the temperature on the day of the jump was well above freezing. And he claimed that the Detroit River was frozen solid and that a hole had to be chopped in the ice through which he plunged. Four minutes passed without any sign of Houdini, and the police were of the opinion that he had perished in the icy water. After five minutes a lifeline was thrown in and reporters hurried back to their papers with the news that the Great Houdini had failed his final test. After eight minutes, all hope had been abandoned, when suddenly, Houdini's head appeared from beneath the waters and he was pulled to safety.

Later, Houdini explained how he had survived so long under the icy waters. When he plunged into the water, a strong current caught him and carried him along under the ice. Suddenly he realized that he couldn't find the hole in the ice through which he had originally plunged. Free of the cuffs, he remained calm and noticed that there was a tiny airspace between the ice and the water. By floating on his back he was able to breathe the air in the space and save himself until he found the hole again. In the Kellock biography, where the Houdini legend reaches its fullest flower, the tale is embellished even further, with Bess waiting anxiously in her hotel room as she hears newsboys in the street crying, "Extra! Extra! Houdini Dead! Extra! Houdini Drowned in River!" Bess sends out for a paper only to have Houdini burst in the door. "His head was still dripping and he was blue with cold, but he was alive." It was also told that in anticipation of just such a wintertime bridge jump, Houdini had been practicing by filling the oversized bathtub of his New York home with water and blocks of ice and submerging himself in order to accustom his body to such low temperatures. There may be at least a partial element of truth in this part of the story, for the old Houdini home, which is still standing at 278 West 113th Street in New York, contains such an oversized tub (with the initials H. H. set in the tile above it) where Houdini undoubtedly practiced holding his breath under water in preparation for his many underwater challenges.

By pointing out the ways in which the legend of Houdini differs from the actual events of his life, I am in no way attempting to discredit the real accomplishments of this remarkable man. His actual exploits performed day in and day out over a period of forty years are enough to ensure his greatness. My purpose is to try to unearth some clues as to how the Houdini legend developed. The fact that this legend continues to grow proves its power and appeal. The almost totally fictionalized George Pal movie of 1954, starring Tony Curtis as Houdini and his wife Janet Leigh as Bess, has added to the legend, as did the theatrical musical *Man of Magic*, produced in London's West End. E. L. Doctorow's 1975 best seller *Ragtime* includes Houdini as a major character, also in highly fictionalized form and, at the time of this writing, at least two other movies about him, one for theatrical release and another intended for television, are in preparation. All of these will add to the Houdini legend as well as to our historical knowledge of the man.

I'm reminded of something Houdini wrote in his book *The Unmasking of Robert-Houdin*, which reveals his philosophy on the Houdini legend we've been exploring. "The secret of showmanship," he said, "consists not of what you really do, but what the mystery-loving public thinks you do."

In addition to the standard jail and underwater escapes, Houdini devised special escapes that were offered to him as challenges by merchants and local organizations in each city he played. Many of these were very colorful and ingenious in nature, and when it was announced from the stage and in advertisements that a particular challenge would be met later in the week, it would often bring patrons back into the theater to see Houdini for a second time. There were literally hundreds of these challenges. Many of them were variations of the packing box escape, with local firms building a crate, normally used to transport whatever merchandise they manufactured. The

When, in 1908, another name appeared *above* Houdini's on a marquee, he reasoned the public had tired of his handcuff escapes and challenges. He created a new escape in which he was submerged in a water-filled galvanized container. The Milk Can Escape was a sensation and put Houdini, once again, at the top of the bill.

Houdini didn't limit himself to on-stage theatrics. His off-stage exploits often brought him the publicity he always sought. His interest in aviation led him to succeed in the first sustained airplane flight in Australia on March 16, 1910, at Diggers Rest for which he received this trophy.

result was publicity for the firm as well as for Houdini's performance. Houdini also escaped from paper bags (without tearing the paper), zinc-lined piano boxes, padded cells, U.S. mail pouches, coffins, straitjackets of many different designs, a large football made by a local sporting goods manufacturer, a roll-top desk, various burglar-proof safes, wet packs used to subdue the violently insane, a plate glass box made by the Pittsburgh Plate Glass Company, a diving suit, and various types of steel boilers.

Perhaps Houdini's most surrealistic escape (not without its biblical overtones) was performed in Boston in 1911, when he was shackled and then chain-laced inside the embalmed body of a giant sea monster weighing several tons. This creature had been beached near Cape Cod and was trucked to the theater for Houdini's feat. Houdini accepted another equally dramatic challenge on February 14, 1911—to escape while lashed to a cannon with a burning fire set to go off in twenty minutes! The challenge grimly reminded him that "if you fail to release yourself within that time you will be blown to Kingdom Come." As usual, he did not disappoint his audience—he released himself with three minutes to spare.

All of these challenges were genuine in that the restraints were honestly built by the challengers in order to defeat the escape artist. The often melodramatic ideas for the escapes were usually Houdini's, and a local merchant or civic group was approached to formally offer Houdini the challenge and to build the particular restraining device to his specifications. Houdini was not in business to fail, and he didn't accept challenges he was not absolutely sure he could meet.

Houdini's entire career was a constant struggle to keep on top and to keep his name perpetually in front of the public. When he created a feature that resulted in packed houses, he was immediately followed by many imitators attempting to cash in on his success. When this happened, there was nothing he could do but drop that feature from his act and try to come up with something even more sensational. And somehow he always did.

Houdini had made his early fame as the Handcuff King, but by 1908 vaudeville was glutted with challenge handcuff escape acts, and Houdini was forced to drop the cuffs from his program. Something had to be done: he was failing to draw full houses, and at one theater, early in 1908, another name appeared above his on a theater marquee. Houdini reasoned that the public was getting tired of the cuffs and the various challenges and that they now accepted that he could get out of anything. He needed something different, a new feature to draw them into the theaters. And so he created the milk can escape, in which he was submerged inside a giant galvanized iron can. The can was then filled to the brim with water and the lid was padlocked to the top of the can. Audiences were reminded that "failure means a drowning death." The milk can escape proved the sensation he hoped it would be and, once again, Houdini was "next to closing" (the coveted feature spot) on vaudeville bills all over the world. Houdini took the can with him in 1908 on his tour of England and Germany, and it remained a feature of his act for the next four years. By 1912, the catalogues of magic supply houses were full of versions of the milk can escape, and once again Houdini had to come up with a new, sensational feature: the Chinese water torture cell.

This struggle to keep constantly ahead of his competitors can also be detected in the evolution of Houdini's outdoor publicity stunts. In the first part of his career, his standard publicity pullers were the "naked test" jail break and the bridge jump. Soon other performers started doing similar feats, and so

Houdini introduced the underwater box escape. When the box escape also began to be duplicated, Houdini created what was perhaps his biggest crowd puller of all, the straitjacket escape, which he performed hanging upside down, suspended several stories above a city street!

Houdini's outstanding showmanship was not confined to his escapes alone. The magic portion of his stage act also contained that unforgettable quality of performance that made people talk about it even if they had not actually seen him in person. During the season of 1918, for instance, Houdini appeared at New York's gigantic Hippodrome Theatre, and boasted that on the largest stage in the world he was performing both the smallest and largest feats of magic. At one point in his act, Houdini swallowed two hundred separate needles and one hundred and ten feet of thread. Then, after having his mouth examined to prove that nothing was concealed inside, he pulled up the thread with all of the needles threaded at intervals along it. On the same program he made a five-ton elephant disappear. At another time, when playing Hammerstein's Victoria Theatre in New York, Houdini featured the illusion of walking through a brick wall. These feats (except for the needles, which was a standard part of his repertoire) were performed for only a short time, but it was enough that he had done them. They became important parts of the legend.

Sometimes one of Houdini's "extracurricular" activities brought him as much publicity as his sensational escapes. One of these was his brief flirtation with aviation. While touring Germany in 1909, Houdini became interested in flying and (for $5000) bought his own plane and tried learning to fly it. Airplane flight was still in its infancy in those days, and so it was a miracle to make a sustained flight of only a few minutes. Houdini had a long-standing booking to appear in Australia, and when he sailed there, early in 1910, he took his plane with him, along with the French mechanic who had taught him to fly. The rest is aviation history—on March 16 at Diggers Rest, Australia, Houdini made the first sustained airplane flight on that continent. Five days later he set a new time record, staying in the air seven minutes and thirty-seven seconds at an altitude of almost one hundred feet. During the tour, Houdini also learned to drive a car. After leaving Australia, he neither drove nor flew again.

Houdini made his Australian flight in this German biplane maintained by French mechanic, Brassic, who had taught Houdini to fly.

The Aerial League of Australia
(N.S.W. SECTION)

"WHAT THE WORLD IS DOING IN AERIAL
CONQUEST"

TOWN HALL, FRIDAY NEXT, APRIL 29th, 8 p.m. *1909*

Brilliant Cinematograph views of the World's Recent Great Aerial Achievements
including FIRST FLIGHT IN AUSTRALIA BY MR. HOUDINI
(to whom the League's Trophy will be presented)

Exciting Demonstration of Flying Models by Commonwealth Prize Entrants.

Admission : ONE SHILLING.   League Members Free.   Booking Plan at Paling's, 6d. extra.

Join the League and encourage Australia's Aerial Defence.   Membership Fee, Five Shillings per year
with Free Admission to all Entertainments.
GEORGE A. TAYLOR, Hon. Sec., 74a Pitt Street.

**Photographs of Houdini's aerial accomplishment
were included in lectures on the new sensation,
flying (inscribed 1909 date is incorrect. The
year was 1910).**

**Houdini tried his hand at the movies making a
thirteen-episode serial, *The Master Mystery* and
four feature films, *The Man from Beyond* and
Haldane of the Secret Service for his own
production company and *The Grim Game* and
Terror Island for Paramount-Artcraft.**

Another fascination of Houdini's for several
years was the infant art of the motion picture.
Always with an eye for good publicity, Houdini had
made it a practice to have his more spectacular
outdoor escape feats recorded on film. During his
Australian tour, movies of several of his bridge jumps
opened the act before Houdini, in the flesh, made his
entrance. Some of his airplane flights were also
filmed. It was inevitable that he would eventually go
to Hollywood to become a film star. Ironically,
Houdini, a great mythmaker, was unsuccessful in
coping with the greatest mythmaker of its time, the
movies. His hair dyed black and wearing make-up
that today seems grotesque even by early silent film
standards, Houdini proved a wooden actor, adept at
recreating his most daring escapes for the camera, but
plodding and uninspired in dramatic scenes and
embarrassingly ill at ease in love scenes. He made a
thirteen-episode serial (*The Master Mystery*) and four
subsequent features (*The Grim Game* and *Terror Island*
for Paramount-Artcraft and *The Man from Beyond* and
Haldane of the Secret Service for his own independent
production company), but none of them were great
successes. Somehow the Houdini charisma and
showmanship, so powerful in the live theater, did not
project from the silver screen.

**With his hair dyed black and wearing makeup
too heavy even for silent films, Houdini proved
a wooden actor unable to reach his audience. In
romantic scenes, he was embarrassing.**

An exciting moment in *Terror Island*.

In spite of their overall ineffectiveness, the Houdini movies did have their moments, and of course it is exciting to be able to see the master escape artist actually doing some of his most physically grueling feats. Houdini's rescue of the heroine from the rapids of Niagara Falls in *The Man from Beyond* is a thriller even by today's movie standards and compares favorably with the somewhat similar rescue on the ice in D. W. Griffith's classic *Way Down East*.

The midair collision of two airplanes in *The Grim Game*, actually an unforeseen accident that was captured on film and incorporated into the movie, is a thrilling screen moment and offers another illuminating example of Houdini's genius for building his own legend. The original idea for the scene was that Houdini would transfer from one plane to another dangling from a rope some 3,000 feet in the air. The two planes accidentally collided and plummeted to earth. Miraculously, no one was injured but the resulting footage was proclaimed in the movie ads to be "The Greatest Thrill in the Greatest Thrill Picture Ever Made!" Here is Houdini's telling of the story:

I was 3,000 feet up in an airplane circling above another machine. The plan was for me to drop from my plane into the cockpit of the other by means of a rope. I was dangling from the rope end ready for the leap. Suddenly the two planes crashed together, the propellers locked, and we started plunging downwards towards the earth—and Eternity. I was helpless—but strangly unafraid. A lifetime passed in an instant. The crash will come. I shall be gone. But

An actual collision of two airplanes occurred during the filming of *The Grim Game* and was incorporated into the film. Houdini was presumed to have been in the collision but was actually safe on the ground.

HOUDINI IN "THE GRIM GAME" A PARAMOUNT-ARTCR

it is not all. There is another life. There must be! was the comforting thought in my head. But fate ruled otherwise. By a miracle we righted into a half glide, and though they were smashed into splinters by their terrific impact with the ground, I was miraculously unhurt.

The story is retold without so much dramatic detail in the Kellock biography, but we are told of Bess and Houdini's airplane mechanic, Brassac, rushing in a car to the site of the crash—a swamp—and pulling the uninjured but half suffocated Houdini from the mud.

The real story, called one of Houdini's "best-kept secrets," was that he was not in the crash at all. A few years ago, the director of the film, Irvin Willat, described what happened: The script did call for Houdini to make the death-defying leap and, characteristically, he was perfectly willing to do it. Willat, however, had other ideas. He wasn't about to risk the life of his star in a dangerous stunt. "Houdini thought he was going to do it," said Willat, "but he was a very intelligent man and gave me no argument when I told him he wasn't." The man dangling from the rope was actually a young stuntman named Robert Kennedy, one of a group of World War I fliers who worked on airplane films in Hollywood after the war. (He is still alive and living in California.) Even though it was the stuntman who actually performed the feat, the story of the midair collision, but with Houdini as the central character, was too good not to be incorporated into the legend.

Houdini as he appeared in a tense scene in *The Grim Game.*

Houdini made a practice of being friendly with local officials eliciting their cooperation in his publicity stunts. Posing for pictures with fire and police chiefs was standard practice. Houdini would take advantage of any event that would lead to good publicity. In Kansas City, he and Hardeen posed with the fire department and a group of midgets.

Kansas City
... also Honolu...

6 Inquiry into the World Beyond

After his movie career was over, Houdini continued to tour in vaudeville, and the fact that many in his audience had also seen him on the screen probably helped at the box office. His features were still the water torture cell on stage, and the upside-down straitjacket escape as an outdoor crowd-puller. But his interest turned to something new, the possibility of surviving after death. "There is another life, there must be!" read the fictitious account of the air crash. And it was this theme that became the predominant one for the last six years of his life. Perhaps this was prompted by the death of his beloved mother, a blow from which many felt he never fully recovered, or by his strange friendship with Sir Arthur Conan Doyle, an impassioned champion of spiritualism. At any rate, Houdini became increasingly obsessed with the possibility of survival after death. Even the advertisements from his second to last feature film, *The Man from Beyond* (written by him and produced by the Houdini Picture Company) have a picture of Houdini pointing and asking the question, "Dare you say there is no life after death?"

This question, while undoubtedly of deep personal concern to Houdini, supplied him with the last great crowd-puller of his long career. Houdini, both in England and the United States, investigated hundreds of so-called mediums. He found that all were either totally self-deluded or outright frauds. I feel that Houdini really wanted to believe in a level of reality beyond the one we normally experience, but that he could find no evidence for belief in the spirit phenomenon he was witnessing. He probably also remembered his early starving days in show business, when he had used similar techniques to bamboozle a gullible public. Even when Lady Conan Doyle, an undoubtedly sincere believer, apparently contacted Houdini's dead mother through "automatic writing," Houdini found little in the message indicating that it was anything more than the ramblings of a self-deluded mind.

Disillusioned by the fraud and gullibility that he saw around him, Houdini launched into a crusade against spirit mediums and, in 1922, at a time when

Houdini was introduced to many of the mediums he investigated through Sir Arthur Conan Doyle, a champion of spiritualism. When Houdini's condemnation of fraudulent spiritualists became strident, Conan Doyle found it impossible to maintain their friendship. Conan Doyle always believed Houdini himself had supernatural powers. London, c 1920.

"Spirit photography" was one of the many mediums' tricks exposed by Houdini. In this widely-circulated photograph, Houdini appears with a myriad of "spirit" faces.

his career seemed once again to be slipping, his exposés of spiritualistic fraud again established him firmly at the very top of big-time show business. Houdini was a showman—he knew that he had found something like the challenges, the straitjacket, the milk can or the torture cell that would put him back into the headlines and fill theaters.

Houdini had started a serious investigation of spirit mediums as far back as 1920 when, during a tour of England, he met Conan Doyle and through his introductions attended literally hundreds of séances. By 1922 the denunciation of mediums had become a regular part of Houdini's stage act. At the same time, he helped set up and was a member of the *Scientific American* committee to investigate spirit mediums. The committee offered a $2,500 prize to any medium who, after being scrutinized by the committee, and naturally by Houdini himself, was found to be genuine.

With his usual flare for showmanship, Houdini came up with an act exposing the mediums that proved to be provocative entertainment. A committee from the audience was invited to the stage and blindfolded to simulate the darkness of the spirit medium's séance room. Then Houdini performed a séance in full light using all of the fraudulent mediums' standard tricks. The blindfolded committee, of course, was completely baffled while the audience saw how everything was done and how easily the "sitters" had been hoodwinked. In each city where Houdini played, he denounced and exposed local mediums and, in his spare time, he lectured to universities and police departments on psychic frauds.

Now nearing fifty years of age, he was pulling just as big headlines with his mediumistic exposures as he had years before by wriggling out of straitjackets or being tossed manacled into rivers. He made national headlines by posting a reward of five thousand dollars to any psychic who could produce physical phenomena which he could not duplicate by natural means. Inevitably, Houdini's friendship with Sir Arthur Conan Doyle, who had become as impassioned a spokesman for spiritualism as Houdini was against it, came to an end.

By 1924 the heyday of American vaudeville was drawing to a close, and Houdini knew it. For the first time in his career, Houdini didn't play in theaters—instead he was booked early in the year by the Coit-Albee Lyceum bureau for a series of twenty-four lectures in the Midwest. During the same year his book *A Magician Among the Spirits* was published. It

During a vacation with the Houdinis, Sir Arthur Conan Doyle requested Houdini to attend an "automatic writing" session with Lady Conan Doyle, who claimed to have contacted Houdini's mother. Though convinced of her sincerity, Houdini found nothing in the message "received" by Lady Conan Doyle to indicate it was in any way a communication from his dead mother.

June 25

TELEGRAMS:
CROWBOROUGH.
NAT. TEL. No. 77.

WINDLESHAM.

CROWBOROUGH.

SUSSEX.

My dear Houdini

That is very interesting. I am glad you got some results. It is certainly on the lowest & most mechanical plane of the spiritual world, or border line world, but at least it is beyond our present knowledge.

I am amused by your investigating with the S.P.R. Do they never think of investigating you?

My Crawford photos — the best of them — are away. I'll send them when I hear how long you will be in town. They are too precious to have lying around.

But I have something far more precious, two photos, one of a goblin, the other of four fairies taken in a Yorkshire wood. A fake! you will say. No, sir, I think not. However all inquiry will be made. These I can not be allowed to send.

All remembrance to the ladies.

Yours very sincerely

A Conan Doyle.

During the years of their friendship, Conan Doyle and Houdini exchanged many letters each promoting his side of the spiritualism argument.

was a scathing and well-documented exposure of most of the famous mediums of the day.

Nineteen twenty-four also proved a banner year for Houdini's exposure of several mediums who applied for the $2,500 award offered by the *Scientific American* committee. One such man was Nino Pecoraro, who produced phenomena while bound with seventy-five feet of rope. Houdini tied him up so that he couldn't escape, and no phenomenon occurred. Another medium was Joaquim Argamasilla, a young Spaniard who claimed to be able to see through solid metal. Houdini easily produced the effect and performed it later as a favorite parlor trick.

By far the most famous psychic to lock horns with Houdini was "Margery," the Boston medium. "Margery," whose real name was Mina Crandon, was the beautiful and charming wife of a prominent Boston surgeon, and certainly one of the most versatile mediums to ever appear on the psychic scene. Margery held séances in her posh Boston home just off Beacon Hill, performing for friends and believers, but never for money. During the sessions she levitated tables, produced psychic thumbprints in soft wax (that matched neither hers nor any of the sitters), materialized various ectoplasmic forms, and rang an specially made "bell box"—a bell wired to batteries inside would ring when the cover was depressed, apparently not by Margery. The fact that the Margery controversy still rages among believers, and that books are still being written about her, establishes her firmly as *the* psychic superstar of her day. After some fifty sittings with the medium, the *Scientific American* committee was so convinced that they were about to give her the $2,500 prize. At this point Houdini was called in. At his first sitting, the bell box rang and a "spirit trumpet" apparently floated in the air. No one could actually see the trumpet, but Margery's spirit guide "Walter" *said* it was floating. And when "Walter" (his voice coming from the medium) asked where he should hurl the trumpet, Houdini said, "toward me," and that is where it landed with a clatter. The other members of the committee were as astonished as ever. Houdini was not. Subsequent sittings served to confirm his suspicions. Houdini had felt the medium extend her foot to press the top of the bell box. He also showed how, under cover of darkness, and having momentarily released her hand from the person next to her, Margery had placed the trumpet on her head dunce-cap fashion, and flipped it off in the direction Houdini indicated.

Here Houdini appears with the "spirit" of Abraham Lincoln. Earlier, Houdini had sent photographs claimed by a medium to be the visual spirits of President Lincoln and his wife, to Lincoln's son for verification. Robert Lincoln said they were indeed pictures of his parents but taken in this earthly life, not sent from another world.

Houdini decided to design a device that would prevent the clever medium from engaging in any further séance-room deceptions. The result was the famous "Margery Box," a large case with a sloping front in which the medium could sit in a chair. There was a hole in the top for her head and two holes in the sides through which she could put her hands to be held by sitters on either side. In previous sittings, one of the stipulations had been that one of Margery's hands would be held by her husband, Dr. Crandon, while the other hand could be held by Houdini or any other sitter. The purpose of this was to put Margery's hands under complete control so that she could engage in no chicanery in the pitch-

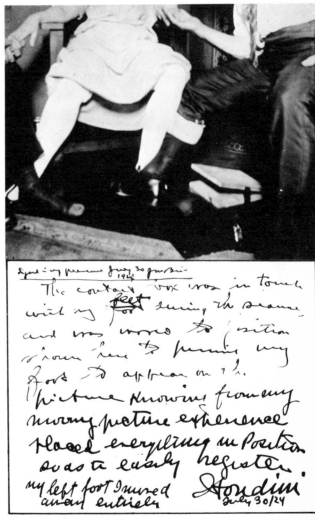

The famous medium "Margery" was a strong match for Houdini. In this photograph, taken during a séance, Houdini, as he explains in the adjacent note, felt the medium extend her foot to press the "bell box."

Houdini found his exposure of fraudulent mediums could be provocative entertainment and he devoted part of his performances to showing his audiences the various means by which they could be taken in by psychic frauds.

dark room. So, if Dr. Crandon was cooperating with his wife, she could have released her hand and engaged in any kind of trickery necessary for her to achieve her spirit manifestations. Houdini eliminated this possible chance for fraud by having someone else hold the medium's other hand while she was in the box he designed.

From the time of the introduction of the special box, the Margery investigation degenerated into a series of accusations and counteraccusations. When the lights came on after the first test séance, it was found that the top slanted part of the box had been broken open and that the medium could easily have leaned forward and rung the bell box with her head. Margery, backed up, of course, by "Walter," attributed this miraculous happening to the spirits, and alleged that Houdini had wedged a small piece of rubber eraser under the top of the box so that it was difficult to ring anyway. Houdini dismissed this as an attempt to discredit him and, as a man who had been escaping from boxes all his life, set about reinforcing his "Margery Box" so that the medium could not escape again. At the next séance, nothing happened, except that a small folding ruler was found in the box and Houdini was accused of planting it. A further séance yielded no results. Naturally, Margery did not get the *Scientific American* award and Houdini did get plenty of newspaper publicity.

With typical dispatch, Houdini published a pamphlet entitled *Houdini Exposes the Tricks used by the Boston Medium Margery,* and, just for good measure, included a chapter exposing the so-called X-ray vision of the Spanish psychic, Argamasilla. Houdini sold this book on his eight-week lecture tour the next fall and took the Margery Box along with him to demonstrate how the medium could have maneuvered the ruler up through the neck hole of the box and, by holding it in her teeth, managed to ring the bell box. Houdini also performed his entertaining routine with the blindfolded committee in which he performed various "spirit manifestations" while his hands and feet were apparently "controlled" by the sitters.

In the spring of 1925, Houdini opened at the New York Hippodrome to begin what was to be his last vaudeville tour. His act was made up mostly of spirit exposés featuring the Margery Box. Before he arrived in each town, he sent his own undercover team of psychic investigators ahead of him. These investigators would attend séances and determine the methods used by the mediums. Later Houdini would expose these methods on stage, naturally with much newspaper publicity. Sometimes Houdini himself would attend séances in disguise, only to snap on a flashlight in the darkened room exposing the trickery and revealing himself as having caught another medium.

It is interesting to speculate for a moment about the results that Houdini's crusade against fraudulent mediums has had on the progress of American spiritualism. To the "true believers," not even the clearest explanation of fraud is acceptable. The literature of the spiritualist movement is full of examples of mediums caught redhanded in boldfaced chicanery, but who the believers still insist were genuine on the occasions when they were not caught. There is clearly no answer to give to this argument, for it is based on faith and not reason. Houdini's crusade was never against spiritualism as a faith or as a religion, but against the dishonesty and deception which was frequently practiced under its name.

There was, however, one very real result of the Houdini crusade—the decline of the physical medium. The psychic who floats tables and spirit trumpets, produces writing on slates and materializes the ectoplasmic forms of his sitters' departed loved ones is very rare today, and this has been the case ever since Houdini's investigations. There is a very good reason for it. As Houdini proved over and over again, it is too easy to get caught. A grab at an ectoplasmic form in the dark may result in a handful of luminous cheesecloth, or a flashlight directed at the floating trumpet may show it connected to the end of a collapsible "reaching rod." You may be sure that any medium today who is bold enough to produce physical manifestations does it under the carefully screened conditions of a "spiritualists' camp" or under circumstances where all of the sitters are well known as unquestioning believers who can be absolutely sure not to act up.

Most of the great mediums of the last fifty years have given up the more spectacular levitations and materializations and adopted the less vulnerable field of "voice mediumship." Going into a trance, they would contact their spirit guide on "the other side" (deceased American Indians have been particularly popular as spirit guides). Then, with the guide's help, the medium would contact various spirits and deliver their messages. Unlike with the physical mediums, there was nothing to catch and, at least in some cases, these mediums (like Lady Conan Doyle) were genuinely sincere persons who believed they were making other-worldly contact.

I myself wanted to find out if spiritualists could actually materialize a departed relative or friend or if this was just another magician's illusion. I had heard of a spiritualist camp in Indiana where a materializing medium still lived. An intrepid nineteen-year-old, I hitchhiked to the camp, gaining entrance by saying I was a member of the Spiritualist Church of Toronto. After a quick interview with the medium and a $25 payment, I was admitted to a room lined in black velvet with three red bulbs providing the only lighting. After a very spooky prayer service, the medium retired to a three-sided curtained closet and the voice of "Tinkerbell," her spirit guide, emerged. The lights were extinguished and we were called up one by one and asked to talk to our dead friends and relatives.

By the time my turn came, I was scared stiff. I'd seen, or thought I'd seen, misty white forms in the room, and my crying, near-hysterical companions at the séance really convinced me that something might be happening. I stood up and walked forward. "Tinkerbell" asked whom I wished to speak to. I said that I didn't know. She said, "Your name is Doug?" "Yes." "You were named after your Uncle Doug?" I again agreed, surprised. "Is he in the spirit world?" This was my chance. I said "Yes," although my uncle was alive and living in Montreal.

Suddenly I heard a voice a lot like my Uncle Doug's. We talked for a few minutes about general topics—school, my mother, and so on. All the while there was a misty white form in front of me. By the time I sat down I was very scared, and quite convinced, so convinced that as soon as the séance was over I ran to the nearest phone booth and called home to see if Uncle Doug were still alive. He was. The séance was a fraud. I figured that the medium had wheedled information from me at the interview. I learned that night of the tremendous effect that the power of suggestion can have on one's mind and emotions.

I still try to remain open to the existence of phenomena beyond our scientific explanations. There have been and will continue to be occurrences caused by subtle laws of nature not yet understood. Perhaps someday, someway, spirits will be called up.

Today the most well-known psychic is the brilliant young Israeli magician, Uri Geller. Through clever misdirection, Geller has been able to bamboozle scientists at prestigious laboratories, such as the Stanford Research Institute, into believing that he can bend metal objects, start broken watches and read the contents of sealed envelopes. Although he claims that his miraculous powers came from flying saucers rather than spirit guides in the great beyond, Geller has been found out on several occasions and has been exposed both in books and in the press with great accuracy as to his methods. Nevertheless, his coterie of true believers insist that "at least part of the time" he is genuine. I can't help but wonder how Houdini would have reacted to Uri Geller.

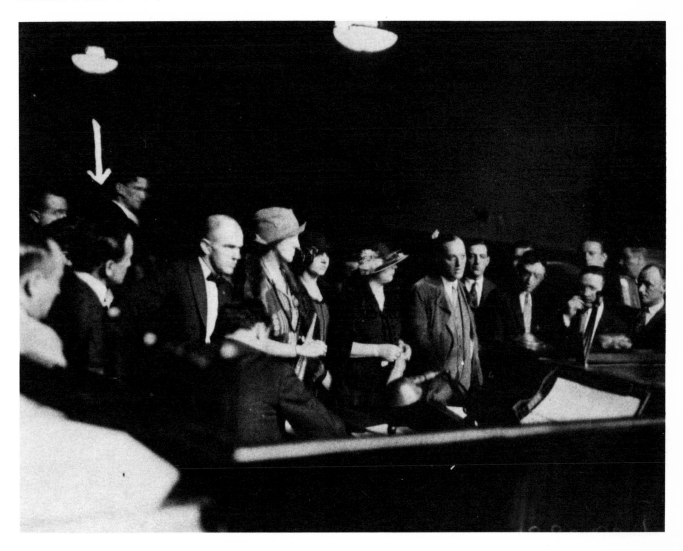

Houdini appeared before a Congressional committee as a witness in an attempt to outlaw fortune telling in the District of Columbia. The law did not pass.

The End of a Life, The Beginning of a Legend

By the time Houdini had finished his 1925 tour, he realized that as a form of American mass entertainment, vaudeville was virtually dead. It had largely been replaced by a medium in which Houdini had achieved no outstanding success—the movies. But Houdini, the eternal showman, was not to be conquered by changing times; he had other plans. In the summer of 1925 he was planning what appeared to be his most ambitious theatrical venture: a two-and-a-half-hour show made up of the greatest features of his career. The show would be divided into three parts. Act I would be magic and illusions. Act II would be devoted to his most famous escapes, opening with the Metamorphosis (for which Bess would once again act as his assistant) and closing with the water torture cell. Act III would be devoted to the spirit crusade that had become an overwhelming passion with him and was gathering as much favorable newspaper publicity as anything else had in his long career.

The big show proved to be a profit-making success, and during his first season Houdini played thirty-six weeks in legitimate theaters across the country.

During the first year of touring with his big show, Houdini took time out to testify in Washington before a House of Representatives committee on a bill that would ban fortune-telling in the District of Columbia. In May of 1926 he returned to Washington again to testify for the bill and demonstrate fraudulent mediums' tricks. The hearings received nationwide news coverage, but the bill did not pass.

Almost immediately Houdini was embroiled in another psychic controversy with an old adversary, Hereward Carrington. Carrington was a so-called psychic investigator who had written several books on the subject and whom Houdini considered an opportunist who would say anything that would sell the most copies. His latest venture was promoting a Hindu wonder-worker named Rhamen Bey, who was appearing in what remained of vaudeville. Bey's big effect was to be "buried alive" on stage in a sealed coffin with sand shoveled on top of it. Later, he managed to stay in the box for one hour, part of the time submerged in water. Houdini insisted that there was nothing supernormal about the feat and proceeded to prove it. On August 5, 1926, he remained for one hour and thirty minutes in a sealed iron coffin submerged in the swimming pool of the Hotel Shelton in New York City. Houdini immediately put out a dramatic new poster: "Buried Alive, Egyptian Fakirs Outdone."

In 1958, the Amazing Randi, who has continued in the Houdini tradition as an escape artist and exposer of psychic frauds, broke Houdini's record by staying submerged in a sealed box of the same size for two hours and thirty minutes. It should be pointed out that Randi not only weighed less than Houdini, but was less than half Houdini's age when he attempted the feat. His method, though, was the same as Houdini's: relaxation, stillness and short breathing.

I myself am very interested in practicing body and mind co-ordination. Houdini used calisthenics and breathing exercises. I find the Transcendental Meditation program is very effective in integrating mind and body. TM is a natural and effortless mental technique that removes stress from the nervous system, provides great relaxation to the body and expands consciousness. The result is a clear, powerful mind with complete integration of mind and body, very useful for those physically difficult illusions.

That summer of 1926 Houdini was very busy planning his next season's show and working on the idea of a "University of Magic." But soon a series of freakish and unforeseen events cut his plans short.

In October, Bess became sick with food poisoning and, between lack of sleep over his wife's illness and the general problems of getting the tour underway, Houdini worked himself into a condition of extreme fatigue and exhaustion. On October 10, while doing the water torture cell escape, one of his ankles snapped as he was raised aloft above the water-filled tank. But Houdini did not stop. There were audiences to be satisfied, and thousands of tickets already sold. The show had to go on, and it did. Houdini devised a special support for his ankle and the tour continied.

On October 21, Houdini was playing in Montreal. He was backstage in his dressing room preparing for the show when there was a knock at the door. Two college students from McGill University had come to see the great Houdini and especially to find out for themselves if one of the well-circulated stories about the illusionist was true: It was said that Houdini had such mastery over his body, such control over all of his muscles, that he could sustain punches to his stomach without injury. When asked about this by the boys Houdini agreed that he was able to do this. Suddenly, before Houdini had time to

HOUDINI COLLAPSES HERE

DETROIT TIMES

Only Detroit Newspaper Carrying International News

EVENING

Universal Service and Complete Sport. Dispatches

27TH YEAR, NO. 25   DETROIT, MICHIGAN, MONDAY, OCTOBER 25, 1926   TWO CENTS

Mayor Hears Voice Known to World

HOUDINI, ILL, GOES UNDER KNIFE

HOUDINI UNDER KNIFE HERE

Harry Houdini, master magician and mystifier, was operated on in Grace Hospital, this afternoon for an acute attack of appendicitis. The operation was performed by Dr. Charles Kennedy.

Houdini was forced to cancel his engagement at the Garrick after giving only one performance. He appeared Sunday night, despite the fact that he was in great pain and running a temperature of 104.

Houdini arrived here Sunday afternoon. He had wired ahead to have a doctor meet him at the Garrick dressing room. Dr. Leo J. Dretka examined him and diagnosed his illness as acute appendicitis.

Because there was a packed house, Houdini insisted on going on. Dr. Dretka was forced to leave to catch a train for Montreal. Today the "master mystifier" was in so critical condition that immediate operation was had to be...

(Continued from Page One) ago when here with a broken ankle in St. Mary's Hospital. His condition is the second entertainer.

(Concluded on Next Page, Col. 8.)

Houdini is the second entertainer seriously ill more than three weeks mouth. Frank Tinney, who became for two weeks at least.

HOUDINI'S CRISIS DUE TONIGHT

DETROIT TIMES

Only Detroit Newspaper Carrying International News

EVENING

Universal Service and Complete Sport Dispatches

HOME EDITION

THE WEATHER

Detroit and vicinity: Tonight and to morrow mostly cloudy; probably showers tonight and cooler tomorrow. Fresh to soft southwest winds, shifting to north and northwest; tomorrow and diminishing

HOME FINAL

27TH YEAR, NO. 28   DETROIT. MICHIGAN, THURSDAY, OCTOBER 28, 1926

BIRTHDAY CRASH KILLS 2, 1 DYIN

DETROIT TIMES

Only Detroit Newspaper Carrying International News

EVENING

Universal Service and Complete Sport Dispatches

TH YEAR, NO. 28   DETROIT. MICHIGAN. THURSDAY. OCTOBER 28, 1926   PRICE TWO CENTS

Wife Stricken as Houdini Nears Crisis

Harry Houdini, famous magician, is still in a critical condition in Grace Hospital and the crisis of his illness has not been reached yet, attending physicians stated today.

The official bulletin said:

"The patient had a rather restless right. His condition, although still critical, continues good. Temperature 100.4, pulse 4, respiration 32."

Mrs. Houdini and her niece, Miss a Sawyer, are under the care physician as the result of the strain caused by the magician's illness. They are confined to their rooms at the Hotel Statler.

The crisis is expected tonight, the fourth day following his operation for a ruptured appendix, with resultant peritonitis.

Surgeons explained it usually takes four days after such an operation for the resultant poisons gathering in the abdomen to be taken up by the blood stream and spread throughout the body.

Immediately after such operations, the patients, as is the case with Houdini, usually show gradual improvement until the fourth day when the poisons begin to spread.

Mrs. Houdini has received the following telegram from Howard Thurston, magician, who is playing Syracuse, N. Y., this week:

"Read Houdini is not worse. His splendid physique, free of alcohol and nicotine, with his natural fighting power, will be great aids to the physicians in his recovery. Sympathy from Mrs. Thurston and myself.

"Howard Thurston."

Thurston is keeping in constant touch with Houdini's condition.

Houdini was stricken here Sunday night after his opening performance at the Garrick Thea His two week's engagement been cancelled.

In Loving Memory of

Harry Houdini

Eleventh Most Illustrious President

of the

Society of American Magicians

who bowed to the mandate
of the Mighty Magician
October thirty-first, 1926.

"GOOD-BYE, OLD PAL"

HOUDINI'S NEW ADVENTURE

The Sphinx mourned Houdini's passing with the publication of Harlan Tarbell's cartoon of Houdini joining the greats of magic who had gone before him.

brace himself, one of the students punched him hard in the stomach. Houdini recovered from the force of the blow, and the students left.

Houdini, as we have found, always made one hundred percent sure of the success of each of his feats. It is very odd that he would let two strange men into his dressing room and then let one of them punch him. But this is what happened on that fateful day in October of 1926, and only Houdini knew why it happened.

He dismissed the incident. But, unknown to him, the unexpected blow had ruptured his appendix. Through sheer willpower he continued to perform in ever-increasing pain, but after a performance in Detroit on October 24 (performed in great agony and with a temperature of 104 degrees) he collapsed in the wings. He was rushed to the hospital, where an emergency operation revealed a gangrenous appendix and advanced peritonitis.

The world was shocked at the news of Houdini's condition. Here was a man who had spent his whole life proving that his body could overcome the impossible challenges of man and of nature. He had escaped death hundreds of times in front of thousands of people. In the eyes of the world, he had obtained a certain kind of immortality. But in the end, like all mortal men, his body lost the final struggle with life. He fought valiantly to live for over a week but, in those days before modern antibiotics and wonder drugs, the struggle was a hopeless one.

On October 31, 1926, Halloween, the most well-known magician who had ever lived passed quietly away. Just before Houdini died, he whispered a message to his wife, who was at his bedside, and said that if it was possible for man to return from the dead, he would send this message to her. In the years that followed, his admirers throughout the world wondered whether the great magician could perform his greatest escape of all—to return from beyond the grave.

The world mourned the death of the man who had given so many people delight and amazement, who had put wonder and magic into so many lives. Houdini the man, the magician, was dead. His earthly career had ended, but his legend would continue to grow.

HOUDINI LETTER ASKED JEWISH B

Magician's Body Rests in State At Club Today

Two years ago Harry Houdini, master magician, accompanied by his friend, Loney Haskell, walked into No. 1, the parent lodge of the Elks. To the secretary Houdini handed an envelope.

"Not to be opened until after my death," he said.

Sunday night, folowing the sad news of the death of Houdini in Detroit, Loney Haskell walked again to the Elks Club. There the letter was opened.

"Rabbi Tinter of Mount Zion Temple married me,' said the letter. "His father, Rabbi Mortiz Tintner buried my mother. He was a life-long friend of my own father, Rabbi Weiss. I wish Rabbi Tintner to say the last farewell over me, the man who married me to the woman I have never ceased to love." And then the desire to be buried from the Elks Club.

There was more in the letter. His wish to be buried beside his mother in his own family plot in Cypress Hills, Brooklyn, and that a bronze casting of his own death mask already in his home, be made and placed on his monument.

At 10.30 o'clock tomorrow morning, Rabbi Tintner, in the Elks Club, at 108 West 43d St., assisted by Dr. Drachman, will conduct the services.

Covered with flowers the casket will be placed on a catafalgue in the Elks club today. Before it in tear-dimmed homage will reverently pass all theatrical New York. And amid the mountain of flowers th one deepest-love of all—a scroll bearing in tracery of white violets the word "Husband"—the final gesture from his heart-broken widow, Mrs. Beatrice Houdini, who collapsed upon her arrival here yesterday.

At the Elks services Thursday morning Loney Haskell will speak as representative of the Jewish Theatrical Guild; Henry Chesterfield of the N. V. A.; Frank Du-bog of the Society of American Magicians, of which the dead master was president and fraternal brothers of Houdini in St. Cecile lodge, F. & A. M. and the Elks dge No. 1

Harry Houdini

HOUDINI TO BE BURIED TOM

Body Brought Here By Widow Lies in State in Chapel

By JEAN VERNON.

For the last time tomorrow crowds will gaze upon Harry Houdini, master magician, not in mystification, but in farewell. His funeral services will be held at 10:30 a. m., at the Elks' club, at 108 West 43d st. Burial in Machpehla cemetery at Cypress Hills, L.I., will follow.

The late Harry Houdini

Meanwhile his body has lain in state at the West End Funeral chapel, at 200 West 91st st. It was taken there yesterday morning after the private car in which his widow, Mrs. Beatrice Houdini, has arrived from Detroit reached New York City.

Dr. William Stone of 48 West 88th st. met her at the train. In a state of collapse she was taken to his automobile in a wheel chair, and thence drove to the home of Houdini's brother at 278 West 113th st. She is resting there under care of her physician unable to see the throngs of friends and admirers of her husband who beg to offer a word of consolation.

Dr. Leopold D. Waiss, Nat J. Weiss and Theo Hardeen visited the undertaking establishment yesterday. Their brother's body lay in state in the solid bronze casket that had accompanied him on his travels during the last few years— the very casket in which he had frequently encased himself under water for as much as seventy-eight minutes at a time.

Its massive lid was covered with a blanket of purple violets and gar-

lands of southern smilax. The heavy scent permeated the somber chapel. Across the coffin lay a scroll bearing, in tracery of white violets, the word "Husband."

Services tomorrow will be conducted by Dr. Drachman and Dr. Tintner of Mount Zion temple. Loney Haskell will speak as representative of the Jewish Theatre guild; Henry Chesterfield, of N. V. A., and there will be speeches from a member of the Society of American Musicians and fraternal brothers of Houdini's in St. Cecile lodge, F. and A. M., and Elks lodge No. 1.

HOUDINI, great magician, liked to visit newspaper offices, and show how he could untie any knot with his hands behind his back. He was a useful man exposing frauds, including one that pretends to bring the spirits of the dead back to talk childish nonsense to those still living.

Now he is gone. Old death has tied for him a knot that not even Houdini can untie.

Houdini

Houdini did not seek to disturb the practice of professional "magicians." He was one of them himself. He held that they presenetd a legitimate form of entertainment and he served as a constant stimulus to them through his own popularity and what goes under the name of moral support. It was a business which he thought worth encouraging and which he never was interested in disturbing. His own tricks were a part of it. Them he kept to himself, performing them in an amused, almost ironical fashion, as though he were enjoying the gullibility of the public. One had the impression that he found as much pleasure in playing that game through to the finish as any man who ever attempted it.

But the line between legitimate tricks and exhibitions which were ascribed to an outside power Houdini drew hard and straight. On that line he stood, alone, and any man who crossed did so at his own peril. Houdini was ready for him and the assault was always direct and severe and determined. The man was ruthless His energy was amazing, his persistence without limit, his capacity and resourcefulness never really extended. He must have loved the tremendous figting he was constantly engaged in. He would go out of his way to seek out and rundown a faker. He would engage in a trans-Atlantic debate with a Lodge and, not satisfied with that, would go to London for the chief purpose of meeting his enemy face to face and renewing the combat. He thought nothing of standing up in front of a delegation of spiritualists at a committee hearing in Washington and tellin them bluntly that they were all liars and rascals. He constantly defied hem, dared them to prove their assertions, flaunted their claims and waved thousand-dollar bills in their faces as reward if they would pull the wool over his eyes. If any of them ever succeeded, it is not in the records.

So he stands, an engaging personality, with far more of intelligence than any other in his business and not a little intellectuality. What a gusto for living he had! And what a amazing way of taking the public into his confidence until the public thought it was understanding—only to be dazzled as Houdini would switch back to more tricks and everybody else knew were tricks but which, of course, were always to those who saw them the last word in black magic.—Greensboro News.

Services at Elks Club by Jewish Theatrical Guild, N. V. A., Masons and Magicians.

N.Y. Times Nov. 3 26

Funeral services for Harry Houdini, noted magician who died on Sunday in Detroit, will be held tomorrow morning at 10:30 at the Elks' club-house in West Forty-third Street, when his associates on the stage and in the realm of magic will join to pay him tribute. Interment will be in the family plot at Machpelah Cemetery, Cypress Hills, Queens, in accordance with the magician's request that he be buried at the right side of his mother and that her letters to him be placed in his coffin.

Rabbi Bernard Drachman and Rabbi B. A. Tintner will officiate at the Elks' Club services. Brief eulogies will be delivered by Loney Haskell, representing the Jewish Theatrical Guild, and Henry Chesterfield, Secretary of the National Vaudeville Artists. Ritualistic rites will be conducted by the New York Lodge No. 1, B. P. O. E.; the St. Cecile Lodge of Masons and the Society of American Magicians.

The honorary pallbearers will be E. F. Albee, J. J. Murdock, Martin Beck, William Morris, L. Lawrence Weber, Lee Shubert, Mark A. Luescher, Charles Dillingham, Richard E. Enright, Adolph S. Ochs, William Johnson, Adolph Zukor, Orson Munn, Arthur Prince, Bernard M. L. Ernst, Professor Brander Matthews, Joseph F. Rinn, Sophie Irene Loeb, Bernard Gimbel, Francis Werner and Oscar Teale.

The pallbearers will be members of the magician's troupe who appeared with him in performances for many years.

The body of Houdini arrived in New York from Detroit yesterday morning and was taken from Grand Central Station to the West End Funeral Chapel, 200 West Ninety-first Street, where it will remain until tomorrow. Accompanying the body were the widow, Mrs. Beatrice Houdini; his sister, Gladys Houdini; his brothers, Theo Hardeen and Nat Weiss; James Collins, technical assistant to Houdini for twenty years; Sophie Rosenblatt, for many years the nurse of the magician, and H. Elliott Stuckel, his business manager. A large gathering of friends and relatives met the funeral party at the station.

It was said yesterday that plans for Houdini's body to lie in state had been abandoned when such procedure was found not to be in sympathy with the wishes of his family.

Says Four Know Houdini's Secrets.

CHICAGO, Nov. 2 (P).—Four friends of Houdini, the magician who died Sunday, know the secret of his magic, Leonard Hicks, a hotel operator here, said today after reading a report that Houdini died without revealing the secrets of his success.

Mr. Hicks claimed a lifelong friendship with the magician, during part of which he said he was associated with Houdini in the theatrical profession, and said the others to whom the secrets are known are Houdini's brother, known on the stage as Theodore Hardeen; James Collins, who was Houdini's assistant for sixteen years, and James Vickery, who was his assistant for fourteen years.

"Trick Coffin" to Bring Houdini's Body Back to His Home in 113th St

Detroit.—In a bronze, air-tight coffin recently constructed for one of his myriad tricks, the body of Harry Houdini, the magician, will leave here tonight for New York. It will probably be taken to his Harlem home at 278 W. 113th St.

The "Handcuff King," known the world over, died here Sunday afternoon, a little more than a week after he became ill with appendicitis, which developed into peritonitis.

Until near the end, Houdini confidently believed he would "get out of this the way I get out of everything else." It was that confidence which

Harry Houdini

him to go through two stage per-lances after his illness took the which later proved fatal.

he magician, however, admitted to brother, Theodore Hardine, Sunmorning, "I guess I am all gh fighting."

few hours later, at 1.26 p. m., uttering an incoherent refero Col. Robert Ingersoll, the late

taken to a circus. The magician of the troupe attracted him. By an accident he "saw through" one of the tricks, and from then on there was no magical Santa Claus for Harry.

Two years later he watched a traveling showman walk a tightrope and hang by his teeth from a cable. Harry tried it in his backyard, and lost five teeth.

At the age of 8, young Houdini joined a traveling circus and became known as "Eric, Prince of the Air." He was a contortionist, wire walker, acrobat and sleight of hand performer. One of his tricks was to bend backward and pick up a needle in the skin of his eye socket.

Becomes Escape King

One night, in Coffeyville, Kan., a sheriff volunteered to tie Houdini and suddenly snapped a pair of handcuffs on the youth's wrists. They were the first handcuffs Houdini had ever seen, but he was free in 11 minutes.

From then on it was as a handcuff expert that Houdini was known. He toured this country and Europe. Here are some of his stunts:

He broke out of the dread Siberian prison van in Moscow.

He leaped, heavily handcuffed, from a Detroit bridge into icy waters and released himself.

He jumped into San Francisco Bay with more than 75 pounds of ball and chain locked to his body and his hands cuffed behind his back.

He escaped from a plate glass box in Boston and did not scratch the box.

Emerges From Cell

He emerged smilingly from the murderer's cell in the United States jail at Washington which confined Guiteau, assassin of President Garfield.

He escaped from a packing box, to which was attached 200 pounds of iron weights, in New York Bay.

For a time he acted in motion pictures and wrote numerous books on the magic art.

Then he became interested in alleged Spiritist manifestations, and with the experience of years of showmanship which made him the equal

---

#| Round the Town.

N.Y. Telegram mail Nov. 2 1926

By S. Jay Kaufman

Houdini's Hobby.

The death of Houdini was one of the much talked of things yesterday. In one club we heard a tribute which is a sort of resume of the Houdini character. "I began in vaudeville about ten years ago and Houdini was on the same bill. He was the headliner and we were only a 'fill-in' act. He helped us with our costumes, scenery and at the end of the week when he heard that we didn't have money enough to go on to the next town he paid our fares. Later I learned that one of his hobbies was helping beginners."

DAILY MIRROR, TUESDAY, NOVEMBER 2, 1926

Houdini

Harry Houdini's long and colorful life ends. Millions will be sorry he has gone.

It is not belittling the magician to call him a master showman. He was a sincere and conscientious performer, who strove seriously and successfully through many years to perfect himself in a novel and difficult calling.

Houdini's last appearance was made with his fatal illness already upon him. The audience must not be disappointed; he was true to stage tradition.

To have entertained a whole world, as Houdini did, is no small matter. And his exposures of spiritualistic trickery will cause his name to be long remembered.

6   **EVENING GRAPHIC**   TUESDAY, NOVEM...

PUBLIC STIRRED BY HOUDINI'S DEA
DEMANDS DOCTORS REVEAL TREATM

Widow Collapses, Throngs Weep as Body Arrives Here

New York halted in its election bustle today to pay tribute to Harry Houdini, who died in Detroit following an injection of serum.

His body reached here on a private car and was met at Grand Central station by throngs of people. Between Albany and this city Mrs. Beatrice Houdini, the widow, collapsed and had to be taken from the train in a wheel chair.

Throngs Show Grief

Scenes of genuine grief marked arrival of the train, which had been met at Albany by a theatrical delegation headed by Henry Chesterfield, secretary to the N. V. A. Hundreds of persons were massed on the platforms, with heads uncovered. There were many eyes wet with tears.

As the coffin bearing the remains was borne through the station hurrying crowds stopped to bare their heads and follow the sad procession with their eyes. The body was taken to the West End funeral parlors at 200 West 91st St.

Daughter Also in Party

The party which accompanied the body East consisted of the widow, her daughter, Gladys; Theodore Hardeen and Nathan J. Weiss, brothers of Houdini; a niece, Miss Julia Sawyer, and Miss Julia Karchere, a cousin of Mrs. Houdini; H. Elliott Stuckel, personal manager of the magician; James Collins, his assistant and Sophie Rosenblatt, nurse.

In the crowd which awaited the body here were the representatives of many organizations, as well as relatives. Mrs. Balbina Rahner, mother of Mrs. Houdini, was one of the first admitted to the private car. She was accompanied by Mrs. Theodore Hardeen and Louis C. Krousu, a nephew.

Publisher Demands Truth About Houdini's Death

WESTERN UNION
TELEGRAM

SUPERINTENDENT OF GRACE HOSPITAL
DETROIT MICH

MORE THAN ONE MILLION READERS OF MY PUBLICATIONS ARE ANXIOUS
TO KNOW HOW HOUDINI WAS FED DURING HIS ILLNESS AND OTHER
DETAILS OF HIS TREATMENT THAT HAVE BEEN WITHHELD FROM THE
PUBLIC ARE YOU WILLING TO GIVE US THESE FACTS OR EVEN PART
OF THIS INFORMATION TO SATISFY THIS TREMENDOUS AUDIENCE

BERNARR MACFADDEN
PRESIDENT MACFADDEN PUBLICATIONS

While the city was paying its respects to the dead man a demand was increasing for a full investigation into the circumstances surrounding his death. It is believed he died from surgical superstition and food administered to his system when the life forces were at their lowest ebb.

In behalf of more than a million readers of the Macfadden Publications, Bernarr Macfadden, publisher, today adressed a telegram to the superintendent of Grace Hospital, Detroit, Mich., where Houdini died Sunday afternoon following two operations and the injection of a mysterious new serum, demanding to know how Houdini was fed during his illness and other details of his treatment hitherto undisclosed.

Text of Telegram

Mr. Macfadden's telegram in full follows:—

Superintendent of Grace Hospital, Detroit, Mich.:—

More than one million of my publications are anxious to know how Houdini was fed during his illness and other details of his treatment that have been withheld from the public. Are you willing to give us these facts or even part of this information to satisfy this tremendous audience?

BERNARR MACFADDEN,
President, Macfadden Publications.

Houdini Loses

HARRY HOUDINI, the world's most noted magician, is dead.

He knew how to escape from *knots, locks and boxes.*

He didn't know how to escape *from the doctors.*

It is a great pity that this foe of sham was sacrificed because of the sham of the medical profession.

When the American public realizes the fallacy of the present system there will be an uproar that will shake medical incompetency to its foundation.

The sooner that happens the better it will be for the health of every one.

Shelton's Charge

Herbert N. Shelton, naturopath, in pointing out the ignorance of medical and surgical practitioners, which has resulted in many deaths of public figures lately, declared today that nature provides a protective gland when the appendix bursts, and if left alone the poison would be carried out of the system in the same manner all poisons are carried out.

Houdini Died Convinced That No

HARRY HOUDINI,
Master of magic and "stunts," who was a great enemy of unscrupulous charlatans who prey upon public credulity.

HOUDINI S...
The magician demonstrates to a co... how a "medium" is able to ring a bell an... other queer "manifestations" with H...

Houdini's death brought headlines in newspapers across the country. His body was brought to New York from Detroit in a trick coffin coincidentally left behind when his other props had been shipped east (which believers in spiritualism accepted as proof positive of a knowing world beyond). Other stories related Houdini's conviction that spiritualism was a fraud. Thousands lined the streets to watch his funeral and there were outcries that more should have been done to save his life.

DAILY NEWS, TUESDAY, NOVEMBER 2, 1926

WANTED: MORE HOUDINIS

The late Harry Houdini will be missed.

Plenty of able showmen remain to carry on the Barnum tradition that the public loves to be fooled. To find all of these, you don't have to go into the stage wings or under the big tops. Look closely and you will see a number of them functioning in politics, business, the legal and medical professions, the newspaper game, here and there in the sciences, and almost everywhere in the arts.

The late Harry Houdini

Harry Houdini was different. He cheerfully admitted that he was a faker, and the best one ever born. He hated crooks who pretended to be witches and wizards, and who made money out of their lies. He devoted his last years to the tracking down and unmasking of every faker he could find in that richest fakers' field of all, spiritualism. He saved to the public much money which the table tippers would otherwise have converted into ectoplasm.

FRIDAY
NEW YORK

Houdini Rites At Elks' Club Before 2,500

Church, Theater, Fraternal Orders Join in Tribute as Magician Is Buried in Special Casket He Asked

Throngs Wait in Street

Letters From His Mother Put Into Grave With Body of Actor Who Fought 'Frauds'

The church, the theatre and fraternal orders paid tribute yesterday to Harry Houdini, whose funeral services were held with elaborate ritual before 2,500 persons in the auditorium of the Elks' Club, 108 West Forty-third Street.

When the last strains of Chopin's Funeral March had died away, twenty-five automobiles of mourners formed a cortege which proceeded to Machpelah Cemetery, Cypress Hills, Queens. There final rites for the magician were pronounced by Rabbi B. A. Tintner, of Congregation Mount Zion, and Rabbi Bernard Drachman, of Congregation Zichron Ephraim, ih East Sixty-seventh Street.

Houdini was laid to rest in a special coffin by his expressed desire, in the presence of Elizabeth Houdini, his widow, Gladys Weiss, his sister, Nat Weiss, his brother and Theodore Hardin, a half-brother.

Hundreds Wait to See Casket

While hundreds stood outside New York Lodge No. 1, B. P. O. E., rabbis and representatives of the Jewish Theatrical Guild, the National Vaudeville Artists, Inc., St. Cecile Lodge of Masons and the Society of American Musicians eulogized Houdini as a Jew, a showman, a magician of genius and a humanitarian exposer of pretenders to supernatural powers.

Rabbi Drachman and Rabbi Tintner spoke of Houdini as "one who hated to bring tricks and religion under the same head," "a Jew of imperishable value" and a "tender and affectionate husband, who never forgot that his father was a rabbi."

"A God-given genius in his profession," said Henry Chesterfield, secretary of the National Vaudeville Artists, Inc., in extolling Houdini. "He respected religion and he respected spiritualism, but not the deception of false mediums." Mr. Chesterfield recalled Houdini's great sympathy for beggars and his work to make many of them self-supporting.

"In vain we call upon him," said Loney Haskell, spokesman for the Elks, stretching forth his hands over Houdini's coffin, which bore the words "Husband" and "Brother," interwoven with flowers. The coffin contained letters from the dead magician's mother.

Could Escape Detection in a Fair Test of Queer Phenomena

New York Eve Journal Tuesday Nov. 2 1926

MS WORK. his hands are held at the time. An legerdemain, Houdini was able to do gs with facility.

ANOTHER TRICK OF MEDIUMS. The illusionist demonstrates the manner of fashioning a paraffin hand by a fraudulent medium can create all sorts of queer effects.

HOUDINI AND PRESIDENT ROOSEVELT. A fellow voyager with the late Colonel Roosevelt, Houdini mystified the ex-President by producing on a slate a map of the River of Doubt, although such a map had not yet been published.

Broadway M

as Passing of King of Magic

(NEWS photo)

THOUSANDS packed street as funeral of Harry Houdini, wizard, was held yesterday at Elks club, West 43d st. Heads were bared as casket was removed. —*Story on page 41.*

A HOUDINI

Harry & Bess pose with members of the Rahner family, nd

...and with the Weiss family, nd

Contrary to fictionalized accounts, the families of Harry & Bess were fond of one another. In 1909, the Houdinis took their mothers together to Europe.

CRAPBOOK

On the beach, 1915

On the beach, nd

The Dancing Houdinis

The Houdinis, at home and abroad...

Harry & Bess, nd

Harry & Bess in their early years, 1900

Harry & Bess, London, 1907

Bess, New Orleans, 1907

The Houdinis, Egypt, 1910

The Houdinis, Ceylon, 1910

The Houdinis, Middle-East trip, 1910

Terrace of Hotel Beau Rivage Monte Carlo Dec. 1913

Hotel Beau Rivage Monte Carlo Dec. 1913

The Houdinis,
Monte Carlo, 1913

Monte Carlo Dec. 1913

Harry & Bess, Coney Island, 1913

Harry & Bess, Nice, 1913

Harry & Bess, nd

The Houdinis, nd

The Houdinis, nd

Feeding the pigeons, nd

Aboard the S.S. Imperator, 1921

Enroute to Europe, nd

Harry & Bess, nd

on our way to
San Diego Calif.

Enroute to San Diego, California, nd

The Houdinis playfully posing as if in a movie
scene, during his film-making days.

Harry & Bess, nd

Off-stage, Houdini was not the serious man known to the public, nd

Houdini in Paris, probably 1920

Prat maón iú eumma suit

Houdini in Paris

Houdini's last look at his mother was as their ship sailed for Europe. He was to return grief-stricken over her death only three weeks later.

The Houdinis
didn't mind a
little advertising,
even at
Christmas time.

Houdini was always a very sentimental man,
sending Bess love notes...

THE
COPLEY-PLAZA
BOSTON

July 24/1924

my Sweetheart Wife

We leave this eve
midnight and walk
into your arms in
morning 6 A.M.

Hope you are feeling
good + that I have
a Bessyfull of

love awaiting me

You husband to eternity + a day
+ then on   Houdini

FLOWN

...and making fun of their little spats...

My Sweet Lone maker—

If you knew
with what joy I am
sending this to you—
you would come up
stairs and give me
a kiss, & wonder if
I am going to have
a bite of lunch.
Dash is going to call.
& motor me to the
city of strife—
yours without
a struggle
Harry Houdini

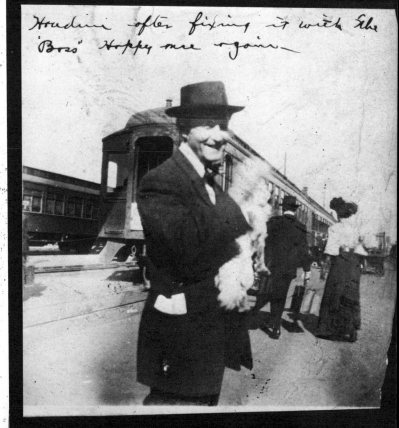

Houdini after fixing it with the
'Boss.' Happy once again—

Houdini trying to [...]with the [...] promising [...] good etc.

1901 wedding

1901. Houdini and wife married [...] years

...and writing her stories.

Short Story
   that lasts
     a blissful
     long time,

But —
   This too will pass away.

By
Father Time

Written by Houdini
1915

What are these two girls looking at?

This is a "What these two girls are looking at".

Atlantic City 1915

Broke *married 23 yrs*

married 21 yrs.

On endearing personal photographs through the years, the Houdinis often sentimentally noted their wedding anniversaries:

1901, Seven years married
1912, Eighteen years married
1915, Twenty-one years married
1917, Twenty-three years married

And what is this girl looking at?

Gaze below gentle reader and behold prince Charming.

And what happened?

Turn softly the pages fear of frightening 'em.

O, Mrs Houdini

Coney Island 1912
18 years married

1918, Twenty-four years married

1925, Thirty-one years married

Houdini was a major star by the time he & Bess celebrated their twenty-fifth wedding anniversary and many of Hollywood's luminaries attended the lavish dinner they gave.

Mr. and Mrs. Houdini's Silver Wedding

Houdini clowns with Fatty Arbuckle who parodies the Needle Trick, nd

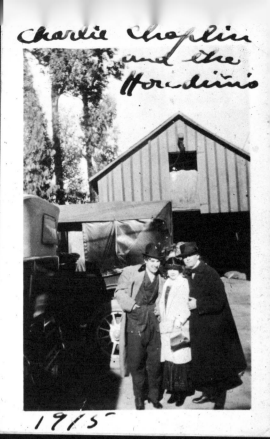

Charlie Chaplin and the Houdinis

1915

The Houdinis had many close associates in the literary and entertainment worlds, many friendships founded during his days in Hollywood. Below: Houdini with Fatty Arbuckle on far left, Buster Keaton second from left, nd

The Houdinis with Charlie Chaplin, 1915

Houdini with Charlie Chaplin, 191_

Houdini with Cecil B. DeMille, nd

The Houdinis with Mr. & Mrs. Jack London, 1915

Houdini with
W.C. Fields, nd

Houdini / W.C. Feilds

Houdini with Jack London, 1915

On the set with Gloria Swanson & Tom Meigham, nd

HOUDI
GREATEST

I'S TEN

LLUSIONS

Throughout his life Houdini performed hundreds of mysteries, from small close-up sleight-of-hand effects to escapes and huge illusions. In order to get a better look at Houdini's magic I have chosen what I consider to be his ten greatest illusions, and have described them as they appeared to Houdini's audiences in the early 1900's.

Houdini's ten greatest mysteries were: Metamorphosis; the Challenge Handcuff Act; the Naked Test Prison Escape; the Straitjacket Escape; the Overboard Box Escape; the Milk Can Escape; the Needle Trick; Walking Through a Brick Wall; the Chinese Water Torture Cell; the Vanishing Elephant.

METAMORPHOSIS

"Metamorphosis," the rapid substitution of one person for another inside a locked and roped trunk, was perhaps Houdini's greatest mystery. It was performed by Houdini throughout his career and it was the fact that he had such an incredible illusion in his act (the rest was stock magic and apparently not impressive) in the early days of his career that kept him working. Since Houdini's performance of Metamorphosis it has become one of the classic illusions in magic and is the effect that also launched my career as a performer and first brought me to the attention of important booking agents. In fact, this is still my favorite illusion. I perform it in every show and it never fails to get the largest audience response. The wonder of Metamorphosis lies not only in the mystery of how it is done, but in the fact that it can be done at all, with such speed that one person actually seems to change into another. It is one of those effects which has elements of both an escape and a magical illusion, and whether the audience accepts it as one or the other depends very much on how the individual performer presents it.

Houdini apparently was performing the trunk substitution as far back as 1892 when he was appearing in the "Brothers Houdini" act first with his partner, Jack Hyman, and later with his brother Dash. The effect came into its own after Houdini married Bess and added her to the act, for the exchange of the performer and his petite wife was a much more startling and appealing effect than the exchange of one "brother" with another.

Exactly how Houdini began performing the trunk substitution is unsure. Box effects had been around long before Houdini appeared on the scene. The original box trick was first performed in England by John Nevil Maskelyne, the founding father of England's greatest dynasty of magicians, on June 19, 1865. It was presented by him for many years thereafter and Maskelyne offered a reward to anyone who could fathom the secret. The illusion, in one version or another, found its way into the programs of many performers of the day, and many box illusions, working a variety of different ways, appeared in the catalogues of the magic dealers. In most versions, the performer would be locked inside the box (sometimes tied inside a sack) and the box would be covered with a screen. The performer would then appear from behind the screen. Sometimes he would go back behind the screen only to be found in the box

again. Alexander Herrmann presented a version billed as the "Asiatic Trunk Mystery." What was peculiarly "Asiatic" about escaping from a trunk is not known but he featured it as an "original Oriental sensation." Maskelyne incorporated a box escape (evolved from his original box trick) in his celebrated magical sketch, "Will, the Witch and the Watch," presented by him over 11,000 times between 1873 and 1916. Walter B. Gibson says Houdini first learned of the illusion from the catalogue of a dealer named Sylvester in Chicago who supplied appliances to bogus spirit mediums. The Sylvester outfit was much too expensive for Houdini, so he bought another from a performer who had one for sale at a lower cost.

I don't know if Houdini was the first to introduce the fast substitution into the box illusion, but it is very likely that this was the case. In many Houdini vaudeville programs the effect is modestly described as the "Exchange of Human Beings in a Locked, Sealed and Corded Trunk" but, in a very interesting program quoted in the Christopher biography, the description is more flamboyant: "Metamorphosis. Two human beings transported through space and walls of steel-bound, oaken boards, outstripping the rapidity of thought, after being bound, gagged and sealed by a committee selected from an audience."

This program from Houdini's first (unsuccessful) attempt to produce, in 1914, a "magical revue" instead of his standard escape act, is illuminating in that it further reveals Houdini's "challenge" approach to magic. In the same program, less escape-oriented illusions are also described in the same way, constantly emphasizing that girls are vanished "in midair in center of stage, away from all curtains, and in full glare of the light," and that girls appear "under strictest conditions possible. Everything open and above board." As I have said before, I do not feel that this challenge approach is the best way to present classic magic, and it may help to explain why Houdini's 1914 magical revue was not a success.

Metamorphosis is presented by almost all performers today, myself included, in the following way. The magician's lady assistant, with wrists tied or in cuffs, is sealed into a bag which is then put into the trunk or box. The trunk is then tied with rope or chained or otherwise securely locked. The performer then stands on top of the trunk holding a tube of

Theo Weiss, later to be known as Hardeen, posed beside the "Metamorphosis" trunk when he was part of the "Brothers Houdini".

cloth around him and exchanges places with the girl in a matter of seconds or less (in the exchange that I perform, I am out of view for less than a second when the girl appears in my place). In another version, the trunk is put in a curtained cabinet and the performer's head is pushed through the front curtains. His head dips inside and the girl's head pokes through in his place. In yet another version, a large cloth banner is momentarily lifted in front of the box when the exchange takes place.

One of the reasons the effect is such a strong applause-puller is that its climax is, oddly enough, not a complete surprise. The audience suspects the outcome, but knows that it would be impossible if it were to actually occur. In my own presentation, I have found that a small additional surprise at the end adds to this effect, which is the strongest applause-puller I perform. When I emerge from the bag at the end, I have made a complete change of costume. The audience is astonished and the illusion receives excited applause.

The costume change is an interesting twist on the illusion that contemporary audiences seem to like. It adds an additional punch after they think the trick is over. When I first started performing the illusion, I was very proud of myself for the idea of the costume change. I could not resist adding icing to the cake by having my assistant's costume change as well. I soon discovered that audiences failed to applaud because they were confused and, at least momentarily, thought it was another girl. With the single costume change that problem was solved and that is the way I have been performing it for several years. I discovered later that my idea of changing costumes was not as original as I had thought and that at least one performer, Leon Mandrake, had for many years been changing from black tails into a white Palm Beach suit and emerging from the untied bag calmly puffing on a cigarette. It was my first realization that truly original ideas in so ancient an art as magic are very rare, and that many a brilliant inspiration was also thought of by some other performer years before.

From a study of reviews of Houdini's act as far back as 1899 we can see some differences between the way Houdini presented the effect and the way it is usually seen by audiences today. Unlike all presentations today, it was the magician, Houdini, who was sealed in the trunk and got out while the assistant, Bess, appeared in the bag at the end. This would seem to be a far less effective *magical* climax, as the audience is ready to applaud the person who emerges from the bag and the effect is stronger if this is the magician rather than his assistant. When we realize that Houdini's strong point was escapes rather than magic it seems that perhaps *for him* this approach was better and that audiences would expect him to get out of rather than get into the trunk. The Christopher biography relates an early occurrence in Houdini's career when he was doing the trick in the usual way and ending up inside the bag. For some reason, his assistant, Dash, was unable to escape from the trunk and the illusion ended in humiliation. From that point on, says Christopher, Houdini vowed that the trick would not go wrong for *he* would be the one to escape.

A clever Houdini touch involved the borrowing of a coat from one of the members of the committee. Houdini would first have his wrists tied behind him. Then he would borrow the coat (if it belonged to a policeman and had a prominent silver star affixed, so much the better) and step inside the cabinet. Seconds later he would reappear, his wrists still tied but *wearing the coat.* After the knots on his wrists were once again examined, the trunk would be introduced and Houdini (still wearing the coat and with his wrists tied) would be sealed in the bag and put inside. The trunk would be placed in the cabinet and Bess would explain what was to happen. "I will step into the cabinet and clap my hands three times—then notice the effect." No sooner were the claps heard than Houdini rushed out, not wearing the coat and free of his bonds. When the trunk was unroped and the bag untied, Bess was found inside with *her* wrists tied and wearing the committeeman's coat.

It is significant that Martin Beck, in his correspondence with Houdini, always referred to Metamorphosis as the "trunk escape," for that is apparently the way Houdini presented it and why, for his personality, it was such a strong effect. When I perform the Metamorphosis, it is presented more as a Secondary Reality fantasy rather than a Primary Reality escape. The trunk, bag, and cuffs are examined by a member of the audience, but this is incidental to the real effect, which is that one person magically and instantaneously changes into another.

The feeling I get when I perform this illusion is like no other experience. First I am standing on top of the trunk. I can see the audience and the lights as I raise the curtain around my body. The next thing I am conscious of is crouching in a sack inside the trunk with a new costume on and a pair of handcuffs tightly chained around my wrists. There is no recollection of any perception in between. I have done the illusion so many times, and it is so fast, that my mind and senses completely transcend the physical technique and it really feels like real magic to me, as well as looking like real magic to the audience.

This illusion is a good example of my belief about practicing the techniques of magic. When practicing, the difficult must become habit, the habit easy, and the easy beautiful. Only then does it look and feel like real magic. Only by practice can the technique be transcended and the effect be made to look like magic.

HOUDINI

Text continues on page 146.

HOUDINI IN COLOR

I. Houdini was at the top of his career when this lithograph was published. It was not necessary to label it with anything other than his name.

> Strobridge Lithographic Co., Cincinnati, 1911
> Doug Henning Collection, New York

II. The "Metamorphosis" remained a part of Houdini's act throughout his entire career. First performed with his brother, Theo, about 1893, the illusion, with Bess as Houdini's partner, was continued through the years and was part of his final tour in 1926. It is performed today by Doug Henning.

> National Printing & Engraving Co., Chicago, c. 1895
> Jay Marshall Collection, Chicago

III. Success finally came to Houdini with his promotion, by theatrical entrepreneur Martin Beck, as an escape artist. European and American audiences thronged to see him extricate himself from all manner of restraints.

> Russell & Morgan Printing Co., Chicago, 1906
> Jay Marshall Collection, Chicago

IV. Always publicity conscious, Houdini made the most of a minor challenge from a German policeman, bringing to court—and winning—a suit for apology. Houdini made it international news and promoted the incident with this lithograph.

> Atelier J. Zier, Leipzig, 1902
> Walter Gydesen Collection, Chicago

V. The Circus Busch was, and is, one of the top European circuses and Houdini performed with them often over a period of many years. His water torture cell escape had its first performance there in the fall of 1912.

> 1907

VI. Houdini was a headliner in both Europe and America performing his famous water torture cell escape, the needle trick, and the milk can escape.

> Handbill, January 6, 1913

VII. A strenuous feat for even a young man, the Chinese Water Torture Cell escape was still being performed by Houdini at age fifty-two, during his final tour. It was performed by Doug Henning on his television special in December, 1975.

> Strobridge Lithographic Co., Cincinnati, 1914
> Houdini Magical Hall of Fame, Niagara Falls, Canada

VIII. One of Houdini's favorite portraits with his beloved mother was handcolored and in a small stand-up frame. On the back was a request to anyone finding the portrait to communicate with Houdini.

IX. Houdini was first president of the Society of American Magicians and, for many years until his death, proudly carried an honorary membership in that organization and was one of its most influential members. These are some of the SAM membership cards he saved and one belonging to his widow Bess who remained a member after Houdini's death.

HARRY
HOUDINI

THE HOUDINI'S

ORIGINAL INTRODUCERS OF
METAMORPHOSIS

THE GREATEST TRUNK MYSTERY THE WORLD HAS EVER SEEN

EXCHANGING PLACES IN 3 SECONDS

BEATRICE
Queen of MYSTERY

IV.

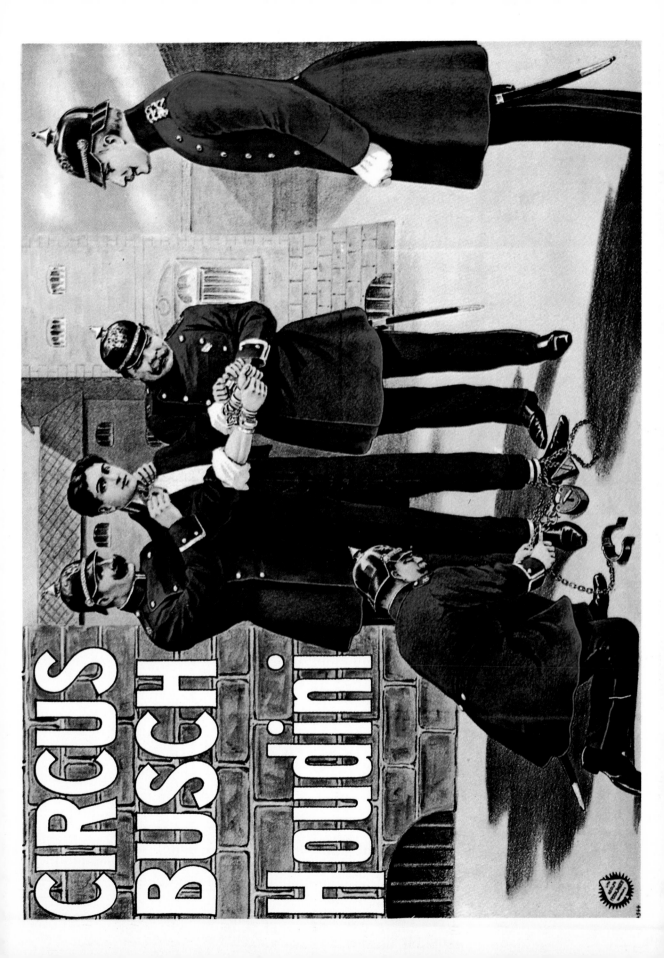

" 'Tis not in mortals to command success, but we'll do more—deserve it."—*Addison*

THE

CARDIFF
EMPIRE

QUEEN STREET

MOSS' EMPIRES, LIMITED.

PROPRIETORS · · · · · · · ·
Managing Director · · · · · · Mr. FRANK ALLEN.
Acting Manager · · · · · HERBERT J. TAYLOR.

MONDAY, JAN. 6th, 1913 and TWICE NIGHTLY
AT 6.45 AND 9.0 DURING THE WEEK.

THE WORLD-FAMOUS SELF-LIBERATOR!

HOUDINI

Presenting the Greatest Performance of his Strenuous Career. liberating himself
after being Locked in a

WATER TORTURE
CELL

Houdini's own Invention, whilst Standing on his
Head, his Ankles Clamped and Locked above in
the Centre of the Massive Cover.   A Feat which
borders on to the Supernatural.

£200 Houdini offers this sum to
anyone proving that it is
possible to obtain air in
the upside-down position
in which he releases himself from this WATER-
FILLED TORTURE CELL.

CASELLI SISTERS
Vocalists and Dancers

HAPPY TOM
PARKER
COMEDIAN AND DANCER

PETER & POTTS
The Comedian and the Call Boy

New Series of Pictures
on the
AMERICAN BIOSCOPE

THE GREAT
WEILAND
COMEDY JUGGLER

G. W.
HUNTER
PATTER COMEDIAN

FERRY CORWEY
THE MUSICAL CLOWN

COOPER & LAIT

In their Latest Vaudeville Mixture. by FRANK PRICE.

GALLERY	BALCONY	PIT	STALLS	GRAND CIRCLE	FAUTEUILS	PRIVATE BOXES
2ᵈ	**4ᵈ**	**6ᵈ**	**1/-**	**1/6**	**2/-**	**5/-**
3d.			Tip up Chairs	Seats Numbered and Reserved	Numbered and Reserved	7, 6, 10 6
Seats not Guaranteed		No money returned.			The right of refusing admission reserved.	

WESTERN MAIL, LTD., CARDIFF.

VIII.

IX.

X.

Houdini
the mysteriarch

Ah! Ah! I see, whence Houdini
claims his power!
The Man of mystery, is now
disclosed!
Don't try to blind again, with
a flowing shower
Of superfluous tricks,— you
are deposed!
The Devil himself, is helping
you along!
In deception's path — but
people do not see.
Are you the Devil's son?
What? I'm wrong?
Then whence to you, comes
all this mystery

H. WHITAKER
HARROW RD
LEICESTER

XI.

B.A. ROLFE

Presents

HOUDINI

IN

THE MASTER MYSTERY

By
Arthur B. Reeve
and Charles A. Logue.

Now Showing
THE GREAT
HOUDINI
in the Monster Serial
THE
MASTER MYSTERY

B.A. ROLFE PRODUCTIONS

OCTAGON FILMS, INC.

HARRY GROSSMAN, General Manager

Eighteen East Forty-first Street - - New York City

THE WORLD FAMOUS
HOUDINI

THE FIRST
HUMAN BEING
TO SUCCESSFULLY
ESCAPE FROM
A REGULATION
STRAIT JACKET
AS USED ON THE
MURDEROUS INSANE

XIV.

HARDEEN

Inherits his Brother's Secrets

"FOURTH: I give, devise and bequeath to my brother, THEODORE, Professionally known as "HARDEEN" all my theatrical effects, new mysteries and illusions and accompanying paraphernalia, to be burnt and destroyed upon his death."

Houdini

HOUDINI'S WILL

Makes possible the continuance of HOUDINI'S MASTER MYSTERIES

HOUDINI

SEE DEATH-DEFYING FEATS BY THE MASTER OF ESCAPE!

THE SENSATIONAL
HOUDINI
WATER TORTURE ESCAPE

XVIII.

Remember: This will be a "live" broadcast of a breathtaking feat never attempted before under these circumstances.

X.   Houdini saved everything presented to him by his admirers. This illustrated poem was given to him on one of his British tours.

XI. One of the publicity handouts used by Houdini on his vaudeville tours was this cut-out lock made of paper. Inside was a publicity biography of Houdini and a picture.

XII. Having spent a lifetime accepting challenges, Houdini could not resist conquering the then-new "movies." He made several adventure films, among them *The Grim Game, Terror Island, The Man from Beyond, Haldane of the Secret Service* and *The Master Mystery* series.

   Publicity folder, 1919

XIII. *The Master Mystery* was a film serial in which Houdini performed his dramatic escapes within the frame of an adventure story. His acting abilities, however, were extremely limited and his on-stage charisma did not come through on film.

   Press book, 1919

XIV. Houdini usually performed his straitjacket escapes outdoors to publicize his local performances rather than in jail cells as this poster implies. Hanging upside down from public buildings, over the heads of the crowd, was one of his favorite methods of drawing attention.

   Strobridge Lithographic Co.,
   Cincinnati, 1912
   Houdini Magical Hall of
   Fame,
   Niagara Falls,
   Canada

XV. "Buried Alive" was a feat that had intrigued Houdini for many years. He had proved his ability to sustain himself underwater for up to 1½ hours and planned his new escape spectacular for what proved to be his last tour.

   Otis Lithograph Co.,
   Cleveland, 1926
   Houdini Magical Hall of
   Fame,
   Niagara Falls, Canada

XVI. After Houdini's death, his name continued to capture the public's attention. His brother Theo, as "Hardeen," did not hesitate to promote the Houdini legend in his own publicity.

XVII. Even today the name Houdini is an interest-catcher. Here it is used in a promotion for a paper company.

XVIII. On December 26, 1975, Doug Henning performed his own version of Houdini's water torture escape. It was presented by the Mobil Oil Corporation live on NBC television and seen by fifty million people—more than saw Houdini in his lifetime.

   Artist: S. Chwast, 1975

THE CHALLENGE HANDCUFF ACT

The escape from handcuffs was a minor part of the repertoire of magicians for almost a century before Houdini. It was Houdini, however, who introduced the element of challenge into the act (together with Metamorphosis) that launched him into the ranks of big time show business.

In Houdini's words: "Returning to the subject of my career, I assert here with all the positiveness I can command that I am the originator of the Challenge Handcuff Act, which consists in the artist's inviting any person in his audience to submit handcuffs of his own from which the performer must release himself. And it is proper that I should add at this point that I do not claim to have conceived and originated the simple handcuff trick. Every novice in this line knows that it has been done for many years, or so far back, as the lawyers say, 'that memory runneth not to the contrary.' "

It is probable that in his very early days Houdini included an escape from trick cuffs in his act. A combination magic book and catalogue of tricks issued by Houdini in 1898, when he was trying anything he could think of to make a living in magic, lists "spirit handcuffs" for $10. These gimmicked cuffs were the invention of Samri S. Baldwin, the "White Mahatma," who used them, according to Milbourne Christopher, in a séance sequence in New Orleans as early as 1871. Houdini was sufficiently desperate at that time in his career to also offer in his catalogue the secrets of the challenge handcuff art (as much as he knew about it at that time) and of Metamorphosis, both "price on application."

It is likely that early in his career Houdini made some fundamental discoveries about standard handcuffs that inspired him to add the "challenge" element to the act. He learned first that most handcuffs have relatively simple locking mechanisms that can often be opened, once you have mastered the technique, with bits of wire or a spring steel as easily as with keys. He also learned that there were relatively few standard makes of cuffs and, most importantly, that nearly all cuffs of the same make and model (prior to 1920) opened with the same key. With these facts in mind, Houdini began collecting handcuffs and the keys that would open them.

In those early days when Houdini was touring what was still almost the frontier, in a circus or medicine show, it is likely that the cuffs presented to him were of a few simple makes. As his career advanced and he became famous as the "Handcuff King," he had to be ready for any challenge and *any* type of cuff no matter how special or bizarre. Luckily, by then he had developed methods to deal with these difficult handcuffs, and his knowledge of locks, which he never stopped studying, had become encyclopedic.

There is no one "secret" to Houdini's handcuff escape act, for there were literally dozens of methods for getting out of cuffs and each set presented a different challenge. Many books, even one by Houdini, have been written on the methods of handcuff escape; it is a complex and very specialized subject.

A few observations should be made on the "challenge" aspect of the handcuff act. Let's face it, not many people have handcuffs lying around the house. If they were motivated enough to go out and buy cuffs to challenge Houdini (as Martin Beck is said to have done before he offered to book him into the Orpheum circuit), they would in almost every case be regulation cuffs. The only people who would have handcuffs would be police officers and, naturally, police departments used regulation cuffs. To make sure that no other special cuffs were brought in without his having a chance to figure out how to deal with them, there was always a notice in his program which specified: "Everyone has the right to test Houdini by bringing their own handcuffs under the conditions that the handcuffs brought must be a recognized Police Regulation in perfect working order and one that has not been tampered with." The importance of these stipulations can be seen from two entries in Houdini's early diaries:

March 28, 1898—Smith's Opera House, Grand Rapids—1st week magic act, handcuffs and box. Gave exhibition Friday to packed house. Police brought 14 styles cuffs. Jan. 9, 1899—Chicago, Ill.—Mid Musee—Evanston officer Waldron fixed cuffs and put them on me. SOAB. Gained a lot of notoriety got an extra week out of it.

L 302-60

SOME OF THE PRINCIPAL HANDCUFFS USED BY THE
POLICE DEPARTMENTS THROUGHOUT THE WORLD

D is the American Bean Handcuff.
E is the American Bean Giant Handcuff.
F is the Bean Prison Leg-iron.

G is the American Army Handcuff.
H is the American Prison Adjustable Leg-iron.
I is the American Guiteau Handcuff.
J is the American Jersey Handcuff.
K is the American Lilly Iron.

The fourteen styles of cuffs brought by the police were regulation ones and Houdini was prepared to get out of them. What he was not prepared for was that Policeman Waldron would be so devious as to "fix" the cuffs he put on him by putting birdshot in the lock, thus jamming the mechanism. Houdini had to be sawed out of the cuffs and *The Chicago Journal* of January 12, 1899 headlined "Was An Unfair Test: Magician Houdini says Sergt. Waldron Played a Joke on Him". After that humiliating experience, Houdini always specified that cuffs must be *in proper working order*, which meant that they must be locked and unlocked in front of him.

In order to make sure that he could include the challenge feature in each performance, Houdini regularly planted cuffs with members of the audience to be brought on stage when he called for them. These were not specially gimmicked in any way, but were regulation cuffs. He simply could not be sure that the average member of his audience would have cuffs in his possession with which to challenge him.

There were, of course, many challenges with specially made cuffs designed specifically to thwart Houdini. There was also a statement in Houdini's program to take care of such eventualities.

SPECIAL NOTICE:—Houdini is open to accept any rational challenge from anyone, but stipulates that if accepted, twenty-four hours must be given so that such test or challenge may be duly advertised.

SOME HANDCUFF SECRETS EXPOSED.

One of the means employed of imitating the handcuff performance is to allow members of the audience to hand up locks on specially prepared neck, wrist or ankle irons, the secret of which is that the performer does not have to unlock any of the locks, but simply removes a false rivet and so releases himself. A glance at the accompanying diagram will quickly explain everything. The dotted line A shows where the rivet is held in place, and it is so constructed that it can only be removed with the use of a pair of pliers.

L   The French Handcuff with letter lock.
M   The Russian Leg-irons.
N   The Egyptian Hand and Leg Iron.
O   The Latest Russian Manacle.

P   is a South German Handcuff.
Q   is the Berliner Handcuff.
R   is the Houdini Bell Lock Handcuff. It contains a bell which
    rings when the handcuff is locked or unlocked.
S   is a Spanish pair of manacles.
T   are a pair of thumb screws which were used in the Bastile in
    Paris.

It should be obvious that this twenty-four hours also gave Houdini time to devise a way to most effectively meet the challenge.

No discussion of the challenge handcuff act should lose sight of the fact that it was not an easy act to do and required fantastic ingenuity and skill. The kind of challenges that Houdini regularly had to deal with can be seen from an account of one of his most famous escapes. In March 1904, the *London Daily Mirror* offered Houdini a unique challenge. Representatives of the newspaper said they had discovered a blacksmith who had devised a cuff that no man could pick. It was said that it took five years to construct it. Before an audience of four thousand at the London Hippodrome, Houdini was locked in the cuffs and entered his cabinet. After half an hour, Houdini requested a pillow to kneel on, but this request was denied. Twenty-five minutes later he asked for the cuffs to be temporarily removed so he could take off his coat. Since he had never seen the cuffs unlocked, this request was also denied. Houdini then, in full view of the audience, opened a penknife with his teeth and cut off the coat. Again he entered the cabinet and finally, after seventy-five minutes, he emerged free. The audience cheered as the committeemen lifted him to their shoulders and paraded him about the stage. Tears were rolling down his cheeks.

While it is unthinkable that a canny showman like Houdini would ever have accepted such a highly

149

35

HOW TO ESCAPE FROM THE GERMAN TRANSPORT CHAIN.

The way the transport chain should be fastened on the wrists.

The German transport chain is used by the German Police almost exclusively for transporting prisoners.

The chain has two rings, one for each hand, one being located at the end of the chain and the other in the centre. One lock is utilized for securing both hands. In the illustration you will note that the chain entwines both wrists, which rest one above the other.

After the chain has been fastened on your wrist as in the illustration, the first movement is to bring the arms akimbo, thereby causing one hand to lay lengthwise on the

Pulling the first band out by sheer strength, using the teeth as an aid.

Freeing the second hand with the aid of the one that was first slipped out of the chain.

other, i.e., the fingers of both hands pointing toward the elbows, and by sheer force of strength you extricate yourself from the chain one hand at a time.

publicized challenge without knowing *exactly* how he would meet it, the incident graphically illustrates how, through his showmanship, he was able to transcend the puzzle of *how* his escapes were done and move audiences to near hysteria over the fact that he was able to do them. As a memento of this spectacular escape, the original cuffs were presented to Houdini, as well as a solid silver replica of them.

Both of these sets can be seen in the Houdini Magical Hall of Fame at Niagara Falls, Canada, a "must" visit for anyone interested in the great escape artist. It should be added that, though there has been great conjecture among magicians, no one knows how Houdini escaped from the "Mirror Cuffs," as they came to be called.

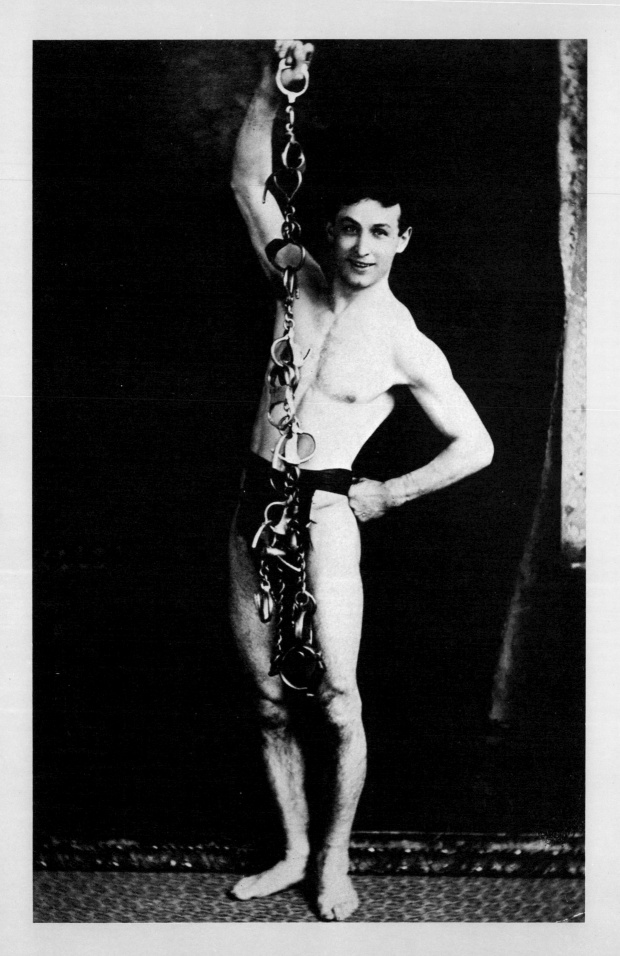

THE NAKED TEST PRISON ESCAPE

Few of Houdini's publicity stunts captured the public imagination more than the hundreds of escapes he made from prisons and jails all over the world. Even if a known criminal escapes from jail, he somehow becomes a momentary hero in the eyes of the public. Houdini exploited this public feeling about prisons and turned it into newspaper headlines in each city he played.

Houdini got his first important newspaper coverage from this stunt in Chicago in 1898 and, in the years to follow, it became his standard means of garnering wintertime headlines (the bridge jumps were for the warm months).

January 20, 1904, Sheffield, England. Houdini was stripped and his clothes were locked in one cell while he was triple-locked in another that had been occupied by Charles Peace, a notorious burglar and murderer, a few years before. Houdini escaped, retrieved his clothes and appeared dressed in five minutes. January 6, 1906, Washington, D.C. He escaped from the cell of the U.S. jail where Guiteau, "the assassin of President Garfield, was confined until he was led forth to be hanged." Stripped and searched, Houdini was locked in one cell, his clothes in another. He escaped, retrieved his clothes and switched eight prisoners around in other cells in the block. Twenty-one minutes after, he appeared in the warden's office fully dressed. March 19, 1906, Boston. Houdini was stripped and searched and locked in a cell on the second tier. He escaped, retrieved his clothes from a locked cell on the first tier, scaled the prison wall and called the prison superintendent from Keith's Theatre, all in a period of about twenty minutes. The next day a diagram of Houdini's movements in this mystifying escape appeared in the Boston papers.

Here is where Houdini's background as a magician came in. Houdini had one of the largest libraries on magic in the world and was a tireless student of magical methods. Just because Houdini's personal performing style was more suited to escapes than to magic does not mean that he did not have a vast knowledge of magic principles. To ask how Houdini concealed the picks or keys on a particular occasion is like asking how a skilled magician made a coin or playing card disappear. There are literally hundreds of different methods. As in the case of any knowledgeable magician, an important part of Houdini's skill was in picking the particular method of concealment and of misdirecting his audience's attention from the method that fitted the specific occasion. What method Houdini used on any particular jail break we will, perhaps mercifully for the Houdini legend, never know.

HOUDINI LOCKED IN.

Unlocks Prison Cells, Handcuffs, and Padlocks.

BUT NOT A CLOSET DOOR.

Held Him Fast—Locked in a Telephone Box and Couldn't Get Out.

Houdini, the magician who laughs at locks, was the victim of a joke yesterday morning that proved he is only human after all.

It was about 1 o'clock when E. P. Wilkins, a traveling man stopping at the Savoy, entered the rotunda of the hotel in company with three or four friends. As they were walking toward the counter they noticed a man go into the telephone box. Having been to the Orpheum, Mr. Wilkins recognized the person telephoning as Houdini.

Procuring a key, Wilkins stole softly to the door of the closet and locked it. "Now we'll have a matinee for our special benefit," he said, rejoining his companions.

Having finished sending his message Houdini hung up the 'phone, and turned to leave. But the door wouldn't open. He pulled and tugged at it in vain. "Some infernal fool had locked it." He kicked at it and banged on the glass, attracting the attention of several men loitering in the hotel.

These gathered about the little office and grinned sardonically. "Hi," said one, "you are Houdini, who defies any padlock, handcuff, roped trunk or prison cell. This is nothing but a modest little telephone door—it ought to be child's play for you to get out of there. Come on."

But the magician only kicked and banged and swore the louder.

"I saw he was getting angry," said Mr. Wilkins to a Globe reporter last night, "so I unlocked the door and let him out. He could hardly talk, he was so mad.

" 'What fool trick is this?' he said.

" 'Now, Mr. Houdini,' said I, 'be a good fellow. We were at the theater tonight and saw you unlock combination handcuffs without touching them with your fingers; we saw you escape from a trunk locked and bound with ropes, and we have heard of you walking out of a prison cell that was barred and double locked. Let us lock you in there again and see you come forh. Surely—' But Houdini waited to hear no more.

" 'If you want to engage me to unlock telephone closet doors you'll have to see my manager.' "

And Houdini walked away in a huff.

FATALLY SHOT.

Millionaire Wright Lies at the Point of Death From a Gun Wound.

Chicago, April .—Rufus Wright, treasurer of the millionaire bicycle tire manufacturing concern, Morgan & Wright, was shot and fatally injured late this afternoon in the rooms of Mrs. Louise Lottridge in the Leland hotel.

The affair is shrouded in much mystery. Mr. Wright himself declares it was an accident, but the police do not credit this entirely from the nature of the wound. Mr. Wright has a gunshot wound in the left side of his neck, where it was practically impossible for him to wound himself. Mrs. Lottridge insists, however, that Mr. Wright told the truth.

Wright is entirely paralyzed on the left side, and the physicians in attendance hold out little or no hope of his recovery, saying that it is probable that he will die during the night.

Mrs. Lottridge was a Miss Backus of Hamilton, Ont., when she married Mr. Lottridge several years ago. They came to ("). .

Why is Houdini, the great, like love? Because, forsooth, he laughs at locks.

Chief of the Secret Russian Police **LEBEDOEFF** has **HARRY HOUDINI** stripped stark naked and searched then locked up in the Siberian Transport Cell or Carette, May 10/1903 in Moscow and in 28 minutes **HOUDINI** had made his escape to the unspeakable astonishment of the Russian Police.

ПОЛИЦ
УПРАВА

Russia.

THE STRAIGHTJACKET ESCAPE

Houdini's escape from a regulation straitjacket of the type used "on the murderous insane" was one of his most spectacular feats. It was also less of a mystery than anything he did. This was for a very good reason. Houdini discovered that it played better that way.

Houdini claimed that he got the idea for the escape after visiting an insane asylum in St. John, New Brunswick, in 1896. He saw an inmate struggling in a straitjacket and visualized the possibilities of the jacket as an escape test. Houdini described the experience: "Entranced, I watched the efforts of this man, whose struggles caused the beads of perspiration to roll off from him, and, from where I stood, I noted that, were he able to dislocate his arms at the shoulder joint, he would have been able to cause his restraint to become slack in certain parts, and so allow him to free his arms. But as it was that the straps were drawn tight, the more he struggled, the tighter his restraint encircled him, and eventually he lay exhausted, panting and powerless to move."

From this description comes an often repeated element of the Houdini legend, that he escaped from the jacket by actually dislocating his shoulder in order to obtain slack. That Houdini actually could do this is doubtful, and I suspect that this harrowing physical feat must be classed with picking up the pins with the eyelids and untying the knots with the toes. It was, however, necessary to obtain some slack. Houdini gained this by utilizing his tremendous chest expansion, which he had developed by doing underwater escapes and by straining as much as possible against the body straps as they were being buckled. It is most important that when the jacket is put on, the arms be crossed one above the other and not folded. Then the real work begins. Houdini explained his technique in a 1908 issue of his *Conjuror's Magazine:* "The first step necessary to free yourself is to place the elbow, which has the continuous hand *under* the opposite elbow, on some solid foundation, and by sheer strength, exert sufficient force at this elbow so as to gradually force it up toward the head, and by further persistent straining you eventually force the head under the *lower arm,* which results in bringing the encased arms in front of the body.

"Once having freed your arms to such an extent as to get them in front of your body, you can now undo the buckles of the straps of the cuffs with your teeth, after which you open the buckles at the back with your hands, which are still encased in the canvas

Toledo
Jail

HOUDINI

sleeves, and then you remove the straitjacket from your body."

At first, Houdini made the escape inside a curtained cabinet, but the audience did not recognize the real difficulty of the escape. His brother Hardeen ("Dash") discovered the real way to sell the escape while appearing in 1904 at the Swansea Empire Theatre in Wales. His first escape from the jacket, performed inside the cabinet, did not register with the audience. They believed he received outside assistance. Hardeen offered to repeat the escape in full view and did so, creating a sensation. From then on, both Houdini and Hardeen performed the stunt in full view so that the audience could appreciate their struggle. Escaping from a regulation straitjacket requires tremendous skill and physical stamina. Once Houdini's audiences realized this they were able to applaud his triumph.

In later years, Houdini was to perform the straitjacket escape not only as part of his stage act, but as one of his most sensational outdoor publicity stunts, hanging from a building or suspended from a crane high above a busy street and releasing himself in an upside down position.

Walter Gibson points out that for these outdoor publicity escapes, Houdini used a regulation jacket but one designed for quick action with slightly longer sleeves and single straps instead of multiple ones on the neck, chest and body. While this was still a very real struggle, Houdini was able to cut the escape time down from a quarter of an hour of hard struggling on stage (some special challenge jackets took as long as an hour and a half!) to about three minutes hanging upside down.

The Ladies' Home Journal for May, 1918   *131*

The Last Four Pages: Edited By The Office Dog

How I Get Out Of A Strait-Jacket

Revealed For The First Time In "Close Up" Pictures And Explained

By Harry Houdini

A WORD OF EXPLANATION

ALL of Mr. Houdini's "escapes," as they are called in the language of magic, are made in a closed cabinet in which, tied and shackled, he is placed by assistants. For The Ladies' Home Journal he made this "escape" before a camera and the eyes of one of the editors of this magazine. Obviously not every move made by him could be photographed, but the pictures shown here, together with the details given in his article, form a disclosure of his feat of "escaping" out of a strait-jacket—the first "exposure" that Mr. Houdini, the greatest living American magician, has ever made in his quarter century of "escapes," and even now only with the permission of the American Society of Magicians.
— THE EDITORS.

WHILE visiting a famous asylum for the insane in Europe, many years ago, I was shown an unfortunate patient who had been condemned to the strait-jacket for his own safety. I was witnessing his efforts to free himself, when I saw at once how he might accomplish this were he able to perform a simple feat of contortion that I had always been able to do. I thereupon persuaded the head physician of the institution to sell me a strait-jacket, and when I got home I endeavored to "escape" from it and succeeded. Since then I have repeated the performance all over the world.

I generally have myself suspended by the ankles, in a strait-jacket, from some high building or lofty height, and then extricate myself in mid-air, so to speak. All my public escapes from a strait-jacket have been made by me high in the air for two reasons: first, the sensationalism of the feat, to be sure; but, secondly and more important, for the reason that, being so far up, with the crowd below me rather than on a level with me, as was the case of the camera in the present picture, it is impossible for the people to follow the movements employed by me to effect the "escape." I might just as well get out of the jacket in a cabinet.

1

Note My Square Shoulders and Expanded Chest as the Soldiers Pull Tight the Straps of the Jacket at the Back

A strait-jacket is made of canvas to which heavy smooth leather is riveted at such points as the wearer would naturally strive to employ his teeth upon in order to tear the fabric. The jacket fits closely from the neck to the lower hips. The sleeves are longer than coat sleeves by several inches and are closed, the ends continuing on the one with a heavy strap, and on the other with a strap that finishes with a buckle.

The jacket buckles all the way down the back and another strap from the hem in front passes between the legs and is caught in a buckle in the hem of the garment at the back. When worn the arms are placed in a "folded" position and the straps extending from the closed sleeves are drawn tight and buckled at the back.

IN PICTURE No. 1 the soldier is pulling the strap at the back tight, and in this instance he certainly pulled it tight! In Picture No. 2 please note the positions of my folded arms in relation to each other. When the jacket was put on me and strapped I squared my shoulders and distended my chest and stomach. When I am "hanged" to a derrick at some great height I flex my shoulders, contract my chest and stomach, and a certain looseness of the straps results. At this point I employ a "talent" which from boyhood I have been able to do at will and at ease: I dislocate both shoulders! Without the leverage afforded me by clinging with my hands I do precisely what the small boy does when he "skins the cat" on the trapeze in the back yard.

If you will compare the position of my arms in Picture No. 2 with their position in Picture No. 3, you may be able to trace the first movement. The last movement I do very quickly with a jerk of head, neck and dislocated shoulders. The result is a freedom of my arms, as in Picture No. 4. Then I reach up my back and, though my hands are still inclosed in the sleeves of the jacket, I fumble the back buckles loose, as in Picture No. 5. This done, I am entirely free, as in Picture No. 6. [Allowing for the time required for the photographs, it took Mr. Houdini just forty-seven seconds to escape from the strait-jacket.—THE EDITOR.]

NOTE—In the next issue of THE HOME JOURNAL Mr. Houdini will explain how he "escapes" from his rope ties in less than a minute.

PHOTOGRAPHS BY
WHITE STUDIO

3

I Have Dropped My Shoulders and Deflated My Chest; Note the Changed Relation of the Arms

5

It's Easy Enough Now to Reach Up and Unfasten the Buckles at the Back of the Jacket

2

This is the First Position. Observe the Placement of the Arms in Relation to Each Other Here

4

I Have Put My Head Through My Arms and They are Free

6

And So, in Less Than a Minute I Am Free. Simple, Isn't It?—When You Know How

THE OVERBOARD BOX ESCAPE

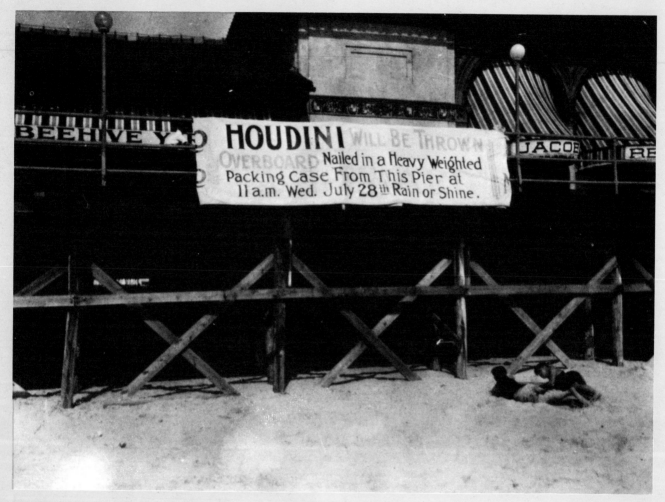

I suspect that if the average person were asked, "What did Houdini do?", his answer would very likely be, "He was thrown in the river in a box and escaped". This escape (the mythological roots of which are examined elsewhere in this book) was important because it resulted in Houdini finally getting publicity stories in the New York papers that had previously ignored his stunts. He announced that he would be manacled and nailed into a packing box weighted with two hundred pounds of lead. The box would be lowered into the East River, and he would make his escape underwater. On July 7, 1912, a huge crowd gathered to witness this death-defying escape, but the New York Police were reluctant to allow a vaudeville performer to commit suicide from one of their piers. Undaunted, Houdini hired a

tugboat and invited the press aboard. He was hand-cuffed and leg-ironed and locked in the box, which was then lowered into the water. Houdini made his escape in fifty-seven seconds and the box, still tightly nailed shut, was hauled out of the murky waters. When the box was pried open, the manacles were found inside.

Houdini repeated the escape nightly at Hammerstein's Roof Garden where a 5,500-gallon tank was specially built so that he could perform it. Later he was to perform it at the New York Hippodrome (which had a more permanent tank as part of its stage equipment) in conjunction with the Vanishing Elephant.

Houdini's notes contain dozens of ideas for box escapes. What method he used at a particular time is

HOUDINI.
1914

HINZ '71

a matter of some conjecture. One thing is certain, whatever method Houdini chose to use for a particular underwater escape, it had to be simple and absolutely sure. By the time Houdini signaled his assistants to lower the box into the water, it was absolutely necessary that, inside, he be completely free of all the manacles and that his method of escape from the box be checked out so that he knew he could get out with certainty. After the box was below the surface and water was gushing in through the airholes was no time to take care of last-minute details. The box that Houdini used for the under-

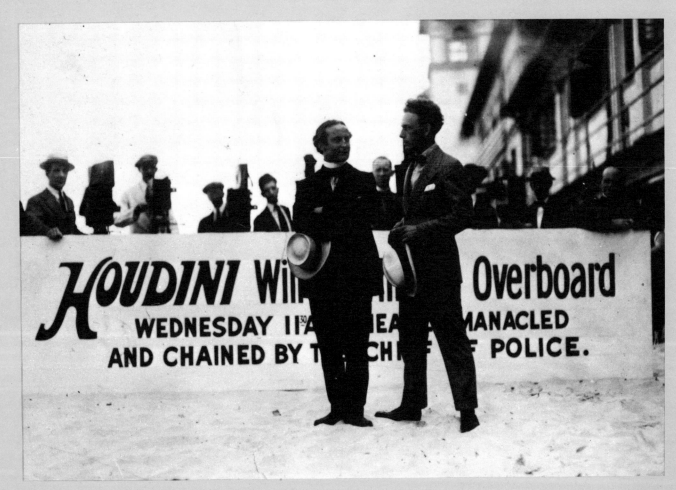

water escape was of his own construction. While it could be thoroughly examined by the committee, it was not a "challenge box" constructed by some local firm like the boxes that Houdini regularly escaped from in his stage act.

With typical flamboyance, Houdini called this escape "my challenge to death." There is no doubt that it is dangerous, and at least one escape artist has drowned attempting it. It is certain that Houdini, always a thoroughgoing professional, took no unnecessary chances.

THE MILK CAN ESCAPE

By 1908, handcuff acts were a dime a dozen. Anyone who had the money for a set of keys was doing a handcuff act. As a result, even Houdini (who did the first and best of such acts) found his career was sagging. An item in Houdini's diary early in 1908 read, "Arrived in Cleveland seven o'clock. Am not featured. Is this week the first step toward oblivion? No attention paid to me." His fears were unfounded for, in less than a month, he had built the Milk Can Escape and tried it out on Bess ("She saw me do the can trick, thinks it is great. I offered her ten dollars if she could tell me how it was done. She failed to fathom trick. GOOD.", his diary reports). He presented it for the first time at the Columbia Theatre in St. Louis on January 27, 1908. By featuring an escape that was performed underwater, Houdini brought to the stage the element of danger that had been present in his bridge jumps, and his audiences were reminded that "failure means a drowning death."

Another highly dramatic element was inherent in the Milk Can Escape and Houdini, with his usual sensational sense of theater, made the most of it. It was the idea of time running out as Houdini was submerged in the water-filled can.

A large galvanized iron can similar in shape to the cans in which milk was regularly delivered was minutely examined by a committee from the audience. While Houdini left the stage the can was filled to the brim with twenty-two pailfuls of water. Houdini returned wearing a bathing suit and entered the can, into which he just fit. Houdini would *suggest* an informal contest with the audience. He invited them to see how long they could hold their breath while he was underwater, demonstrating that he could hold his breath longer than a normal man. When Houdini disappeared from view beneath the water, most spectators tried holding their breath with him. Most could hold their breath for no longer than half a minute, while Houdini remained submerged much longer (for about a minute and a half). Then Houdini would be handcuffed and again disappear beneath the water with extra pailfuls being added to fill the can to the very top and compensate for any that had been spilled during the previous demonstration. The lid was then fastened on with six heavy-duty padlocks and the can was placed in the cabinet. Seconds ticked off as a spotlight concentrated on the front curtains of the cabinet and the pit orchestra played that popular favorite of the day,

Asleep in the Deep. After a minute and a half, an assistant would appear with a fire axe and nervously peek into the curtained cabinet. After two minutes many in the audience were afraid he was going to have to use it. After three suspense-filled minutes, Houdini would emerge dripping wet from the cabinet to what was usually an ovation from the vastly relieved audience. The milk can could once again be examined and it was still locked.

Houdini performed the Milk Can Escape as a regular part of his act from 1908 until 1912, by which time there were, as usual, many imitators. As in his other feature escapes, he would occasionally add special touches to the standard effect to get extra publicity. In some cities when a publicity tie-in could be arranged with a local dairy to "challenge" him, Houdini would escape from the can filled with real milk. On at least one occasion, Houdini nearly drowned in the milk can! In Leeds, a brewer filled the can with beer and Houdini, a teetotaller was overcome by the fumes.

Later, when a number of performers copied this mystery, Houdini had an iron-bound chest built and escaped from the locked can inside the locked chest.

By 1912 Houdini had devised a new feature to replace the can in his act, but the can continued to be featured by his brother, Hardeen, until shortly before his death at the age of sixty-nine on June 12, 1945.

On special occasions, the Amazing Randi, the outstanding escape artist of today, has performed the mystery using the original apparatus.

THE CHINESE WATER TORTURE CELL ESCAPE

By 1910, once again plagued by imitators, Houdini was searching for a new and even more sensational escape than the Milk Can which, for the past two years, had helped maintain his position as a top vaudeville headliner. Houdini created such an escape with his Chinese Water Torture Cell and it was to remain a regular feature of his programs for the duration of his career. It combined the thrilling underwater feature of the milk can with building of suspense as time ran out. Two additional features made the escape even more sensational. Houdini was locked into the cell (his ankles in massive padlocked stocks) in an upside-down position and, more importantly, the front of the cell was made of glass so that the audience could actually see Houdini under the water until the last second when the curtains of his cabinet were closed. The dimensions of the cell were such that it seemed impossible for Houdini to turn himself around even if he were able to free himself from the stocks, which were examined and secured with borrowed padlocks. (In March 1911, Houdini performed the escape in the form of a playlet for an audience of one spectator who paid one guinea for his seat. This was a form of copyrighting to register it with the Lord Chamberlain, as Houdini did not believe in patenting illusion secrets. The first public performance of the Torture Cell was in 1912 at the Circus Busch in Germany.)

One of the best descriptions of Houdini's performance of the escape is the account of a "committeeman" in the March 1913 issue of *The Magician Monthly*, a popular British magic magazine of the day.

HARRY HOUDINI'S LATEST AND GREATEST ESCAPE. A Committeeman describes the 'Water Torture Cell'

I cannot recollect exactly when or where I first saw a performance by Harry Houdini. The nearest I can get to it is to say that it was a good many years since at one of the West End variety theatres. But my recollection of the performance itself is still vividly clear. A certain London newspaper had issued a challenge to Houdini to escape from a specially constructed pair of handcuffs. He had accepted the challenge and this was the performance at which he was to attempt the escape. My seat was in the front of

the stalls, and I was able to watch the performance closely. Did Houdini succeed? Yes; but only after an hour's nerve breaking work. My sympathy, together with that of thousands of others present, was with him to the full when, at the very moment of triumph, he broke down and cried like a child.

That was a long while ago. But somehow or other I have never seen him again until the other evening at the Finsbury Park Empire. Again I was seated in the front of the stalls. When the curtain rang up on his number and he stepped on to the stage and bowed to the cheering audience, I watched him intently. A little older looking; a touch of grey in the hair; a tighter line of mouth. But still the same man; still the challenger—inviting, welcoming, opposition—even eager for it as becomes the born fighter. And if ever there was a born fighter Houdini is one! There is a suggestion of the great Napoleon about his head and the carriage of his body. "You in front," he seems to say, "which of you are my friends and which my enemies? Which believe in me and which do not? But it matters little. I am what I am; I do what I say I do. It is Harry Houdini who stands before you."

The man has personality. The mere sight of him stirs you; there is an electric feeling in the air. And when he speaks, the grip he already has on you grows tighter. As the words, well chosen, deliberate, full of meaning, come forcefully from his lips, you listen as to a master. Of what does he speak? Of the business that has brought this great audience to the theatre—of his forthcoming escape from the "Water Torture Cell."

Aided by his assistants he exhibits the cell. The construction of it is simple, so simple that the merest child in the audience can understand. Each part is shown separately. The glass front is explained. It is necessary because of the danger of a mishap during the "escape." Houdini might faint, or his nerve might suddenly give out. Is he to drown, then, to make a Finsbury Park Empire holiday? No: the watching assistant would smash the glass, and the life of the great magician would be saved. For once, and for the first time, he would have failed "to make good." But the defeat would not be final. The next evening would see another attempt which would surely be crowned with success.

And now Houdini invites a committee of the audience to step on to the stage. Several respond and among them myself. I want to see the man closer and I want to inspect the apparatus in detail. I do both.

Houdini smiles as I walk round the cell and examine every part of it. "Are you quite satisfied?" he asks. "Quite," I reply. But another member of the committee is more sceptical. "What's this for?" he inquires. Houdini explains. "What about the flooring?" the man next says. "Any trap doors?" Houdini shrugs his shoulders, and answers, "Choose any part of the stage you like, and I'll have the cell removed to it." The man quickly responds with, "Very well, then let's have it here."

The cell is removed to the position indicated. "I am ready," cried Houdini. "Begin!" He bends down, and his feet are locked into the roof of the cell. "Are you satisfied that I am secure?" he asks the committee. One man answers before the rest of us have a chance to. "No, I am not," says the sceptical member. "Let me try the key." He does so. He does more; he locks and unlocks the fastenings; he pulls Houdini's feet to and fro; he sounds the woodwork on every side. At last, in grudging tones, he announces, "All right; you can go ahead."

Meanwhile the cell has been filled with water. This is done in full view of the audience. Bucket after bucket of water is poured into it by the assistants. Gradually it fills. The audience watch the water line rise until it is level with the top of the glass front. Is there room for anything more?

There has got to be room for Houdini! He is lifted from the stage, and then lowered head downwards into the cell. The water flows out to make room for him. At last he is completely submerged. Hurriedly the roof is clamped to the rest of the cell; and hurriedly curtains are drawn round him. But not too hurriedly. The sceptical member of the committee has every chance—and takes advantage of every chance—to see that there is no possibility of deception.

We surround the curtains, and watch them closely. The orchestra plays. I smile as I recognize the air; it is "The Diver." Seconds that seem as long as minutes pass. "What of the Diver?" I ask myself. "How fares he in the Water Torture Cell?" A few more seconds, and the curtains move. We jump to our feet. Suddenly the curtains are torn asunder, and Houdini leaps through them. He is dripping with water; his eyes are bloodshot; a speck of foam is on his lips. But he is free!

And that—and that only—is what the audience have been waiting for. "He's done it," "He's escaped," "He's free!"—these cries, and others to the same effect, arise from all parts of the house. Then follows a great shout of general applause. And then a short speech by Houdini. Very short. For he has done all that he promised to do. The deed speaks for itself. Words are not wanted. The few he speaks are hardly more than a graceful farewell to his audience.

We committeemen leave the stage together.

"What do you think of it all?" I ask the skeptical member. "It knocks me," he replies, "fair knocks me." I laugh, and remark, "A wonderful escape! How does he do it?" The skeptical member shakes his head, and says "Lord only knows! I don't! And yet I watched him as a cat does a mouse. Yes, it fair knocks me!"

In 1975 when I was approached by NBC to do my first hour-long television special, I proposed that we feature a streamlined version of the Torture Cell on the show. Since I consider myself primarily a magician rather than an escape artist, I had devised a magical twist on the escape but I told neither NBC or Mobil Oil (the sponsor of the show) that this would be the case. My idea was to have the safety man, who holds the ax to chop in the cell in case anything goes wrong, wear a hooded costume. At the end of two and a half minutes, the curtains would be dropped and the cell would be seen empty. I had vanished! The hooded figure (who had been in full view throughout all of the proceedings of locking me upside down in the water-filled tank) would remove his hood—and it would be me. I felt that this surprise finish would make the effect more of a magical illusion and would also get away from the idea that I was trying to top Houdini, something I could not and would not want to do.

We realized that for the requirements of modern-day television a somewhat modernized version of the cell would be necessary. Our cell, rather than sitting on the stage floor itself, was on a high platform that could be seen under at all times. The tank, which held two hundred gallons of water and weighed over a ton, had glass on all four sides, rather than just the front, so the television camera could see into it from any angle. Finally, in addition to the locks, we had the stocks secured by an examined solid steel bar that was screwed through them from side to side and was then bolted in place. It was quite different from Houdini's original escape but was equally dangerous and maintained all of the sensational suspense elements of the original.

When I first cast eyes on the completed cell, I realized for the first time what I was in for. "How could he have done that?" I commented. "He must have been crazy!" That was the beginning of three long months of daily rehearsal before I presented the escape on live television to an audience that was actually seeing the escape at the very same time as it was being performed. Evidence that Houdini's great feature is still as sensational a draw as ever, is that the television show was one of the highest-rated specials of the year and pulled an audience of over fifty-one million viewers.

My version of Houdini's Metamorphosis had launched my professional career as a magician. Now on my first big television special I was performing another Houdini illusion. The experience served only to increase my admiration for the man. Each time I was immersed in the cell, I realized that I was taking a chance with my life. The only thing between me and drowning (hopefully my watchful assistants could have prevented that, but you never know) was my ability to hold my breath long enough to make my escape. One of Houdini's most brilliant bits of advertising was a challenge that he always posted when performing this effect. It read: "$1,000 Reward. Houdini offers this sum to anyone proving that it is possible to obtain air in the upside-down position in which he releases himself from this water-filled torture cell." I can assure you that his money was safe. There is no way to breathe when your head is five feet under water!

For the first few weeks of rehearsal, we took the precaution of placing a scuba tank at the bottom of the cell, and on several occasions I had to use it. I remind myself that in Houdini's day such safety devices had not been invented. I also ponder that Houdini was performing the feat regularly seven nights a week, with matinees on Wednesdays and Saturdays, when he was almost twenty-five years older than I. When I performed this live on my TV show, I was twenty-eight years old, and, even though I was young and in excellent shape, I was quite apprehensive the day of the show. It was being aired live, and there was no time for even a small delay.

I felt myself being raised upside-down and saw the audience still and hushed in expectation. I heard myself take four deep breaths and then, as the warm water surrounded my head, I heard the deepest silence I have ever experienced. I felt euphoric, but at the same time very alone. Looking out I could see blurred lights and colors but could make out nothing real. I relaxed to conserve air and waited for the locks to be fastened and the curtain to go up so I could begin my escape. I felt my air running out and my chest getting tight when I saw a blur of red. The curtain was up. Realizing I must work with complete economy of movement but very quickly, I began my escape. I was successful, but if I had been in the tank a few seconds longer I would surely have blacked out. I was thrilled and honored to have done Houdini's most dangerous illusion. If you really want to appreciate Houdini's genius, try doing his escapes.

THE NEEDLE TRICK

In the rather rarefied air of the world of magic historians there seems to be a minor controversy as to where Houdini learned his famous needle-swallowing trick. One thing is sure—he learned and occasionally performed it early in his career as a young dime-museum performer. In his later career it became a feature of his act, sharing the billing with such heavyweight mysteries as the Vanishing Elephant and the Chinese Water Torture Cell. One theory, advanced by the late Al Flosso, one of America's greatest magicians and a personal friend of Houdini's, was that Houdini had seen the trick performed by "Maxie, the Needle King," a fellow sideshow attraction, and that Maxie taught him the method of performing it. Since Flosso came from the same sideshow background, this has the ring of truth to it. Milbourne Christopher reports that Houdini saw the trick performed by a Hindu conjuror on the midway of the Chicago Fair in 1893 and that Houdini traded him a secret for the method. This theory is supported by an item in the catalogue section of *H. Houdini's Magic Book*, published in 1898. "Hindu Needle Trick. There are very few who know the secret of this trick, and I am the only one that sells it. Can't be had anywhere else. Was taught to me by Hindoos at World's Fair in 1893. The trick is to have committee inspect hands and mouth; you then swallow 40 to 50 sewing needles, then a bunch of thread, and bring them up all threaded. One of the best and easiest tricks to do. Secret only needed, $5.00."

Houdini was stretching the truth a bit when he stated that the trick "can't be had anywhere else." *Amateur Amusements*, a magic book published in New York City in 1879, gives the standard presentation and method for this effect, and it has been fully

HARRY HOUDINI DOES HIS NEEDLE TRICK

described in dozens of magic books since that time. Actually, the trick originated in the Orient and, in its original version, was performed with beads and horsehair thread. It is possible that the "Hindoos" did teach him the trick in Chicago. At any rate, it makes a much more glamorous story than learning it from "Maxie, the Needle King."

In his book, *A Magician Among the Spirits*, Houdini describes his presentation of the trick: "In this trick I swallow (if one's eyes are to be trusted) anywhere from fifty to a hundred and fifty needles and from ten to thirty yards of thread; then after a few seconds I bring up the needles all threaded. The length of thread is governed by the size of my audience. For instance, at the Hippodrome, in New York, I used one hundred and ten feet of thread and two hundred needles; at the Berlin Winter Garden one hundred and ten feet of thread and one hundred needles. In the regular size theatres I use about eighty feet of thread and one hundred needles but for ordinary purposes thirty-five feet of thread and seventy-five needles are sufficient.

"So far this trick has never been properly explained but that does not prove that I have abnormal powers. This needle mystery has been examined by a great many physicians and surgeons and in Boston at Keith's Theatre it was presented at a special performance to over a thousand physicians and they were never able to explain it. However, there is nothing abnormal about it. It is nothing more than a clever and natural mystification."

My personal empathic response to the needle trick (and, in fact, to all tricks where the magician puts things into and pulls things out of his mouth) has always been quite negative. I believe that such demonstrations are more disquieting than truly magical. Nevertheless, it is obvious that this must have been a very strong effect as presented by a supershowman like Houdini, and it apparently suited perfectly his style of challenge magic.

In later years, many magicians attempted to "improve" upon the trick by swallowing razor blades as they were more visible in large auditoriums than the needles. To my thinking this is as empathically bad as the needles, or possibly worse, and it should be remembered that Houdini overcame the visibility problem with sheer showmanship and presented the needle trick with great audience impact at the New York Hippodrome, one of the largest theaters in the world.

One of today's best magicians, Marvin Roy ("Mr. Electric"), performs a spectacular and less blood-curdling version of the trick when he swallows dozens of small electric bulbs followed by a length of wire and then pulls them up *lighted* in a long string that stretches completely across the stage.

Miracles of apparent regurgitation are very old and occupy an important place in the primitive magic of China, India and North Africa. Because they have remained a part of the art for thousands of years, I cannot deny that they strike some responsive chord in audiences. I can only say that they are not for me.

WALKING THROUGH A BRICK WALL

When William Lindsay Gresham wrote his 1959 *Biography of Houdini*, he subtitled it *The Man Who Walked Through Walls*. The paperback edition of Milbourne Christopher's 1969 biography of Houdini has a stylized illustration on the front cover of Houdini walking through a brick wall. The appeal of this illusion to the public imagination is obvious. The effect is simple and direct. The performer apparently does exactly what he says he is going to do. At one moment he is at one side of a solid brick wall. A moment later he is on the other.

As Houdini presented the illusion at Hammerstein's Roof Garden, the audience saw bricklayers erect a wall about nine feet high on stage. The wall was constructed on a steel beam on rollers about two inches high (obviously no room to pass underneath). A large canvas was laid on the stage with a rug on top, and the wall was positioned running front to back on top of the rug, proving that no trap doors could be used. Houdini, wearing a long white smock over his clothes, took a position at one side and a small three-fold screen about six feet high was placed around him. A similar screen was placed on the other side of the wall. Houdini would wave his hands above the screen, shouting "Here I am." The hands would disappear behind the screen as he shouted, "Now I'm going," and in a few seconds, "Now I'm on the other side." The screen that had hidden Houdini was removed and he was gone. Immediately the screen on the other side was removed. There was Houdini, smiling to acknowledge his applause. What was amazing about this illusion was that everything was without preparation and could be completely examined. It was a real wall and was seen being built. There were no traps in the canvas or the rug and, to make things even more impossible, it was performed surrounded by a committee from the audience which watched at close range to make sure that Houdini did not in some way slip around the back of the wall.

This wonderful illusion was purchased from a British magician named Josolyne; Houdini had bought the performing rights from him. In the original effect an assistant magically passed through a plate of steel. Houdini, with his typical sense of what would intrigue an audience, made two important changes. He replaced the steel plate with a real brick wall, something to which the audience could more easily relate, and instead of using a pretty girl assistant, it was Houdini himself who passed through the wall.

Considerable professional controversy arose over this illusion and the great British illusionist and inventor, P. T. Selbit, claimed the feat as his and presented it at Maskelyne and Devant's St. Georges Hall. A letter from Charles Morrit, another major British inventor of stage illusions, seems to indicate that Joselyne did invent the illusion, though Selbit was the first to perform it in England.

This illusion had one great flaw from Houdini's standpoint. While the working of most of Houdini's features was known only to him or his close associates, the secret of the wall illusion was, by necessity, known to the stagehands and others who worked in the theater. Although Houdini performed the trick a relatively few times, the secret soon leaked out and magic dealers were offering full working diagrams for the price of $1. It was also not an original Houdini illusion and he always liked to present his own conceptions, the secrets of which were closely guarded.

Once the secret of any great stage illusion is revealed, it loses its charm and its mystery. I believe this is an effect that could still enchant audiences. Perhaps someday some magician will revive it and evoke a sense of wonder in audiences that have forgotten its exposés in the popular press. There must be something powerful about an illusion that, though performed only a few times, added to Houdini's legend by making him "the man who walked through walls."

THE VANISHING ELEPHANT

Houdini's publicity boasted that he presented "the largest, the smallest and the most perplexing mystery in the world and history of magic." The smallest was, of course, the needles; the most perplexing was the Water Torture Cell and the largest was the Vanishing Elephant. The vanishing elephant seems, at least to me, to be one of Houdini's greatest mysteries in more ways than one. He performed the illusion for nineteen weeks (the longest single engagement of his career) at the New York Hippodrome, one of the world's largest theaters. Literally hundreds of thousands of people saw him do it and it was one of the illusions he performed relatively late in his career (January 7, 1918, was its debut).

Everyone remembers *that* he did it but even if you ask knowledgeable magicians who saw it (many of whom remember that it was not an exceptionally good trick), most of them seem a little vague as to *how* he did it. Gresham in his Houdini biography is reasonably accurate about the great magician's life. He describes the elephant vanish as "not much of an illusion," but then proceeds to give a description of it that is almost certainly not correct. Even Walter Gibson, one of the most knowledgeable men in magic and a friend of Houdini's, gives ways it might have worked but seems somewhat unsure of the exact method. To make the mystery even more tantalizing, some magic historians believe that the elephant vanish was a larger version of a Charles Morritt illusion, The Disappearing Donkey, which he presented in the British music halls at about the same time. It is known that Morritt conceived the idea for Houdini, but whether it was based on the donkey illusion seems somewhat less certain. Anyway, nobody I have ever talked to seems to be able to remember the exact details of the Disappearing Donkey. Thus magic retains some of its mysteries even for those of us who are involved in it professionally.

We do know some things about Houdini's illusion. The elephant entered a large box that was subsequently shown empty. The box was raised on short legs and the elephant could not go down through the stage, for below the floor was the famous Hippodrome tank containing 250,000 gallons of water. In the Hippodrome program the illusion is described, in that special prose that one feels Houdini himself must have written, as "the most colossal disappearing mystery that history records. Dissolving into thin air, on the largest stage in the world, an elephant weighing 10,000 pounds. Before one's very eyes, in a full blaze of light, with bewildering rapidity, this pachyderm monster suddenly eludes the vision."

Perhaps as clear a description of the illusion as we shall find comes from Houdini himself in a letter to Dr. A. M. Wilson, editor of the famous American magic magazine *The Sphinx*.

My Dear Dr. Wilson:

I have been prolonged at the Hippodrome as the vanishing elephant is creating so much talk, and really it is the biggest vanish the world has ever seen.

I have a wonderful elephant, and it is stated she is the daughter of the famous Barnum Jumbo.

I use a cabinet, about eight feet square, about twenty-six inches off the floor, it is rolled on by twelve men. I show all parts, opening back and front. The elephant walks into it, I close the doors and the curtains. (Doors in the back and curtains in the front), and in two seconds I open back and front and she is gone. No special background, in full-glare of the light, and it is a weird trick. In fact, everyone says "We don't see enough of it." They are so busy watching for a false move that, though the trick takes seven or eight minutes, it appears like a few seconds.

The elephant salutes me, says good bye to the audience by waving her trunk and head, turns to me, lifts up her trunk as if to give me a kiss; in fact, I say to the audience, "Jennie will now give me a kiss," but she is really coming to me with her mouth open for sugar, with which I trained her. I introduce her as the first known Vanishing Elephant.

She has a baby blue ribbon around her neck, and a fake wrist watch on her left hind leg, so the audience can see her leg until the last second, when she enters the cabinet. I say, "She is all dressed up like a bride," and that gets a big laugh; for the good-natured beast lumbers along, and I believe she is the best natured elephant that ever lived. I never allowed a hook to be used, relying on block sugar to make her go through her stunt, and she certainly is very fond of me.

She weighs over ten thousand pounds, and as gentle as a kitten.

Everything is in bright light. It is no black art, and it is a wonderful mystery, for an elephant to be manipulated. They move so slowly.

Must close, with best wishes and regards,
Sincerely yours as always,
HOUDINI

When curious people pestered Houdini about the secret of the illusion, his stock answer was, "Even the elephant doesn't know how it is done." On my second NBC television special (December 23, 1976) I presented my own version of The Vanishing Elephant. It in no way resembled Houdini's version because I, perhaps like the elephant, do not know *exactly* how Houdini's version of the Vanishing Elephant was done.

THE LEGEND

OF HOUDINI

The Magician as Mythmaker

Houdini was once quoted as saying, "When I pass on, I would rather have one line in the press than a one-hundred dollar wreath." If somewhere in that "great beyond" with which Houdini was so obsessed during his entire lifetime, he could look back and see that there has never been a year since his death when he didn't have a considerable number of lines in the press, he would, no doubt, be a happy man.

Sir James Frazer speculates in his monumental classic of cultural anthropology, *The Golden Bough,* that many mythological figures were once real people, and that "after death the myth-making fancy wove its gossamer rainbow-tinted web." That web hasn't been woven more tightly about any figure of modern times than it has about Harry Houdini. Relatively few people know specific historical facts about Houdini, but in the fifty years since his death he has become a figure of mythological stature with whom people identify.

I'm using the term "myth" not in the journalistic sense of "untruth," but in the sense of a story about fabulous things which, though perhaps not literally true, have an inner truth in that they help create "a meaningful place for man in a world oblivious to his presence." The myth-making faculty is inherent in human thought, and its products both express and satisfy human need. In this way, art (whether it be the art of the entertainer or any other form) has the power to move us because of its mythical quality—it tells us, without ever saying so in so many words, something that we want and need to hear about our lives and central problems. Myths are somewhat like dreams on a social level of experience. "Myths are public dreams; dreams are private myths," says mythologist Joseph Campbell.

In his book, *Myth and Modern Man,* Raphael Pati examines in detail how a real-life hero can achieve the stature of a mythological or legendary hero. "Despite the well-known phrase about the great man who 'became a legend in his own lifetime,'" he says, "there is no such thing as a true mythological figure who is alive." Thus the physical death of the hero is an indispensable prerequisite for the development of the myth, but this physical death must be of a very special kind and must happen to a very special kind of figure if he is to be guaranteed mythological resurrection. "The speed at which a myth can develop, provided the hero on whom it centers dies at an opportune moment and under favorable circumstances is nothing short of astounding," comments Pati. "If the death of a hero comes at a young age his chances of becoming a myth are enhanced; if he dies a violent death, if his death is surrounded by unusual circumstances, or if he appears to have sought or accepted death in devotion to or pursuance of an ideal, the likelihood of his transformation into a myth is considerable. If, in retrospect, his life can be construed as having had a pervasive central theme which appeals to the survivors, his myth is assured." Although Houdini did not exactly die in the bloom of youth, he also did not die as an old man of natural causes and all the other of Pati's requirements for becoming a mythological figure fit Houdini with astonishing accuracy.

Ever since Frazer's *The Golden Bough* was published at the turn of the century, there has been great interest among students of myths and legend in the recurring myth of the dying and resurrected hero-king. This figure, who Frazer points out was also frequently a magician, was symbolic of the annual cycle of vegetative life—the dying of the corn in the late summer and its resurrection the next spring—that was so important to all primitive people.

E. M. Butler, in her fascinating study of many of the great wonder-working figures of history, *The Myth of the Magus,* further elaborates the mythical requirements of the magician. While her study does not include stage magicians like Houdini (Christ, Merlin, Faust, Cagliostro, and even Rasputin and Madam Blavatsky are among her subjects), her observations apply equally to the great escape artist. Tracing the mythological figure of the magus through all world cultures, Miss Butler notes certain common traits. Among them are supernatural or mysterious origin (where was Houdini born and who was his real father?), special signs at birth (as an infant he never cried and slept only half as much as other babies, the Kellock biography reports), an initiation followed by distant wanderings, a magical contest and a trial, a prophetic farewell (the Houdini legend is full of omens that he, and others, are said to have had of his death), a violent or mysterious death and, finally, a resurrection. The accuracy with which this "myth of the magus" fits Houdini is almost uncanny.

The final chapter of the magus myth, that of resurrection, is a particularly mysterious one in the Houdini legend. We have seen how Houdini's entire life revolved around the death and resurrection theme. From his first fascination with the performance of Dr. Lynn cutting a man to pieces and restoring him, to his constant performance of the ritual of burial and rebirth in his escapes, to the theme of his movie *The Man from Beyond,* and his final obsession with spiritualism and its theme of return from "beyond the grave," this theme seems obvious. Some biographers have dated Houdini's obsession with death from the time of the loss of his beloved mother, but more likely his interest was sparked long before that. From the earliest days of his career, Houdini was constantly visiting the graves of dead magicians and even graves of the relatives of his friends. It is a curious fact that there are more photographs of Houdini standing in graveyards than there are pictures of him on stage performing his act. His diaries are full of notes on people who have died and of his own thoughts about death. Even his vast collection of theatrical programs contains hundreds of penciled notes in the margin, the word "dead" after the names of performers no longer living. It is not surprising, then, that Houdini made a pact with his beloved Bess promising that, if there were an afterworld and if it was possible to return from that world, he would do it. The story of this mysterious pact, and whether he did or did not fulfill it, has been one of the most fascinating, though very confusing, parts of the continuing Houdini legend.

HOUDINI AND HIS WIFE
The widow of the great illusionist continues to get "messages" from her husband by way of mediums. She calls them all nonsense.

In the months following Houdini's death, there was much talk in the popular press of the pact he had made with his widow. Houdini would have been pleased to know he continued to be so newsworthy.

RNAL

America's Greatest Evening Newspaper

2ND SECTION
THIS PAPER NOT COMPLETE WITHOUT FIRST NEWS SECTION

OUDINI MESSAGE

☆ ☆ ☆ ☆ ☆ ☆

oudini Would Make His Spirit Known," Says His Grieving Widow

DINI
d with purported messages from udini eagerly reads the contents

DEVOTED TO HIS MOTHER
Her husband made frequent trips to the cemetery and talked to his mother in her grave, says Mrs. Houdini.

SIR ARTHUR CONAN DOYLE
According to Mrs. Houdini, her husband promised Sir Arthur and a Boston man to come back, if possible.

LADY DOYLE
She fainted when Ho demonstrated his weird disappearing trick.

A Spirit Speaks

In the months following Houdini's death, there was much talk in the popular press of the pact that he had made with his widow. On his deathbed he had reportedly whispered to Bess a secret message that only she was to know. If Houdini could manage to return, he would, conveying that same message to her.

For a while after Houdini's death, Bess offered ten thousand dollars to anyone who could produce the real message. She was besieged by mediums who claimed to have contacted Houdini. None of the messages were correct, and after two years Bess withdrew the offer.

There then appeared on the scene a most important and enigmatic figure—the Reverend Arthur Ford. Ford (who died in 1971) was pastor of the First Spiritualist Church of Manhattan and one of the world's most sensational voice mediums. On February 8, 1928, through the amazing mediumship of Arthur Ford, the first of two important Houdini messages came through. The message, purportedly, was not from Houdini but from his mother, who had died thirteen years before. It was the single word, "forgive." This, indeed, was the word that Houdini had hoped to receive from his mother, although no pact was made between them that she would try to send such a word.

When Ford, through his spirit guide, "Fletcher," talked to the deceased Mother Weiss (who, he said, was standing by his side) and revealed the word "forgive," Bess was, naturally, impressed, and the newspapers picked up the story. Bess commented that there were some trivial inaccuracies in the message—among them that Houdini's mother always called him Ehrich, not Harry, as she had in her spirit-world conversation with Fletcher—but that it was the first message among thousands that had "the appearance of truth."

Impressive as Ford's message seemed at first glance, it was not the real Houdini message. Through the resulting publicity, however, Bess and the newspaper-reading public became aware of the amazing Reverend Ford. The last words of Mrs. Weiss during the séance were, "Since this message has come through, it will open the channel for the other," (Mrs. Weiss had apparently mastered English on the spirit plane, a feat she had not been able to accomplish during her earthly life). The "channel" did indeed seem to be open and it was not long before

Ford, presumably with the help of Fletcher, got to work on the Houdini message. The first word came through in a séance in Ford's home in November 1928. It was "Rosabelle." Fletcher declared that "this is the one that is going to unlock the rest." The rest was revealed in eight séances performed over a period of ten weeks. The final message, as it evolved over that period, was "Rosabelle... answer... tell... pray—answer... look... tell... answer—answer... tell." Lest this seem incomprehensible even for a spirit communication, Fletcher explained that the message was in code. "Houdini says the code is known only to him and his wife and that no one on earth but those two know it." Bess, reportedly convinced and deeply moved, agreed to a sitting with Ford since Houdini, from the spirit world, had urged this meeting at the previous Ford séance. This next séance was held at Bess Houdini's home on January 7, 1929. During the séance, Houdini (through Fletcher to Ford) repeated the message and then interpreted it explaining the code. An account in *The New York Graphic*, a popular sensational scandal sheet of the day, read as follows: "According to the code devised by Houdini some four years ago, the mystic utterances translated signified the single word: BELIEVE." A reporter from the *Graphic*, Miss Rae Jaure, was present at the séance along with other reporters. The story hit the news wires and was front page headlines everywhere. In a more detailed story in *The New York Times*, Bess was quoted: "Since Harry's death two years ago I have received hundreds and hundreds of messages from mediums, but today for the first time the message was repeated exactly by Arthur Ford, minister of the First Spiritualist Church, while in a trance in my home. They are the exact words left for me by Harry, and I am absolutely convinced that my husband talked to me and that there is life beyond the grave..."

The day after the séance Bess issued a statement which was witnessed by three persons who were present at the séance:

"Regardless of all statements to the contrary, I wish to declare that the message, in its entirety and in the agreed upon sequence, given to me by Arthur Ford, is the correct message pre-arranged between Mr. Houdini and myself. (signed) Beatrice Houdini." Witnessed: Harry W. Zander, Minnie Chester, John V. Stafford.

The next day the headlines were even bigger and newspapers across the country devoted not only stories to the event but even editorials, many of them expressing skepticism about the message and sug-

New York Eve Journal Harlem
July 10 — 1928

Vigil for Houdini's Spirit Unbroken

THE LONG VIGIL

Photo by Evening Journal Staff Photographer.
This bust of Houdini, the magician. rests in the home of his widow, at No. 67 Payson avenue, Inwood. The code message he promised to send from the land of the dead has never arrived, though Mrs. Houdini continues her vigil, now in its third year.

CODE WORD WAITED BY WIDOW

Mrs. Houdini Hopeful Dead Husband Will Keep Promise to Send Her Message.

Two years have passed since Houdini, the master magician, died—promising the world that he would communicate with his wife through a code message should he find it possible to span the gap between life and death.

In a sunlit apartment at No. 67 Payson avenue, in Inwood, a silvery-haired woman, the beloved widow to whom Houdini made that promise, when they lived in Harlem, is still waiting for the message from the other world.

Not confidently, but hopefully, is Mrs. Beatrice Houdini waiting. The years have not destroyed her belief that the ten-word code message devised by Houdini may yet come to her.

WANTS TO BELIEVE.

"I want so to believe in a communication with my husband," said Mrs. Houdini, in an exclusive interview with a Harlem-Bronx Journal reporter today. "Every day I get letters from people who say they are able to feel his presence and catch his messages. But they have nothing to show me—no proof. Perhaps they are sincere, these mediums, but they are unconvincing."

Houdini offered $10,000 to anyone who could prove immortality and communication with the hereafter. His widow has perpetuated the award and feels it is a small amount if she can really hear from her husband.

Mrs. Houdini, whose wavy silver hair was brown but two years ago, has no dread of the supernatural. About six months ago, to prove she

Continued on Next Page.

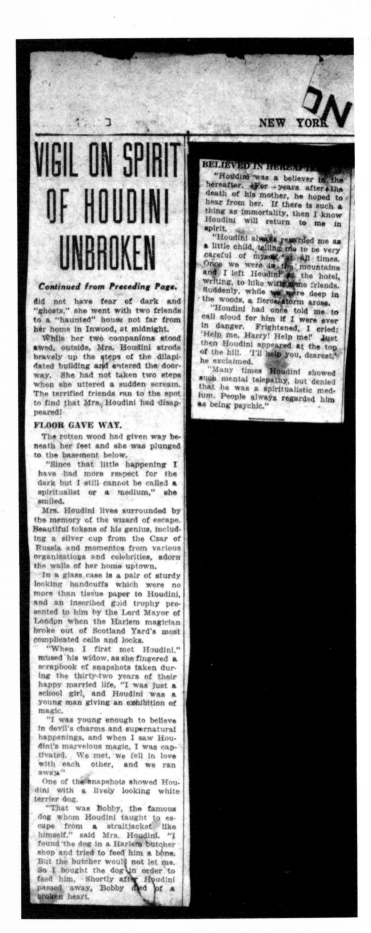

VIGIL ON SPIRIT OF HOUDINI UNBROKEN

Continued from Preceding Page.

did not have fear of dark and "ghosts," she went with two friends to a "haunted" house not far from her home in Inwood, at midnight.

While her two companions stood awed, outside, Mrs. Houdini strode bravely up the steps of the dilapidated building and entered the doorway. She had not taken two steps when she uttered a sudden scream. The terrified friends ran to the spot to find that Mrs. Houdini had disappeared!

FLOOR GAVE WAY.

The rotten wood had given way beneath her feet and she was plunged to the basement below.

"Since that little happening I have had more respect for the dark but I still cannot be called a spiritualist or a medium," she smiled.

Mrs. Houdini lives surrounded by the memory of the wizard of escape. Beautiful tokens of his genius, including a silver cup from the Czar of Russia and momentos from various organizations and celebrities, adorn the walls of her home uptown.

In a glass case is a pair of sturdy looking handcuffs which were no more than tissue paper to Houdini, and an inscribed gold trophy presented to him by the Lord Mayor of London when the Harlem magician broke out of Scotland Yard's most complicated cells and locks.

"When I first met Houdini," mused his widow, as she fingered a scrapbook of snapshots taken during the thirty-two years of their happy married life, "I was just a school girl, and Houdini was a young man giving an exhibition of magic.

"I was young enough to believe in devil's charms and supernatural happenings, and when I saw Houdini's marvelous magic, I was captivated. We met, we fell in love with each other, and we ran away."

One of the snapshots showed Houdini with a lively looking white terrier dog.

"That was Bobby, the famous dog whom Houdini taught to escape from a straitjacket like himself," said Mrs. Houdini. "I found the dog in a Harlem butcher shop and tried to feed him a bone. But the butcher would not let me. So I bought the dog in order to feed him. Shortly after Houdini passed away, Bobby died of a broken heart.

BELIEVED IN HEREAFTER.

"Houdini was a believer in the hereafter. For years after the death of his mother, he hoped to hear from her. If there is such a thing as immortality, then I know Houdini will return to me in spirit.

"Houdini always regarded me as a little child, telling me to be very careful of myself at all times. Once we were in the mountains and I left Houdini at the hotel, writing, to hike with some friends. Suddenly, while we were deep in the woods, a fierce storm arose.

"Houdini had once told me to call aloud for him if I were ever in danger. Frightened, I cried: 'Help me, Harry! Help me!' Just then Houdini appeared at the top of the hill. 'I'll help you, dearest,' he exclaimed.

"Many times Houdini showed such mental telepathy, but denied that he was a spiritualistic medium. People always regarded him as being psychic."

gesting that if Houdini were still alive he would have been able to expose the real story behind it.

The following day the whole thing exploded. *The New York Graphic*, which only the day before had run the front-page headline, "HOUDINI BREAKS CHAINS OF DEATH, TALKS FROM GRAVE IN SECRET CODE," now, in the finest tradition of yellow journalism, headlined "HOUDINI MESSAGE FROM THE GRAVE A HOAX." The story that followed told how the evening before, *Graphic* reporter Jaure had invited Ford to her apartment and he had revealed that the message was a publicity stunt cooked up between Bess and himself to promote a lecture tour the two of them were to make together. The *Graphic* story also said that their reporter had the whole story twenty-four hours before the séance took place.

Ford's encounter with Jaure was reportedly overheard by two *Graphic* staff members who were hidden in the next room. Ford denied being there and said he had been impersonated, in spite of the fact that the doorman of her apartment building identified Miss Jaure's visitor as Ford. Ford produced witnesses who swore he was with them at the time and even a man who said he had impersonated Ford. Bess, along with Ford, branded the *Graphic* exposé as false in every detail. Bess, who was not well and obviously perplexed and disturbed by the controversy that had so suddenly sprung up around her, wrote a letter to the *Graphic* columnist Walter Winchell. Some writers have said that her letter denied there was any validity to the contact with Houdini. This is hardly the case. It is a poignant protest of her own innocence in the matter and a denial of any collusion with Ford. It said in part, "This letter is not for publicity. I do not need publicity. I want to let Houdini's old friends know that I did not betray his trust. I am writing you this letter personally because I wish to tell you emphatically that I was no party to any fraud....

"When the real message, THE message that Houdini and I agreed upon, came to me, and I accepted it as the truth, I was greeted with jeers. Why? Those who denounce the entire thing as a fraud claim that I had given Mr. A. Ford the message. If Mr. Ford said this I brand him as a liar. Mr. Ford has since stoutly denied saying this ugly thing, and knowing him as well as I do, I prefer to believe Mr. Ford. Others say the message has been common property and known to them for some time. Why do they tell me this now when they knew my heart was hungry for the true words from my husband.

"I have gotten the message I have been waiting for from my beloved, how, if not by spiritual aid, I do not know....

"In conclusion, may I say that God and Houdini and I know that I did not betray my trust. For the rest of the world I really ought not to care a hang, but somehow I do; therefore this letter...

"Sincerely yours,
Beatrice Houdini."

At this point, everyone who felt strongly about the matter, or could gain some newspaper publicity from it, got in on the act. Hardeen, Houdini's brother, denounced the séance as a frame-up, and Joseph Dunninger, the mentalist, who knew Houdini, introduced some interesting facts which, as we shall see, made Ford's revelation of the "secret code" less miraculous than it seemed. Bess, who was at that time in her life sick in both mind and body and very confused by the cyclone of which she had become the center, beat a hasty retreat.

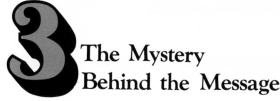

The Mystery Behind the Message

The story is a strange and, at best, confusing one. Speculation on what really happened raises almost more questions than it answers. It is interesting, however, to pose some important questions of our own and see if we can come up with at least a few answers.

Obviously the first question is: Was there a message and did Houdini reveal it to Bess on his deathbed? The Kellock biography, which is based on Houdini's own diaries and Bess's reminiscences, makes no mention of any message or pact. And, as far as I can tell, accounts of Houdini's death that were written at the time he died do not mention the message either. It would seem to be part of the legend that evolved out of later accounts of his death, and out of the reward Bess posted for any medium who could contact Houdini. But I feel that there was a pact between Bess and Houdini that he would try to come back and contact her and other close friends. One such friend was Sir Arthur Conan Doyle, who was a true believer in the beyond. In a letter to Sir Arthur after Houdini's death, Bess indicates that there was some kind of pact between herself and Harry. The letter was written on December 16, 1926, just after Houdini's death, and because it sheds some light on several aspects of the mystery, I include it here in its entirety:

"My dear Sir Arthur:

"Just read your letter and I am indeed sorry my offer of the books is refused. I fully understand how you feel about them, but I also understand whatever you do write about Houdini would be just of your belief and his, and that surely would not be detrimental to Houdini the man or yourself.

"This same subject has been sadly abused by the press. Words were printed that Houdini never said or used. I, who have lived with him so many years, know what his beliefs were. If, as you believe, he had psychic power, I give you my word, he never knew it. Often in the night I would waken and hear him say, 'Mama, are you here?' and how sadly he would fall back on the pillow and sigh with disappointment. He did so pray to hear that sentence from his beloved mother, but as the world did not know of the secret buried in his heart (his Sainted Mother died before he reached her side) he hoped and never, despite what was printed, gave up hope of hearing that one word—'forgive'.

"Two days before he went to his beloved Mother he called me to his bedside (I had been very ill

and forbidden to embrace him, as my illness was contagious), grasped my hand and prayed as only such a loving son could pray. He held my hand to his heart and repeated our solemn vow of our compact. 'Mother has not reached me, dear. I never had that one precious word, but you, dear, must be prepared, if any thing happens, dear, you must be prepared.'

"As my illness was so much more dangerous than his, at that time, and the doctor feared for my life, I naturally laughed at his fears—'Nothing, dear heart, will happen. We will soon be together on our vacation and forget all this illness.' But it did not satisfy him. He again repeated the words in formation—'When you hear those words you will know it is Houdini speaking. The same message will go through to Sir Arthur, but in that formation, only. Never despite anything will I come through otherwise', and with his dying kiss (although we did not know then) I vowed to wait for that, and only that message.

"Dear Sir Arthur, Houdini was a level-headed man. He was deeply hurt whenever any journalistic arguments arose between you and would have been the happiest man in the world had he been able to agree with your views on spiritism. He admired and respected you, therefore, as you say, you would be free to discuss this subject. Do so, surely it cannot harm him. Two remarkable men with different views. It is usually the third party that distorts the word or meaning.

"I will never be offended by anything you say for him or about him, but that he possessed psychic powers—he never knew it. As I told Lady Doyle often he would get a difficult lock, I stood by the cabinet and would hear him say, 'This is beyond me', and after many minutes when the audience became restless, I nervously would say, 'Harry, if there is anything in this belief of Spiritism,—why don't you call on them to assist you', and before many minutes passed Houdini had mastered the lock.

"We never attributed this to psychic help. We just knew that that particular instrument was the one to open that lock, and so he did all his tricks. He buried no secrets. Every conjuror knows how his tricks were done—with the exception of just where or how the various traps or mechanisms were hidden. You, Sir Arthur, could do the same tricks. It was his stunts that were dangerous.—but, it was Houdini himself that was the secret. His personality, his brilliant mind, that carried him through, and perhaps it will be this same Houdini who will come through to you or me.

"Surely, our beloved God will let him bring me the message for which I wait, and not the silly messages I get from the various people who claim they hear from him.

MELBOURNE FLORIDA,
MAY 11TH. 1934.

I SOLEMNLY SWEAR I HAVE NEVER, AT ANY TIME OR PLACE, RECEIVED A LEGITAMATE SPIRITUALISTIC OR PSYCHIC MESSAGE FROM MY LATE HUSBAND, HARRY HOUDINI.

I ALSO SWEAR IT IS MY HONEST BELIEF THAT ALL SO-CALLED SPIRITUALISTIC MESSAGES, BROUGHT TO MY ATTENTION IN THE PAST, PURPORTING TO BE FROM HOUDINI, WERE NOT SPIRITUALISTIC.

Witness *Edw. Saint* (SIGNED) *Beatrice Houdini*

SWORN TO AND SUBSCRIBED BEFORE ME THIS THE 12TH DAY OF MAY A. D. 1934

Bess in later years denied ever receiving a message from Houdini after his death.

"Please believe me when I say that I have taken an oath to tell the world when I do hear from him, also if a message directly to you, with our code comes through. The hour his soul went to his Maker (Sunday at 1:26 P.M., October 31, 1926) and every Sunday at the same hour, I spend with him, alone, in prayer.

"Write, Dear Sir Arthur, just as your heart dictates. My beloved will understand, and no one else counts.

> *"My love to you and yours,*
> *B.H.*

"P.S. One exception to your article enclosed. Houdini's mother never spoke Yiddish, not even Hebrew,—German, French, Italian, Spanish and her own Hungarian only. Is there any objection to me presenting the sketch book of your father or other books to your boys or Billy. Again lots of love to you all.

> *B.H."*

In addition to being a touching insight into Bess's feelings about her husband, as well as showing her denial that he ever believed he had psychic powers (as Doyle and other believers asserted again and again) and her attitude toward his secrets, this letter also reveals one other thing—it tells Doyle that Houdini was waiting for the word "forgive" from his mother. This is, of course, the first Ford message, the one that Bess said was the one out of thousands that had an "appearance of truth."

The second question we must ask has two sides to it: could Reverend Ford have obtained information about the code and the message before his séance with Bess, or is it possible that Ford was a genuine medium (if there is such a thing) and was in fact in communication with the spirits of the dead?

I believe that an open attitude toward the mysteries of the universe is essential for all of us. And I think that Houdini, throughout his crusade against fraudulent spiritualists, kept his mind open to the possibility that somewhere, sometime, such a thing might be possible, and that it is important to retain this same state of mind when examining the work of any psychic. Houdini was never able to find the genuine article, and I feel that this was a great disappointment to him, but in spite of this he never, to my knowledge, said that psychic phenomena were totally impossible. I must say, however, that in view of the facts about the Reverend Ford, which we will examine in the following pages, I personally don't believe that he was a genuine psychic.

If Ford, as I suspect, did not receive the Houdini messages from beyond the grave, then where did he get them?

To arrive at a tentative answer to that question we must remind ourselves that there were two distinct messages produced by the Reverend Ford. The first of these was purportedly from Houdini's mother. The second was supposed to be from Houdini himself. Where Ford might have obtained the so-called secret information for the first of these messages is not very difficult to figure out.

Christopher speculates in his biography that Reverend Ford could have had access to Bess's letter to Sir Arthur Conan Doyle that contains the key word "forgive" even before Ford's séance with Bess. He points out that in Ford's autobiography, *Nothing So Strange*, the Reverend tells of a visit to England in 1927 during which he talked to Doyle several times. It is very possible that Doyle could have mentioned the letter or even shown it to Ford, not deliberately to feed the medium information, but simply to illustrate some point about Houdini. Doyle was above all else a noble man of great integrity, but he was credulous and believed implicitly in the genuineness of Ford. As more facts about Ford's methods are revealed, it appears that Doyle's trust in the spiritualist was perhaps excessive. Even if Ford hadn't seen this letter from Bess to Sir Arthur, there is another, even easier way (also pointed out by Christopher) that Ford could have gotten the information. In an interview in the *Brooklyn Eagle* of March 13, 1927, Bess stated that any authentic communication from Mother Weiss would have to include the word "forgive." It is very likely that Ford was aware of this newspaper interview. Thus he would have been able to deliver the message from Houdini's mother without the aid of his spirit guide, "Fletcher"!

Two remarkable bits of evidence about the Reverend Arthur Ford have come to light since his recent death. Both are revealed in books written by men who are firm believers in the reality of psychic phenomena and of spirit communication. The first of these books is *Arthur Ford—The Man Who Talked with the Dead*, by Allan Spraggett (in collaboration with the Reverend Canon William Rauscher). The second is *The Spiritual Frontier*, by the Reverend Rauscher (in collaboration with Allan Spraggett). It is a credit to both authors that when they discovered their idol to have feet of clay they had the courage to admit it. There are many things that Arthur Ford did for which the authors have no explanation, and which they attribute to genuine psychic powers. They do, however, present overwhelming evidence that at other times he was cheating.

Ford's last great spurt of worldwide publicity took place shortly before his death when, during a televised séance (arranged by Spraggett and Rauscher), he allegedly contacted the deceased son of the late Bishop Pike. In this séance Ford revealed much information that Pike swore could have been learned only through spirit sources. After Ford's death, an inventory of his personal effects revealed that he was a tireless researcher and maintained files of newspaper clippings (obituaries were a major part of them) containing information that might some day come in handy in his séances. Much to the disillusionment of Spraggett and Rauscher, it was found that virtually all of the supposedly unknown information revealed by Ford in the Pike séances was in his newspaper files, carefully underlined. The whole story, with no punches pulled, is fully reported in the Ford biography. An appendix to *The Spiritual Frontier*, titled *The Houdini Mystery Solved*, offers further illuminating information on the working methods of the Reverend Ford.

Now another question comes to mind: Was Mrs. Houdini part of a plot with Ford to gain publicity, or was she somehow duped by Ford into giving him the information he needed for the second séance in which he supposedly contacted Houdini himself? After the publication of the Ford biography in 1973, Rauscher was contacted by a man living in New York named Jay Abbott, who said he could offer some interesting information on the Houdini mystery. It turned out that Abbott (now deceased) was a close friend of both Reverend Ford and Bess Houdini, and had dozens of letters they had written him as well as many other mementos of them. Abbott said that Bess and Ford had been close friends long before the date of the famous séance and frequently went out together. It was Abbott's contention that Ford had duped Bess, and it was only later, after the flurry of publicity over the séance, that she realized it. According to Abbott, Bess told him that one day she was washing her hands when her wedding ring slipped to the floor. Ford, who was there, picked it up. Engraved inside the ring was "Rosabelle," the key to the secret message. This, said Abbott, was how Ford got that needed clue.

There is another theory, popular with those who collect gossip about the magic world, about how Ford could have obtained the contents of the second, and more important, Houdini message. It is popular perhaps because it supplies a spicy element of scandal in the very conservative life of Houdini. This theory is that the message was revealed by Houdini to Daisy White, a lady with whom he was presumably having an extramarital relationship, and that Daisy, in turn, passed the message on to Ford. Probably to the disappointment of those who would like some juicy gossip about Houdini, an examination of the available facts seems to indicate that there is absolutely no truth in the story.

Houdini did know Daisy White, and it is likely that she was attracted to the famous magician. Daisy had worked as an assistant to magician Frank Ducrot and later worked as a clerk for him when he was owner of the famous Martinkas Magic Shop (which years earlier had been owned for a brief period by Houdini). Houdini frequently purchased props at Martinkas, and it is said that he once helped Daisy out of some financial trouble as he had helped literally hundreds of others throughout his life. It is almost certain the relationship with Daisy went no further. It is possible that the flirtatious Daisy would have liked it another way, but Houdini was prudish and ultraconservative and had been happily married to the same woman for over thirty years. He was certainly a poor prospect for any kind of amorous conquest.

Daisy, apparently to see Houdini's reaction, had written him several torrid love letters, as had many other women he had never met but who adored him on the stage or screen. Houdini's vanity never allowed him to throw away any scrap of paper that mentioned his name and so he saved the letters. After his death Bess found them, and Gresham reports that Bess "pitched quite a fit" over them but that Daisy explained to her that it was "all in fun." Christopher says that Bess found, in their safe, a thick packet of letters from various women who had fallen in love with Houdini. "Months later," he writes, "Bess gave a tea party. Most of the guests had never been invited to the Houdini home before. After a pleasant afternoon, Bess stood at the door and gave each of the departing ladies a present tied in a ribbon. Inside were that woman's letters to Houdini." Christopher feels sure that the women's attentions were never reciprocated by Houdini, and Houdini's own enraged reaction to what he considered to be marital infidelity within his own family certainly bears this out. Among Houdini's effects a last letter to Bess was found.

"Sweetheart, when you read this I shall be dead. Dear heart, do not grieve. I shall be at rest by the side of my beloved parents, and wait for you always— remember! I loved only two women in my life, my mother and my wife. Yours, in Life, Death and Ever After."

There is one other explanation of how Ford could have gotten the Houdini message, subsequently revealed in his séance. In order to understand what I believe to be the true story behind the message we must look at two elements of the information that Ford (or was it his spirit guide, "Fletcher"?) revealed. First let us look at the so-called secret code and then at the contents of the message itself.

The key word "believe" (supposedly known only to Bess) was delivered in code—a code that Harry and Bess used in their early days in show business when they did a two-person mind-reading act. We have it on the authority of "Fletcher" that "Houdini says the code is known only to him and his wife and that no one on earth but these two know it." If this is truly what Houdini said to "Fletcher," it indicates that perhaps, busy with other affairs in the land of the spirits, he had not kept up with the growth of his own legend! When the Houdini séance story hit the headlines, Joseph Dunninger was quick to point out that the code had in fact been *published* two years before in the Kellock biography, largely based on the "recollections" of Bess herself! So much for the "secret" code.

Next we must look at the contents of the message. It is even possible to ask the question: Was "Rosabelle believe" actually the secret message? (Houdini scholar Manny Weltman doubts that there was a specific message at all.) We do know that Bess told interviewers that there was only one copy of the message in existence and that was locked in the vault of her bank. She never produced this copy for anyone to see. And Christopher's research reveals a remarkable statement that Bess made to the *New York World* on January 9, 1929, which throws the whole matter of exactly what the message was into considerable doubt: "I had no idea what combination of words Harry would use," she says, "and when he sent 'believe' it was a surprise."

In discussions with people who knew Bess Houdini in later life and with surviving members of her immediate family, I can come to only one sad conclusion. It is that Bess either gave the message to Ford (if there was a specific message) or at least

agreed that Ford had produced the message (even if there was not one).

Why would Bess, the faithful and loving wife of Houdini, have betrayed his trust? One can only speculate. We know that after her beloved husband's death Bess was emotionally destitute and in poor health. Never one to refuse an occasional drink (unlike her teetotaling husband), after Houdini's death Bess began to drink heavily, and a failure to make a comeback in show business with an act of her own as well, a lack of success at other business projects, made her emotional state even worse. She had a drinking companion in Arthur Ford, who had a serious problem with alcoholism throughout his life. After Ford's first revelation of the message from Houdini's mother, Ford and Bess became friends and for a period were known to be social companions. It is said that Ford and Bess had even planned a lecture tour together and to promote this, and gain much-needed publicity, I believe that Bess, sick in mind and heart, agreed to the genuineness of the Ford message. When she later realized what she had done she suffered a complete emotional collapse, and in later years, in a state of greatly improved mental health, she always steadfastly denied that her beloved husband had ever contacted her from the grave.

We will probably never know all the details of this last great Houdini riddle. Each year on the anniversary of Houdini's death, Bess attempted to communicate with him, but with no success. In 1934, after unsuccessful attempts to return to the stage and to enter the restaurant business, Bess moved from New York to Hollywood. There she met a man who was to be a major guiding influence during the rest of her life. His name was Dr. Edward Saint, an ex-crystal gazer and part-time psychic investigator. Christopher points out that, as an old-time showman, "he could talk Bess's language," and he became her business manager and constant companion.

You are invited to attend
Final Houdini Seance
8:30 to 9:00 P. M.
October Thirty-first, Nineteen hundred thirty-six
(Hallowe'en)

EDWARD SAINT
DIRECTOR FINAL SEANCE

Under Saint's expert guidance, a "Final Houdini Séance" was arranged. It was held on October 31, 1936, the tenth anniversary of Houdini's death, on the roof terrace of the Hollywood Knickerbocker Hotel. Invitations, engraved in gold, were sent to a select group of friends, magicians, Hollywood celebrities and the press. The ceremony was elaborately staged, but Houdini gave no indication of his presence, although a sudden rainstorm (some say it was only a mist) was interpreted by a few believers as a sign of some sort. "Houdini hasn't come," said Bess, "I am now convinced that he will never be able to come through. I will extinguish the light on his shrine. My last hope is gone." (A recording of this séance has recently been reissued on an LP record in time for the fiftieth anniversary of Houdini's death.) Before her death (February 11, 1943), Bess told reporters that when she was gone, she'd be gone for good and had no intention of trying to come back.

Each Halloween, on the anniversary of Houdini's death, magicians all over the United States celebrate National Magic Day (established largely through the efforts of Dr. Saint to keep the Houdini name before the public), and invariably many séances are held—more, I suspect, for the publicity value than for any serious attempt to contact Houdini.

I wish to thank all the Individuals and Magic Societies that joined in the Final Houdini Seance which encircled the world, October 31, 1936.

Those names and records will live forever in the Houdini room in the Congressional Library at Washington, D. C.

Since the failure of the ten year test, it is my opinion that all concerned have struck a mighty worldwide blow at superstition.

MRS. HARRY HOUDINI

EDW. SAINT
Director
Final Service

A thank you note sent by Bess for the final Houdini séance, October 31, 1936.

'I Have No Fear of Death'

White-haired, and with illness shrinking her weight to a mere 72 pounds, Mrs. Beatrice Houdini, widow of the famous magician, gave one of her last interviews here today and said, "I have no fear of death, but when I die, even if I should have the supernatural power to come back to the world, I shall never come back." She is shown, at left, with her sister, Mrs. Marie Hinson, who will accompany her to New York.

As her own death approached, Bess continued to express her disbelief in a hereafter.

4 The Undying Legend of Harry Houdini

The myth of Houdini, which is the classic myth of the magician, is as strong today as ever. Albert F. McLean, Jr., in his fascinating book, *American Vaudeville as Ritual,* convincingly argues that vaudeville, as the first American mass entertainment medium, was not only an important social institution but was also "a mythic enactment—through ritual—of the underlying aspirations of the American people". He points out that vaudeville was a major way in which the disruptive experience of migration (from an agrarian culture to an urban one) and emigration (from the Old World to the New) was objectified and accepted. At the center of this ritual of the new urban mythology was the towering figure of Houdini—the hero-magician enacting the same rituals of death and resurrection that had been a part of all cultures for untold thousands of years.

It is interesting that Osiris, one of the earliest and most important of the ancient Egyptian gods of death and rebirth, was put into a box (by his brother Set) which was nailed shut, sealed with molten lead and thrown into the Nile, and that this pattern was repeated with dozens of later gods who were sealed in containers and thrown into the water. As a central figure in the vaudeville ritual, Houdini was symbolically relating exactly the same message as these ancient gods to the people of his time, and I believe this is an important factor in the mythical stature he has achieved.

In the late nineteenth and early twentieth century, people flocked to the cities, from foreign lands, from the farms and from rural towns of America, to start a new life—to be reborn. Houdini told them, through his triumph over seemingly insurmountable obstacles, that this was possible.

Each age recreates the old myths in its own terms and creates its own mythological figures who are embraced by the mass public because they symbolically express the unconscious values of that society. Today, magic is having its greatest renaissance since the time of Houdini. I believe that the reasons are similar. Magic is telling people, as all myths and rituals do, something they want and need to hear. The end message of magic is the same, "You can be born again," but the means of reaching that end are quite different.

Houdini was a part of the American Dream. Like Horatio Alger and Tom Swift, he symbolized the triumph of mind and body over the restraints of the world and delivered to his audiences the unconsciously perceived message that, through pluck and perseverance, through technological knowledge and physical prowess, they could be born again into the new world of urban America.

Today the battles of urban assimilation have all been fought (and have been won or lost depending on one's individual point of view), and the rebirth that magic symbolizes is of a quite different order. It is a rebirth through wonder, transcending one's physical reality and expanding one's consciousness, that will bring, not triumph *over* nature but harmony *with* it.

Cultural anthropologist Joseph Campbell points out that the first function of a properly operating mythology is the mystical function: "to waken and maintain in the individual a sense of awe and gratitude in relation to the mystery dimension of the universe, not so that he lives in fear of it, but so that he recognizes that he participates in it, since the mystery of being is the mystery of his own deep being as well." This, in its own way, is what magic, as a theatrical art, expresses.

Today, many major figures of science have become aware of the wonder that is central to our contemporary experience of the world. Quantum physicist John A. Wheeler eloquently expressed this when he said, "There may be no such thing as a glittering central mechanism of the universe. Not machinery, but *magic,* may be a better way to describe the treasure that is waiting to be discovered by science."

These insights of our present day go far to explain why Houdini, whose name has become synonymous with the sense of wonder, still lives and will continue to live as a figure of popular legend rather than of theatrical history. Like Charlie Chaplin and Mickey Mouse in the movies or Sherlock Holmes in literature, Houdini has become part of the mythology of our time. Fifty years after he vanished from the theatrical scene, Houdini is a figure of ever-growing legend. He is a hero who stands for the conquest of possibility over impossibility and, in this age when man is exploring the outermost regions of space and reaching the innermost realms of the mind, Houdini's message of wonder is more timely than ever.

Dedication

This book is dedicated to the memory of my chosen sister, Barbara.

Acknowledgments

The basis for the directions in this book were originally written by Don Wiener, one of the founders of PRO Chemical & Dye, Inc. (PRO Chem). Over the years, I have always turned to Don for assistance with my personal dyeing experiments and business. So, when I was invited, in 1991, to manage the dye laboratory at PRO Chem and work with Don, I was elated. Don, who had been my mentor and friend for years, was now a daily source of inspiration and enlightenment. He is an important part of this book. The knowledge and experience Don has shared with me, and what I gained from working at PRO Chem, I now share with you.

This book marks an emotional and eventful crossroads in my life. Its publication is the result of the unequivocal support and love of many people: some helped in technical ways, others provided wise counsel or quiet space. Many thanks to my family for their help and wisdom, from the long conversations with my mother, Maurine Noble, to the personal and professional support from my husband, Ron—it has always sustained me. My sincere gratitude to Adelle and Don Wiener, Steve Grunebach, Debi Hogan, Karen Perrine, Vicki Jensen, and Nancy Rodrigues. I thank the late Barbara Eckhardt for her friendship, support, contagious enthusiasm, and—most of all—for sharing her courageous spirit.

A very special thanks to the staff at PRO Chemical & Dye, Inc., whose tireless efforts in helping me track down information and recheck numbers and facts, made this book a reality.

I am fortunate to have textile-artist friends who continue to inspire me with their work and inventiveness; I am indebted to those artists whose exceptional work helps illustrate this book.

My appreciation goes to Melissa Lowe, whose excitement about *Dyes & Paints,* faithfulness to the manuscript, lighthearted approach to editing, and patience during my recovery made working with Fiber Studio Press a pleasure.

Finally, thank you to my students, who asked many questions and also helped answer them. I am grateful to all of you who, like me, get excited over a length of a beautifully dyed cloth.

Contents

Dyes & Paints

A Hands-On Guide
to Coloring Fabric

Credits

Editor-in-Chief .... Kerry I. Smith

Technical Editor .... Melissa A. Lowe

Managing Editor .... Judy Petry

Copy Editor .... Tina Cook

Proofreaders .... Leslie Phillips

Meilssa Riesland

Kathleen Pike

Design Director .... Cheryl Stevenson

Text and Cover Designer .... David Chrisman

Logo Design .... Mint Evans

Design Assistant .... Keather Weideman

Illustrators .... Laurel Strand

Robin Storbel

Photographer .... Brent Kane

*Dyes & Paints: A Hands-On Guide
to Coloring Fabric*
© 1998 by Elin Noble
PO Box 161
East Freetown, MA 02717 USA
Printed in Hong Kong
First Printing 2003
ISBN 0-9728252-07
(previously published by Martingale & Company,
ISBN 1-56477-103-2)

Library of Congress Control Number is available
from the Library of Congress (previously published
1997, TT853.N63, 746.6-DC21, 97-27637 CIP)

• *Dyes & Paints* is the winner of the 1999 INDEPENDENT PUBLISHER BOOK AWARDS for the best "How-To Book".

The Independent Publisher Book Awards are conducted annually to honor and recognize the year's best independently published titles. Conceived as a broad-based, unaffiliated awards program open to all members of the independent publishing industry, the IPPY Awards reward those who exhibit the courage, innovation, and creativity to bring about change in the world of publishing.

⋀ *Aqua Detritus*
by Karen Perrine, 1996, Tacoma, Washington,
34" x 171". **Method**: Fiber-reactive dye on cotton.
Machine pieced, hand appliquéd, and machine
quilted. Photo by the artist.

> Detail of *Aqua Detritus*

Foreword

"Surface design" is a relatively new term for an activity as old as man, the coloring and embellishing of surfaces that are a functional part of daily life. Although technically the definition encompasses any coloring applied to paper, basketry, leather, or even metals, most surface designers today work with fabric. Fiber is familiar, closer to us than any other medium, and color is what we see first. No wonder that coloring fabric has a magical appeal.

Any contemporary gathering of surface designers will include a number of artists, usually women, who discovered dye twenty to thirty years ago during the tie-dye craze of the 1960s and early 1970s. Elin Noble and I are charter members of the club. However we came to get our hands immersed in it, dye has held us captive ever since. We share stories of lengthy searches for cotton fabrics in an era of polyester and remember heroic quests for written instructions. Dyes of dubious provenance and mysterious content were widely available then, but accurate information on what, why, and how was nonexistent. As the tie-dye fad faded, supplies became hard to find and sources disappeared overnight. We often had to begin all over again with a new type of dye, purchased by mail from a post office box in a small town hundreds of miles away. All of us from that era did lots of experimenting out of necessity.

Elin Noble began her colorful journey by accident, discovering dyes in the textile design program at the University of Washington. She was, and is, intensely curious, and dye quickly became her intellectual focus and passion. It became subject to The Elin Method: research extensively, ask lots of questions, read everything available on the subject, experiment exhaustively, keep good records, and teach. Her long friendship and working relationship with Don Wiener, a founder of PRO Chemical & Dye, Inc., has led to invaluable insights into achieving the most permanent, repeatable results, using ingredients efficiently and reducing variables.

To those who are new to dye and to those who are experienced, this book offers the gift of proven methods that speed us to the business of painting glorious cloth. Elin says this book arose from her students' questions. We thank her for her lovingly crafted answers.

Karen Perrine

Preface

I never meant to write a book. My schedule was full with managing the lab at PRO Chemical & Dye, traveling, teaching, and dyeing fabric. But my students kept asking questions (often, in fact, the same questions). This book is the result. It was born of and grew in response to your questions and encouragement.

Many of you, knowing I was working on a book in 1994, wondered what had happened when that book didn't appear. In 1995, several weeks before I was scheduled to work on the photo shoot, I became severely ill with Lyme disease. Initially, doctors could not find the cause of this sudden onset of varied and recurring symptoms. Not knowing what is wrong with you is really quite silencing.

But, thanks to a handful of dedicated people, the crisis passed. My health is slowly returning, which leads me here, to finishing this book (and, of course, the photo shoot). I vividly recall Karen Perrine's enthusiastic and soothing voice when we first discussed my need for help with the photo shoot. She gracefully and willingly offered her artistry, technical proficiency, and inquisitive, "itchy" mind. Karen's enthusiasm and support are important additions to *Dyes & Paints*.

Elin Noble

Introduction

Dyeing and coloring fabric is exciting, captivating, and extremely rewarding. *Dyes & Paints* focuses on the fundamentals of dyeing and coloring 100% cellulose fabrics with fiber-reactive dyes and textile paints. The techniques in this book can be used for coloring cloth or adapted for thread, yarn, ribbon, handmade paper, basket reed, and even wood.

Many people try dye and textile paint because the fabric colors or patterns they want are hard to find. When you are able to color and pattern your own cloth, you are no longer limited to what is in stock at the fabric store. Instead, you can produce fabric of any hue, value, and intensity you desire.

Don't jump into these recipes expecting to reproduce a specific piece or style of hand-dyed or -painted fabric. Textile artists spend years cultivating and developing their technical ability and style. If you find a piece of hand-dyed fabric you love, buy and appreciate it! I continually find lengths of fabric from all over the world that are enriching and exciting. The color, pattern, and drape of these coveted fabrics are wonderful sources of inspiration.

This book guides you through a variety of dye and pigment applications. My aim is to give you a solid foundation for further exploration, especially the information you need for problem solving. There are some processes and technical aspects of coloring fabric that are beyond the scope of this book. For information on other types of dyes, application methods, and dyeing techniques, I encourage you to read the books listed on page 159.

I offer this book as a beginning, rather than as a means to an end. The techniques will give you a foundation, a jumping-off point, for developing your own style of dyeing and coloring fabric. I urge you to experiment and to build on these techniques. I hope that, as you gain experience, the technical processes become second nature, so you can focus on the soul of your work.

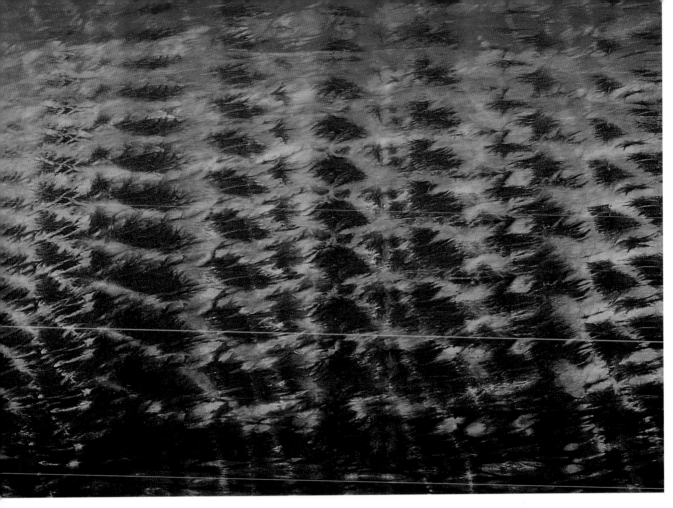

⋀ Untitled yardage

by Michael Mrowka for Lunn Fabrics, 1994, Lancaster, Ohio. **Method**: Fabric bound, then dyed in multiple immersion dye baths. Photo by John Bonath at Mad Dog Studio.

⋖ Untitled yardage

by Michael Mrowka for Lunn Fabrics, 1994, Lancaster, Ohio. **Method**: Fabric folded and clamped, then dyed in an immersion dye bath. Photo by John Bonath at Mad Dog Studio.

⋁ Untitled yardage

by Stacy Michell for Shades, 1994, Marietta, Georgia. **Method**: Fabric dyed with direct-application technique. Photo by the artist.

∧ Untitled yardage
by Michael Mrowka for Lunn Fabrics,
1994, Lancaster, Ohio. **Method:** Fabric
dyed in multiple immersion dye baths.
Photo by John Bonath at Mad Dog
Studio.

＞ Untitled yardage
by Stacy Michell for Shades, 1994,
Marietta, Georgia. **Method:** Fabric
dyed with direct-application technique.
Photo by the artist.

⋀ Untitled yardage
by Stacy Michell for Shades,
1994, Marietta, Georgia.
Method: Fabric dyed with direct-
application technique. Photo by
the artist.

⟨ Untitled yardage
by Michael Mrowka for Lunn
Fabrics, 1994, Lancaster, Ohio.
Method: Fabric bound on a pole,
then dyed in multiple immersion
dye baths. Photo by John Bonath
at Mad Dog Studio.

> *City Light*
by Carol Keller, 1996, Somerville, Massachusetts, 68" x 58". **Method**: Fiber-reactive dye on cotton muslin and cotton sateen. Machine pieced and quilted. Photo by David Caras.

∨ *Encore*
by Janet Steadman, 1995, Clinton, Washington, 64" x 45". **Method**: Hand-dyed cottons by Liz Axford and Connie Scheele. Machine pieced and quilted by the artist. Photo by Roger Schreiber.

∧ *Within/Without 5*
by Liz Axford, 1995, Houston, Texas,
25" x 25". **Method**: Fiber-reactive
dye on cotton. Machine pieced and
quilted. Photo by Hester and
Hardaway.

< *Linear Study #7*
by Nancy Crow, 1996, Baltimore,
Ohio, 39" x 42". **Method**: Fiber-
reactive dye on cotton. Machine
pieced. Hand quilted by Marla
Hattabaugh. Photo by J. Kevin
Fitzsimons.

▲ *Spheres and Atmospheres*
by Rosemary Hoffenberg, 1995, Wrentham, Massachusetts,
61" x 58". **Method**: Fiber-reactive dye on cotton. Photo by
David Caras.

Part I: Basics

Using This Book

This book is organized into three parts: learning about dyes and paints (Part I), using fiber-reactive dyes (Part II), and using textile paints (Part III).

There are two basic methods of applying dyes to fabric: immersion dye bath (also known as vat or exhaust dyeing) and direct application (by hand). This book covers many techniques for and variations of both application methods, in addition to the standard dye bath: value gradation, hue gradation, immersion dyeing with a resist, tie dyeing, fold-and-dip dyeing, hand painting a design, color wash, monoprinting, stenciling, stamping, hand painting with a resist, and stamping with a resist.

Textile paints are usually applied by hand. As with dyes, this book covers many different techniques and variations, including stamping with leaves and shells, stenciling, sun printing, and marbling.

If you are new to coloring fabric, I urge you to read through the book rather than skipping directly to a specific application procedure, which I call "recipes." I know it's tempting to jump ahead, but there is helpful information on every page! Be sure to read "Protecting Yourself and Your Environment" on pages 16–17.

Understanding Dyes and Paints

Fiber-reactive dyes and textile paints color fabric in different ways. This does not mean that one is better than the other—each has advantages and disadvantages, depending on the desired result.

When you apply fiber-reactive dyes to fabric, a chemical reaction occurs and the dye molecules bond with the fabric molecules. The chemical bond cannot be broken or reversed, so the fabric is washfast. To remove color, as in a discharge process, you must destroy the color part of the dye molecule.

No creative artist. can be anything so long as his hands have no share in shaping things.

Goethe

Helpful Hint

Substituting Dyes and Paints in the Recipes

As you work through the recipes, you may want to try stenciling with dye instead of with textile paint or immersing fabric in paint instead of in dye. Go ahead! The key is to match the viscosity of the dye paste or textile paint to the viscosity in the recipe, then set the dye or paint as needed. For example, mix a thick dye paste—the same consistency as textile paint—to stencil dye. Apply the dye paste as you would the paint, then **cure** the dye following the instructions for using thick dye paste. (Remember to wear gloves when using dye paste.) Or try dipping fabric in a bucket of diluted textile paint. Don't be frightened. Improvise, experiment, and enjoy yourself.

Safety equipment for working with fiber-reactive dyes

This type of chemical reaction does not occur with textile paints. Instead, textile paints contain a "binder" or adhesive that attaches insoluble particles of color to the fabric surface. This is an important difference. Textile paints leave an adhesive residue that may make fabric feel slightly to significantly stiffer; this is referred to as changing the hand of the fabric. Dyes do not change the hand of fabric.

Dye molecules are soluble in water (hydrophilic) and form transparent solutions. Textile paints are made of insoluble particles (hydrophobic) and are dispersed in water. While textile paints do not penetrate the fiber, they are available in intense colors—transparent and opaque—and are very easy to apply. The durability of the paint depends on the binder. As a rule, textile paints are more lightfast than dyes, but they have a tendency to "crock" or rub off in the wash.

To help you visualize the difference between dyed and painted fabric, I suggest thinking of the difference between a beet and a radish. Fiber-reactive dyes color fabric all through, like a beet. Slice a beet in half and it is the same color throughout. Textile paints color fabric like a radish—color on the outside fiber, and white, or undyed, fiber on the inside.

Protecting Yourself and Your Environment

If used properly, the fiber-reactive dyes, textile paints, and auxiliary products described in this book present a low risk to your health and to the environment. The dyes themselves are among the safest made; they are nonflammable and nontoxic. There is no need to be afraid of working with fiber-reactive dyes or auxiliary products. Water-based textile paints are even safer to work with than dyes—just don't eat them. (Textile paints do, however, have an odor that some people dislike. If this is a problem for you, work in a well-ventilated area.)

Because no chemical is entirely hazard-free, respect fiber-reactive dye and auxiliary powders, and treat them as chemicals, as you should household cleaning products. Use the following common-sense safeguards:

- Just as some people are allergic to pollen, chocolate, or nuts, some people are hypersensitive or have allergic reactions to dye and auxiliary powders. Avoid unnecessary exposure. Wear a dust/mist mask or respirator (see "Equipment" on pages 34–36) while working with these powders.
- Wear rubber gloves, old clothes or protective clothing, and even old shoes.
- Do not eat, smoke, or drink in an area where dyes and auxiliary products are used.
- Protect your work area with plastic sheeting.

- Do not use food utensils as dyeing equipment if you intend to return them to your kitchen. If you do use utensils from your kitchen, consider them donated to your dyeing. (I use this as an excuse to buy new kitchen gadgets and tools.)
- Wipe up any spills immediately. Liquid dye dries to powder that can be accidentally inhaled or ingested.
- Store dyes and auxiliary products in a cool, dry place, away from food and out of the reach of children or animals.
- Clearly label all solutions and containers of powder. *Do not* remove the supplier's name or hazard-warning labels.

When you have finished a dyeing procedure, you will have colored water left over; this is the exhausted dye bath. The color that is left is not harmful and is safe to discard down the drain into any septic or city disposal system. If you work outside, carry the dye bath into the house to discard it.

All suppliers have Material Safety Data Sheets (MSDS), which are available on request. This information sheet details precautions, potential health hazards, and clean-up information for *industrial* applications. The potential health and environmental hazards of wastewater from most home usage is considered insignificant.

RECOGNIZING AN ALLERGIC REACTION

An allergic reaction to dye is quite rare and is usually not severe. People experiencing an allergic reaction are usually responding to one of the auxiliary products, such as the activator, rather than the dye. Signs of sensitivity include coughing, a feeling of tightness in the chest, wheezing, and contact rash. If you experience any of these symptoms, move away from the area to fresh air. If the symptoms persist, consult your physician.

If you work with young children, have severe allergies, or are pregnant or asthmatic, take extra precautions. If working with young children, mix all the solutions in advance. Make sure the children wear old clothes, old shoes, and rubber gloves. If you have severe allergies or are pregnant or asthmatic, have someone mix the dye and auxiliary powders for you. As an alternative, consider using textile paints to color fabric instead of dyes.

Setting Up Your Work Space

Our mood—including the way we feel about our work space—greatly influences how we work, from the colors we choose to how productive we are. In an ideal world, we would all have a room or space we could set up as a dye studio. But no matter where you work, make sure you feel comfortable, and make sure you have enough space for the amount of fabric you plan to dye.

Fan

Getting Organized

It's a familiar cry, "I don't have enough room for this stuff!" There is no doubt that having to take things out and put them away each time makes starting more difficult. I have a rolling cart that I keep a couple of plastic tubs on; I can collect and roll out my supplies whenever I need them. Try not to squeeze your first attempt at these techniques into a few moments between other activities. If time is short, collect all the things you might need beforehand. When you are ready to start, time is not wasted looking for equipment.

It's best to work away from the primary living areas of your home—for example, in an unfinished basement, laundry room, or garage. You can work outside when the weather is nice. *Do not* work in a living area such as a kitchen, bathroom, family room, living room, or bedroom. This is a simple but important safety precaution (and it prevents accidental stains as well).

Proper ventilation is essential. Mix dyes in a well ventilated, but not windy, area. Create a local exhaust system by using a portable fan in a window. Place the fan so it pulls air from the room, away from you and out the window. Work facing the fan, so air currents are pulled away from your face.

Good lighting is essential. I like adjustable clamp lights; you can move them around so you never have to work in your own shadow.

Place a piece of homosote, foam core, or foam insulation board against one wall and use it for pinning up dyed fabrics.

It is convenient to have a water source, but it is not absolutely necessary. Improvise! You can use buckets and a garden hose with a nozzle.

If you do not have a work table, you can make one by placing a piece of plywood or a door on top of two sawhorses. A padded table with legs is ideal for direct-application techniques, though not essential. To make a padded surface, you need a piece of plywood—a 48" x 24" (122 cm x 61 cm) piece works well for half-yards of fabric—a piece of rug padding, thick felt, or ¼" (6 mm) -thick foam cut 2" to 3" (5 cm to 7.6 cm) larger than your plywood; a piece of muslin cut 6" to 7" (15 cm to 18 cm) larger than the padding; and a staple gun. Wrap the padding and muslin around the plywood and staple, pulling so both the padding and muslin are tight and even. If you don't have enough space to leave a padded work table set up, attach a strap to the back and move it as needed.

For an immersion dye bath technique, protect your table with a heavy plastic drop cloth and newspaper. For a direct-application technique, protect a padded table with plastic sheeting or a heavy plastic drop cloth. If you are pinning or taping fabric for wet techniques such as hand painting or monoprinting, cover the padded table with a heavy canvas drop cloth (rather than plastic). The canvas acts like a sponge, absorbing excess dye. Wash the canvas drop cloth after each use.

Cleaning Your Work Space

Since both dyes and textile paints are water based, you can clean with water. But be careful; dyes and paints tend to stain! Even the most pastel concentration can leave a trace of color on your clothes or work surface. You can usually remove dye and paint stains from your work surface with a bleach-type kitchen cleanser, but clothing stains are permanent. Remember Murphy's Law; if something spills, it's bound to end up where it's not wanted. Cover all your work surfaces and protect your clothes. Better yet, wear clothes you don't mind staining.

Understanding Color

Color is what dyeing and patterning fabric is all about. Because we associate certain colors with certain emotions, we tend to use those colors that make us feel most comfortable. This may be based on pleasant experiences or even on the inherent nature of warm (yellow, orange, red) or cool (blue, green, purple) colors. The challenge is to use colors you do not like. A funny thing usually happens—you end up liking or even falling in love with those colors you used to hate.

Traditional color theory helps us understand color relationships and why different color combinations are pleasing or disturbing. The following is a basic guide to color terms and relationships. For more information on color theory, see "Further Reading" on pages 159–60 and "Color Mixing Fiber-Reactive Dyes" on pages 41–45.

Analogous: Hues that are adjacent to each other on the color wheel. Yellow and orange are analogous colors. You can use analogous colors to produce harmonious color schemes.

Cool colors: A color that evokes cold. Blue and green are cool colors.

Direct complements: Hues that fall directly opposite each other on the color wheel. Blue and orange are direct complements. Direct complements mix to produce harmonious colors in the brown range. Try using a small amount of a direct complement to reduce the intensity of another color.

Hue: A synonym for color, hue is the pure state of a color.

Intensity: The saturation of a hue. The brightest colors are the pure hues on the color wheel. Less intense dye colors are less saturated and contain a small amount of their complementary color.

Monochromatic: Refers to a single color. A monochromatic color scheme consists of different values and intensities of one color.

Primary colors: There are three primary colors: red, yellow, and blue. All mixed colors fall within one of these color families.

Secondary color: A color that is a mixture of two primary hues. Orange, green, and purple are secondary colors.

Split complements: A hue plus two hues on either side of the primary hue's direct complement. Blue, yellow-orange, and red-orange make up a split complementary combination. Split complements often provide a subtler and more harmonious color scheme than a direct complementary scheme.

Tertiary color: A color that is a mixture of all three primary hues. Olive green, rust, and plum are tertiary colors.

Value: The lightness or darkness of a hue.

Warm color: A color that evokes heat. Yellow, orange, and red are warm colors.

What tremendous variations from the smallest shading to the glowing symphony of colour. What perspectives in the dimension of meaning!
Paul Klee

Different fabric weights
and weave structures

Choosing Fabric

This section provides an overview of the types of fabric that work best with fiber-reactive dyes and textile paints, and instructions on how to prepare these fabrics.

The recipes in this book are based on 100% cotton muslin, 45" (115 cm) wide, which is relatively inexpensive and available at most fabric stores. As you gain experience, try different fabric weights or weave structures. Experiment with jacquard, chintz, satin, velveteen, sheer, and embossed fabrics. The variations in weave may inspire designs or be appropriate for specific designs. Refer to "Calculating Measurements for an Immersion Dye Bath" on page 40. As a rule, the more tightly woven the fabric, the darker the color after dyeing.

FABRIC FOR FIBER-REACTIVE DYES

Fiber-reactive dyes are designed to work on 100% cellulose (vegetable) fibers, such as cotton, linen, viscose rayon, jute, ramie, or any combination of these fibers. These dyes also work well on silk, a protein fiber with cellulose dye sites. Many of the techniques I've described in this book can also be used or adapted for other protein fibers, such as wool, angora, mohair, and leather. The application procedures for these latter protein fibers are different than those covered in this book. For additional information, refer to "Further Reading" on pages 159–60 and consult a dye supplier.

Although fiber-reactive dyes do not work on synthetic fibers, they will work (to some degree) on polyester-cotton blends. After dyeing, these fabrics may have a uniformly heathery look or very irregular look depending on the consistency of the polyester-cotton blend. Also, synthetic blends will only dye a light value, regardless of how much dye is in the dye bath.

Stay away from fabrics treated with softeners and permanent-press, stain-resistant, flame-retardant, and water-repellent finishes. These finishes are difficult or impossible to remove and can cause tremendous headaches. My advice is to use another fabric. If you are determined to use a fabric with a permanent-press finish, follow the recipe on page 24.

Most fabric stores offer a selection of 100% cotton fabrics. Your local fabric store may have or may be willing to order fabric that has been specially prepared for dyeing—not treated with any of the finishes described above. Mail-order sources for prepared-for-dyeing (PFD) fabric are provided on page 158. Muslin is available as bleached (white) or unbleached (beige). The base color affects the final dyed color of a pastel shade. For example, use bleached muslin to dye a pastel tint such as sky blue. If you use unbleached muslin, the blue may have a greenish cast.

You may be able to purchase mercerized cotton fabric from your local fabric store. Mercerized cotton yields deeper colors and has improved strength and enhanced luster. It appears 25% darker than unmercerized cotton dyed with the same amount of dye. (Rayon also yields deeper colors.)

Different fibers have different chemical structures and react differently to heat and flame. These different reactions can help you determine the content of your fabric. Separate a couple of threads from your woven fabric. Twist them together so they form a tuft. Use tweezers to hold the tuft at the edge of a match. Note whether the fiber shrinks or melts, then place the tuft in the flame. Compare the characteristics of the flame, smoke, smell, and residue to the following table.

Mercerized versus unmercerized fabric. Mercerized fabric dyes 25% darker.

Determining Fabric Content

Fabric	Flame	Smell	Residue
Cellulose	Burns readily	Burnt paper	Soft gray ash
Protein	Burns only while held in flame, causes an irregular, spurting flame	Burnt hair	Black, crushable ash
Nylon	Does not burn easily, melts and drips	Strong sweet odor	Hard bead/drip shape
Polyester	Melts and burns with flame	Strong chemical odor	Hard bead
Acrylic	Melts and burns with flame	Strong chemical odor	Hard bead

FABRIC FOR TEXTILE PAINTS

Textile paints work on any fiber or combination of fibers, including cellulose, protein, and synthetics such as polyester, acrylic, and acetate. Avoid fabrics with permanent-press, stain-resistant, flame-retardant, or water-repellent finishes. As with dyeing, it is important to thoroughly clean the fabric before attempting to pattern it.

Overdyeing Commercial Fabric

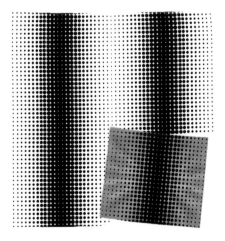

It is fun to experiment with **overdyeing** commercially printed and dyed fabrics. If you overdye different, incompatibly colored fabrics with the same color, you can end up with a harmonized palette.

Dyeing Ribbon, Thread, and Yarn

You may want to dye ribbon, thread, and yarn for quilting or couching.

1. Wind the ribbon around a skein winder or piece of cardboard that is approximately 18" (45 cm) wide. Loosely knot the ends together.

2. Using synthetic or nylon twine, weave a loose figure eight (in and out and back again) through the ribbon. If the figure eights are too tight, you'll have tie-dyed ribbon! Knot the ends.

3. Tie the figure eights every 4" (10 cm) or so. Tying keeps the ribbon from tangling during dyeing.

4. Remove the skein winder or cardboard and dye the ribbon following the tie-dye technique (see page 99). When you rinse and wash the ribbon, agitate by dunking the ribbon up and down or back and forth in the rinse water. If you agitate too much or stir in a circular motion, you'll have a tangled mess.

5. Remove the twine after the ribbon is dry.

Preparing Fabric

Scour your fabric to remove dirt, sizing agents, waxes, and oils before dyeing. Scouring may seem like an unnecessary step, but fabric that is not completely clean will not dye evenly. I recommend that you scour all fabric, even fabric prepared specifically for dyeing, before use. Scouring is an insurance policy worth investing in.

Do not use grocery store detergents for scouring fabric. These have added whiteners and brighteners that go on the fabric unevenly and may make dyeing uneven (especially for pastels). I particularly recommend avoiding powdered laundry detergents with little specks of color.

You can scour fabric by hand or machine. For small amounts of fabric, it's quicker and easier to scour by hand.

RECIPE FOR HAND SCOUR

Read through the directions and assemble all the necessary equipment and supplies before you begin.

Equipment

2-gallon (8-L) plastic bucket or enamel canning kettle

Clothesline and clothes pins (optional)

Dust/mist mask or respirator

Kitchen timer or watch

Long-handled spoon

Measuring cups and spoons or scale

Mixing box (see page 35)

Newspaper

Plastic drop cloth

Rubber gloves

Scissors

Spray bottle filled with water

Thermometer

Supplies

1 yard (91 cm) 100% cotton muslin

¼ teaspoon (1 g) soda ash (see "soda ash" on page 38)

¼ teaspoon (1.25 ml) Synthrapol (see page 39)

Procedure

1. Cover your work table with the plastic drop cloth.
2. Set the mixing box on top of the drop cloth. Cut a small stack of newspapers to the inside dimensions of the box. Place the newspapers in the bottom of the mixing box and spray them with water. If you spill any of the powder during the mixing process, it will stick to the damp newspaper.
3. Measure 1 gallon (4 L) of 140° F (60° C) water into the plastic bucket. *Note:* If your water source is not hot enough, heat water on a stove or hot plate, then turn the heat off after the water reaches 140° F (60° C). Scour your fabric in the pot.
4. Wear a dust/mist mask or respirator and rubber gloves while working with the soda ash powder. Before opening the container, tap the lid so the powder settles to the bottom. Carefully open the container. Measure ¼ teaspoon (1 g) of soda ash powder into the bucket. Recap the container. Stir until the powder is dissolved.
5. Add ¼ teaspoon (1.25 ml) Synthrapol to the bucket. Stir.
6. Wearing rubber gloves, hand wash the fabric for about 10 minutes. Use the long-handled spoon to stir.
7. Rinse the fabric thoroughly in warm or cool water. It should feel squeaky clean.
8. You can use the fabric wet, or you can dry it and store for later use. To dry the fabric, hang it from a clothesline or use a dryer, following the manufacturer's instructions for the appropriate heat setting.

RECIPE FOR WASHING-MACHINE SCOUR

The following recipe is for the extra-large load setting on a washing machine. For smaller loads, see the chart on page 24. Contact your washing-machine manufacturer for your tub capacity (the number of gallons needed to fill the tub, not the total amount of gallons used for a wash load). Compare it to the chart and adjust the recipe if necessary.

Read through the directions and assemble all the necessary equipment and supplies before you begin.

Equipment

| Clothesline and clothes pins (optional) |
| Dust/mist mask or respirator |
| Kitchen timer or watch |
| Measuring cups and spoons or scale |
| Rubber gloves |
| Scissors |
| Thermometer |
| Washing machine |

Washing Machine Tub Capacity

To determine how many gallons or liters it takes to fill your washing machine, set it on small load with nothing in the tub. Let it fill. Measure, with a yard stick, the number of inches or centimeters and record the number. Set your machine on medium load and let it fill. Again, record the number. Continue this process until you have gone through all the size cycles. Allow your machine to cycle through the wash process (or do a load of laundry). Once the machine is empty, fill it one gallon (or liter) at a time from the sink. Count the number of gallons or liters until you reach the numbers recorded off the yard stick. Save this information!

Removing Permanent-Press Finishes

This recipe uses muriatic acid (hydrochloric 30%), a strong corrosive acid. **You must wear a respirator, rubber gloves, and safety glasses and use an exhaust fan while you work.**

1. Pour 2 gallons (8 L) of water into a large stainless steel or enamel pot. Carefully add 1 tablespoon (15 ml) of muriatic acid. To prevent splashing and possible explosion, **always add the acid to the water; never add the water to the acid.**

2. Place the pot on the stove, then submerge your fabric.

3. Heat the fabric to 185°F (85°C). Keep the temperature constant for 20 minutes, stirring the fabric occasionally.

4. Remove the pot from the heat and place it in a sink. Slowly add cold water, allowing the water to spill over and into the sink. Continue until the fabric is cool.

Supplies

10 to 15 yards (9.1 to 13.6 m) 100% cotton muslin for an extra-large load
2 tablespoons (18 g) soda ash (see "soda ash" on page 38)
2 tablespoons (30 ml) Synthrapol (see page 39)

Procedure

1. Cut the fabric into pieces, each 5 yards (4.5 m) or less.
2. Set the washing machine on the extra-large load, hot wash, and warm or cool rinse cycles. Check the water temperature after the machine fills. The water must be at least 140°F (60°C). You may need to heat water on the stove and add it to the machine.
3. While wearing a dust/mist mask or respirator and rubber gloves, add 2 tablespoons (18 g) of the soda ash powder and 2 tablespoons (30 ml) of Synthrapol. Let the machine agitate for 2 minutes.
4. Distribute the fabric evenly around the washing-machine tub.
5. When the machine has completed all the cycles, remove the fabric.
6. You can use the fabric wet, or you can dry it and store for later use. To dry the fabric, hang it or use a dryer, following the manufacturer's instructions for the appropriate heat setting.

Washing Machine Capacity Conversion Table

Machine Size	Water	Fabric
Small	12 gal (45.4 L)	9½ yd (8.7 m)
Medium	14 gal (53 L)	11 yd (10 m)
Large	17 gal (64.3 L)	13½ yd (12.3 m)
Extra-large	19 gal (72 L)	15 yd (13.7 m)

For each yard (91 cm) of fabric, use ¼ teaspoon (1 g) Activator and ¼ teaspoon (1.25 ml) Synthrapol.

WATER-DROP TEST

If you're not sure whether your fabric is completely clean, try this water-drop test. It can save you a lot of headache and heartache.

Using an eye dropper, place one drop of water on the dry fabric. Is it absorbed immediately, or does it sit on top of the fabric before it is absorbed? If it isn't absorbed immediately, there is a residue or finish on the fabric. Scour the fabric and test again before dyeing. Try using hotter water or a longer wash cycle, or try removing the finish as described at left.

Victory of Spirits
by Debra Lunn, 1991, Lancaster, Ohio, 32" x 54". **Method**: Fiber-reactive dye on cotton. Machine pieced, hand quilted, and beaded. Photo by John Bonath at Mad Dog Studio.

> **Detail of** *Victory of Spirits*

Lobby
by Heather Allen, 1992, Asheville, North Carolina, 76" x 90". **Method**: Fiber-reactive dye and textile paint on cotton. Machine pieced and quilted. Photo by John Lucas.

Make a Move
by Angela Holland, 1992, Portland, Oregon, 24½" x 22¼". **Method**: Fiber-reactive dye on cotton. Machine pieced and hand quilted. Photo by David Bachhuber.

On the Edge of Indecision
by Debbie Photopoulos, 1992, Medford, Massachusetts,
60" x 28". **Method**: Fiber-reactive dye on cotton and silk.
Hand appliquéd, embroidered, and quilted. Photo by the artist.

A Summer's Day
by Angela Holland, 1993, Portland, Oregon. **Method**: Fiber-
reactive dye on cotton. Machine pieced. Photo by David
Browne.

28

> *For Christiana Rossetti*
by Elizabeth Owen, 1991, Baton
Rouge, Louisiana, 33" x 29¼".
Method: Fiber-reactive dye on cotton.
Machine pieced and hand embroi-
dered and quilted. Photo by Ron E.
Dobbs.

⌄ *Beware of Falling Rocks*
by Connie Scheele, 1994, Houston,
Texas, 36" x 36". **Method**: Fiber-
reactive dye on cotton. Machine
pieced and quilted. Photo by the artist.

△ *Land, Sea and Sky*
by Linda Perry, 1995, Lexington, Massachusetts, 48" x 60". **Method**: Hand-dyed and commercially dyed cottons, silk, and rayon. Machine pieced and quilted, hand appliquéd. Embellished with metallic leaf. Photo by Joe Ofria at The Image Inn.

❯ *Pathways*
by Alison Goss, 1993, Cumming, Iowa, 52" x 52". **Method**: Fiber-reactive dye on cotton. Machine pieced and quilted. Photo by the artist.

▲ *Views from the Hubble*
by Melody Johnson, 1994, Cary, Illinois,
60½" x 42¾". **Method**: Fiber-reactive
dye on cotton. Machine pieced and
quilted. Photo by the artist.

❯ *Dance Doctor*
by L. Carlene Raper, 1994, Putney,
Vermont, 55" x 75". **Method**: Fiber-
reactive dye on cotton. Machine pieced
and tied. Photo by Jim Thomas.

Pool II
by Karen Perrine, 1996,
Tacoma, Washington,
31" x 50". **Method**:
Fiber-reactive dye and
textile paint on cotton.
Machine pieced,
hand appliquéd,
and machine quilted.
Photo by the artist.

> *David's House*
by Jan Myers-Newbury, 1994,
Pittsburgh, Pennsylvania, 49" x 57".
Method: Fiber-reactive dye on
cotton. Machine pieced and
quilted. Photo by Sam Newbury.

> *Seeing Is Believing*
by Jan Myers-Newbury, 1993,
Pittsburgh, Pennsylvania, 52" x 47".
Method: Fiber-reactive dye on
cotton. Machine pieced and
quilted. Photo by Sam Newbury.

Part II: Dyes

In 1956, Imperial Chemical Industries Limited (ICI) discovered that a dye molecule containing certain chemical groups ("reactive groups") could react chemically with cellulose under alkaline conditions. The dye molecule reacts with the fiber molecule and becomes part of the fiber rather than remaining an independent substance trapped within it.

There are several types of dye available to home dyers. I recommend fiber-reactive dye, which is packaged under a variety of trade names. The most common brand is Procion. The instructions provided in this book are for Procion MX, also known as MX Fiber-Reactive Dye or cold-water dye.

MX Fiber-Reactive Dyes are applied at room temperature. There is no need to slave over a steaming dye bath or to chill your hands in cold water; the optimum dyeing temperature is between 70° and 105° F (21° and 40° C).

Fiber-reactive dyes are available in a wide range of colors. Other types of dyes available for home use may "bleed" or fade with repeated washing and exposure to light. Fiber-reactive dyes are highly concentrated and produce fabric that is resistant to bleeding and fading.

Working with Fiber-Reactive Dyes

There are two basic methods of applying dye to fabric: immersion dye bath and direct application. This book covers many different techniques for each method.

With the immersion dye bath method, fabric is placed in a dye bath containing water, dye concentrate, and auxiliary products for a specific amount of time. The fabric is then removed from the dye bath, rinsed, washed, and dried. The average dye-bath process takes approximately one hour.

With the direct-application method, a concentrated dye-stock solution is applied to the fabric. The dye-stock solution can be thick (like jelly), thin (like water), or any consistency in between, depending on the application technique. The fabric is left to cure for a specific amount of

> Dreams come true: without that possibility, nature would not incite us to have them.
> John Updike

time. Excess dye is rinsed and washed out and the fabric is dried. Depending on the design and amount of fabric, this process takes from five minutes to several hours. Curing takes from four to twenty-four hours.

Equipment

The following is an overview of the equipment needed for working with immersion dye bath and direct-application techniques. A list of what is absolutely necessary is included at the beginning of each recipe. Don't be overwhelmed by the list. You can use many things you already have—old plates and saucers, sponges, pins, scissors, and newspapers—to test the dye techniques before investing in more expensive equipment. Necessity can lead to some interesting equipment and supplies!

It is surprising what useful objects and odd machines you can find in second-hand shops and yard sales. Look in industrial catalogs for strong plastic bins and troughs. Restaurant supply companies are a good source for buckets, spoons, and kitchen tools. Restaurant suppliers usually stock expensive and inexpensive large utensils. When you find interesting items or large items, pick them up. You will never be sorry.

Dust/mist mask: A paper mask is fine if you only dye fabric every once in a while. However, if you plan to do a lot of work with dye and auxiliary powders, I recommend that you purchase a Mine Safety and Health Administration (MSHA)/National Institute for Occupational Safety and Health (NIOSH) approved respirator with cartridges for dusts, mists, and fumes. These are available from suppliers that specialize in dye and safety equipment. Check your phone book for local suppliers or see "Resources" on page 158.

Dyeing Equipment

Dye buckets: Plastic, glass, or nonreactive metal containers (such as unchipped enamel or stainless steel) are preferable. Use a white bucket; the reflection of the dye color is truer. Plastic jelly buckets used in doughnut stores or joint-compound buckets used at construction sites work well. Avoid aluminum, tin, copper, and galvanized-metal containers. The dye will interact with the metal and produce duller colors. Have on hand a variety of one- to five-gallon (4- to 20-L) buckets. For level dyeing, there must be sufficient room in the bucket for the fabric to move freely. In addition, you must be able to stir the fabric without spilling the dye bath.

Fan: You need a large fan that you can position to pull the air away from your face as you work.

Measuring cups: Both plastic cups and Pyrex glassware are suitable. Some suppliers offer plastic safety beakers with markings. It is handy to have cup (250 ml) and quart (1 L) sizes.

I like to use 50-, 100-, and 250-milliliter graduated cylinders for more accurate measurements. Graduated cylinders are available in many sizes from dye- and scientific-equipment suppliers.

Measuring spoons: You need a set of plastic or stainless-steel measuring spoons.

Mixing box: Use a simple mixing box to limit airborne exposure to chemical powders. Cut off the top and one side of a 12" x 12" (30 cm x 30 cm) cardboard box, leaving a small "room" for mixing.

Newspapers: This is important for protecting your work space from stains.

Plastic drop cloth: Purchase plastic by the yard from a fabric store. This plastic does not have fold marks and will lie flat. If you purchase a heavy gauge (8 or 12 gauge and up), it will stay put without pinning. Use masking tape to secure your fabric to the plastic.

Record book: Keep a notebook with all the information you need to repeat a particular dye process. Over time, this book becomes a dyer's most essential piece of equipment! Write down the amount of fabric, dye, water, and different auxiliaries; the number of dye baths (if you are gradation dyeing); the length of time the fabric was in the bath; the curing time; the temperature (for direct-application techniques); and the date. Staple a swatch of undyed fabric and a swatch of dyed fabric next to the information.

Rubber gloves: You can use either disposable latex or reusable rubber gloves. Some suppliers carry reusable gloves that reach above the elbow. (I found shoulder-length gloves at a commercial fishing supply store.) These are great for large dye baths. Make sure the gloves fit well; they should feel like a second skin.

Scale: There are many different types of scales available (for example, kitchen, digital, counterbalance, and triple-beam). Choose a scale that you find easy to use. Make sure that it is accurate. A scale that measures from 1 gram to 2 pounds is handy. Use a bathroom

Keep a notebook detailing your dye processes.

Helpful Hint

Achieving Predictable, Repeatable Results

For predictable dyeing, you must control and repeat as many of the variables as possible. Variables include amount of dye, dyeing time, water, and air temperature, water source, and fabric. For instance, the temperature of cold water in Florida differs from that in Wisconsin, well water differs from a municipal water supply, and winter water differs from summer water. Also, our perception of cold varies from daytime to nighttime, from season to season, from Northeast to Southwest. This book includes specific time, water, and air temperature guidelines. If you follow these guidelines, you should have repeatable results. As you read this book, you may feel that I am repeating myself. You're right! Certain elements, if missed, can take the pleasure out of dyeing. Keep a notebook and record everything about your dye processes. Over time, this notebook will become your most important dyeing tool.

scale to weigh large amounts of fabric. (Weigh yourself while holding the dry fabric; then weigh yourself without the fabric. The difference is the weight of the fabric.)

Stirring tools: You need long-handled spoons (plastic, wood, and stainless steel), wooden dowels and/or chopsticks for stirring the dye bath, and small spoons, iced tea spoons, and swizzle sticks and/or wooden tongue depressors for stirring solutions. You may find that a wire whisk and a rubber scraper or spatula are helpful.

Thermometer: You can use any thermometer, as long as it measures temperatures from 60° to 185° F (16° to 85° C).

Timer: You need a kitchen timer, watch, or clock, preferably with a second hand.

Tools that are useful for specific techniques include: containers or jars of assorted sizes; paper cups or empty yogurt containers; rubber bands, bulldog clips, and pieces of wood; pushpins and/or masking tape; plastic plates or trays; an artists' stretcher frame or embroidery hoop; assorted synthetic artists' brushes and sponge brushes; assorted sizes of squeeze bottles and/or syringes; rubber or acrylic stamps; cellulose sponges; a plant mister or spray bottle; and rags, old towels, or paper towels.

A washing machine and dryer are handy, but you can use a bucket, clothesline, and plastic clothespins. Avoid wooden clothespins, which may absorb dye and stain your fabric. Always clean plastic clothespins before reusing them.

Supplies

I like to mark all dyes and auxiliary products with the date purchased. Each product has an optimum amount of time for use—the shelf life—based on its strength. Some products have much longer shelf lives than others. Be sure to store chemicals in properly labeled containers, and include any hazard information.

Dyeing Supplies

Baking soda (bicarbonate of soda): I use baking soda to make mixed alkali, which fixes dye to fabric. You can buy baking soda from the grocery store. Store it in a cool, dry place. I purchase a new box every year.

Citric acid or vinegar: If you work with silk, you can substitute citric acid or distilled white vinegar for the activator soak or mixed alkali powder in the direct-application dye recipes (see page 125). In general, citric acid is more stable than vinegar when mixed with dyes and produces better results. For more information on working with citric acid or vinegar, consult a dye supplier.

Fiber-reactive dye: The recipes in this book are written for Procion MX Fiber-Reactive Dyes. I prefer these dyes because they are versatile and easy to use, and they produce brilliant colors.

The major differences between brands of fiber-reactive dye are the application methods, temperatures of the dye bath, and the length of curing time. In addition to Procion MX, popular fiber-reactive dyes include Cibacron F (sold by PRO Chem as Sabracron F), Procion H (available in powder or liquid form), and Remazol. To adapt these recipes for use with Cibacron F dyes, modify the dye-bath temperature and curing time. The immersion dye bath temperature for Cibacron F is 105° to 120°F (40° to 50°C). Curing takes twenty-four to forty-eight hours and/or setting with a steam iron.

Most of the recipes in this book can also be adapted for use with Procion H dyes. The immersion dye bath temperature for Procion H is 170° to 180°F (77° to 82°C). The manufacturer recommends that the fabric be cured with steam. Consult your dye supplier for specific recipes and fixing procedures.

Remazol dyes work best with temperatures of 105° to 140°F (40° to 60°C). Consult a dye supplier for specific recipes and fixing procedures. Curing with steam is recommended, but I have been successful using stronger alkali and curing for 24 to 48 hours.

Store Procion MX dyes in a cool, dry place. Keep them in containers with tightly fitting lids. Under these conditions, the optimum shelf life of dye is two years. After two years, the color yield will begin to decline. The dye can still be used, but your results may not be repeatable.

Hand cleaner: The best approach is to wear gloves so you don't dye your hands in the first place! If you need to remove dye stains from your hands, purchase a specially formulated hand cleaner, such as ReDuRan, from dye suppliers. Do not use bleach to remove dye stains. If you make sure the container is closed between uses, the hand cleaner will remain at full strength for many years.

Metaphos: See "water softener." I recommend Metaphos (sodium hexametaphosphate) because it does not contain fragrances or other additives.

38

Presist: This liquid resist is a combination starch-paste (for creating bold patterns) and gutta (for creating fine-line patterns) resist. When applied to fabric and allowed to dry, Presist forms a barrier that inhibits dye penetration. Presist dissolves in the rinse without leaving a residue. Because it is amber, rather than clear, Presist is easy to see. This is my preferred resist for silk painting, beginning projects, and projects that involve children.

Store Presist in a cool, dry place. Keep it in a container with a tightly fitting lid, and do not allow it to freeze. According to the manufacturer, Presist has a one-year shelf life, but I have used two-year-old Presist with great results. Test a sample before using if your Presist is more than one year old.

Print paste: Made from urea, water softener, and sodium alginate, print paste is used for direct-application techniques. You can make print paste from scratch (see pages 56–57), or you can buy a premeasured print mix from most dye-suppliers.

The SH products are recommended for cotton and the F products are recommended for silk. I have found the SH products to be the best all-purpose thickener; they work well on cotton and silk. For more information, consult a dye supplier.

Sabra Silk Resist: Frequently called a water-based, gutta resist, Sabra Silk is a colorless resist that works well for painting on silk or lightweight cotton. Like Presist, it forms a barrier on the fabric to create the pattern. Sabra Silk dissolves in rinse water without leaving a residue.

Store Sabra Silk in a cool, dry place. Keep it in a container with a tightly fitting lid, and do not allow it to freeze. According to the manufacturer, Sabra Silk has a one-year shelf life.

Salt (sodium chloride): Salt is an exhausting agent for the immersion dye bath recipes in this book. It has an electrostatic charge that pushes dye through the water and onto the fiber. Noniodized table salt is preferred but not absolutely necessary. (Iodine is a metal and can sometimes dull colors.) Noniodized table salt is available as kosher salt, canning or pickling salt, and "common" salt. Store salt in a cool, dry place. Keep it in a container with a tightly fitting lid. You can continue to use the salt as long as you are able to dissolve it.

Some dye manufacturers recommend Glaubers Salt (sodium sulfate) for increasing color yield, especially for turquoise dye. I don't feel that the minor color increase compensates for its expense and difficult dissolving characteristics.

Soda Ash: The soda ash (also referred to as the fixative) is a chemical that causes a molecular reaction to take place between fabric and dye. The soda ash is also used to scour fabric before dyeing.

You can use soda ash or sodium carbonate (PRO Dye Activator, washing soda, or sal soda). Do not use washing soda from the grocery store. It contains additives that would be detrimental to the results. I recommend using PRO Dye Activator because it is easy to dissolve.

Store the soda ash in a cool, dry place. Keep it in a container with a tightly fitting lid. You can use the soda ash as long as you can dissolve it. (Once wet, it will resemble concrete and will not dissolve fully.)

Sodium alginate: This is a type of seaweed that thickens dye-stock solution for direct-application techniques. Sodium alginate is combined with urea and water softener to produce print paste. You can purchase sodium alginate as Thick SH or F. It is also sold under the names Keltex, Manutex, and Lamitex.

Store sodium alginate in a cool, dry place. Keep it in a container with a tightly fitting lid. If kept dry, sodium alginate will remain at full strength for many years.

Synthrapol: This is a special cleaning agent known as a "surfactant" (surface active agent). It is used in the scour recipe to prepare fabric for dyeing (see pages 22–24) and in the hot wash after dyeing to remove excess dye. You can also use Synthrapol in the dye bath to help ensure level dyeing.

Synthrapol has a very long shelf life. Over time, it may turn an amber color. You can continue using it even after it has changed color.

Urea: A synthetic nitrogen compound, urea ammonium carbamate is a humectant that prevents fabric from drying during the curing process. Urea also increases the solubility of the dye powder and is especially useful for mixing concentrated solutions of yellow, red, and black. In essence, urea makes the dye think it is in more water than it really is.

Store urea in a cool, dry place. Keep it in a container with a tightly fitting lid. Urea usually has a long shelf life. If you notice an ammonia-like odor after mixing, discard the solution and the urea.

Water: Your water source greatly effects your dye results. Municipal water sources add chlorine to kill harmful bacteria. The amount of chlorine can vary, producing lighter or darker results. MX fiber-reactive dyes perform best when applied and washed off in soft water. Impurities such as calcium, magnesium, iron, and copper take up space in the water, decreasing its ability to dissolve dye or auxiliary products. If you know you have hard water, purchase bottled or distilled water for mixing dye-stock solutions, or add water softener.

Water softener: If you live in an area with hard water, you need to add a water softener (Metaphos or Calgon) to the dye bath. I recommend Metaphos (sodium hexametaphosphate) because it does not contain fragrances or other additives. I also recommend using Metaphos in the print paste; it makes a smoother paste and improves your printing and painting results.

Store water softener in a cool, dry place. Keep it in a container with a tightly fitting lid. You can continue using the water softener as long as you are able to dissolve it.

Dyeing Brighter Colors

Some dyers add Ludigol (PRO Chem Flakes) to the dye-stock solution and paste mix in their direct-application dye recipes for brighter colors. Ludigol is a mild oxidizing agent that absorbs gasses from the air so dye molecules do not react prematurely and become "used up" before permanently fixing to the fabric. Ludigol is optional if you use MX Fiber-Reactive Dyes, but it is necessary if you use Procion H Fiber-Reactive Dyes. Although the recipes in this book do not include Ludigol, you may want to use it if you live in a city with a great deal of air pollution. Add one teaspoon (2.5 g) per cup (250 ml) of prepared urea water or print paste.

Calculating Measurements for an Immersion Dye Bath

The immersion dye bath recipes in this book are based on industrial standards. These standards use the weight of the fabric to determine how much dye, auxiliary products, and water are needed to achieve a certain hue or value. This is referred to as "percent on weight of goods or fabric" (%OWG or %OWF). I translated the %OWG into teaspoons or grams and quarts or liters for home dyeing.

All the recipes are based on 45"-wide (115 cm) 100% cotton muslin. The weight of three yards (2.74 m) of 100% cotton muslin is approximately one pound (454 g). I divided one pound by three to determine the amounts of dye, auxiliary products, and water necessary to dye one yard (91 cm) of cotton muslin.

Because these recipes are based on an estimate of the fabric weight, you may get slightly different results, depending on the type and weight of your fabric. For example, the basic dye-bath recipe is not adequate for one yard (91 cm) of 100% cotton velveteen. Because cotton velveteen is heavier than muslin, you need more dye, auxiliary products, and water to produce the same hue. See the table to calculate the amount of dye, auxiliary products, and water needed for different weights of fabric.

Calculating an Immersion Dye Bath for Different Fabrics

For each pound (454 g)* of dry fabric:

Value	Light		Medium		Dark**	
	English	Metric	English	Metric	English	Metric
Water	2.5 gal	9.5 L	2.5 gal	9.5 L	2.5 gal	9.5 L
Salt	1¼ cups	363 g	1¾ cups	550 g	2½ cups	725 g
Water Softener	1 tsp	7 g	1 tsp	7 g	1 tsp	7 g
MX Fiber-Reactive Dye	1 tsp	2.5 g	5 tsp	12.5 g	2½ Tbl	22.5 g
Soda Ash	2½ Tbl	23 g	5 Tbl	45 g	7½ Tbl	68 g

* Determine the weight of your fabric using a kitchen or bathroom scale.
** For black, double the amount of dye powder and extend the dyeing time to 90 minutes after adding soda ash.

Using Direct-Application Techniques

The direct-application recipes in this book are based on industrial standards. These standards use the strength of a stock solution to determine how much dye, auxiliary product, and water are needed to achieve a certain hue or value. This is referred to as a "percent solution." I translated the percent solution into teaspoons or grams and quarts or liters for home dyeing.

You can prepare more or less dye-stock solution according to the amount of fabric you want to dye. One cup (250 ml) of dye-stock solution colors one and one-half to two yards (1.37 to 1.82 m) of 45"-wide (115 cm) 100% cotton muslin. See "Dye-Stock Solution" on pages 50–51.

Color Mixing

Fiber-reactive dyes produce transparent color. The more dye powder you use, the darker the color. Conversely, the less dye powder you use, the lighter the color. To take advantage of the flexibility of transparent color, you must understand color mixing and the characteristics of each color. If you purchase and learn to blend the seven colors described in this section (your dye color palettes), you can enjoy a wide range of hues and values.

At present, there are fifteen colors of MX fiber-reactive dye manufactured as "self-shade" colors. The term "self-shade" indicates that these colors will dye, *by weight,* the same shade, value, and intensity every time. All other MX fiber-reactive dye colors are mixtures of these colors.

Color mixing is based on blending the self-shade and mixed dyes in different combinations and amounts. You can use a traditional color wheel to help understand the relationship between colors. Pure primaries (red, yellow, and blue) are not available as dye colors. Choose the closest dye colors based on whether you want earthy (rich, dark) or jewel (bright, saturated) colors.

Remember that white does not exist as a dye. It is assumed the fabric is white. As mentioned previously, if your fabric has a yellow, blue, or other tint, it will effect the color of the dyed fabric. This may not be important for medium to dark values, but it is very important for light values.

EARTHY PALETTE

For earthy colors, I recommend Procion Yellow MX-3R, Procion Red MX-5B, and Procion Blue MX-2G 125 or Procion Blue MX-G. These dye powders are usually less expensive than brighter dyes.

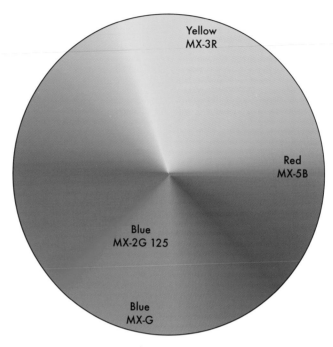

Earthy Palette Dyes

JEWEL PALETTE

For jewel colors, I recommend Procion Yellow MX-8G, Procion Red MX-8B, Procion Blue MX-G, and Procion Turquoise MX-G.

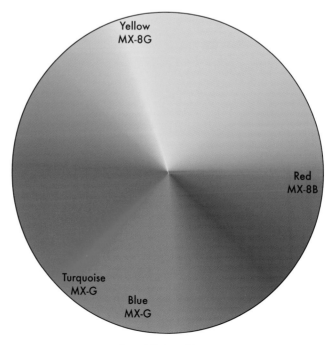

Jewel Palette Dyes

HELPFUL EXTRAS

You can always purchase more colors for easier mixing. For instance, it is difficult to mix a good brown and almost impossible to mix a good black. The first two dyes listed below are also manufactured as self-shade colors.

- Orange MX-2R is a brilliant orange with exceptional coloring power. A little goes a long way.
- Blue MX-R is a sky blue. This is not a strong dye and will not dye a dark value, but it is the only manufactured blue with a reddish cast.
- Black MX-CWNA is a mixed color with a red cast. Black is by far the most difficult color to achieve with MX fiber-reactive dyes. This color is a full saturation of the right hues in proper proportion. If you use too much dye powder, the fabric takes on a reddish appearance, referred to as "bronzing." If you don't use enough dye powder, the fabric dyes gray rather than black.
- Mixing Gray 601, available from PRO Chem, is your neutral gray. No black, in MX fiber-reactive dye, dyes a neutral gray.
- Purple 804, Leaf Green 700N, and Chino 500, also available from PRO Chem, are convenient additions to a dye collection.

Converting Decimal Amounts to Teaspoons

0.875 =	⅞ teaspoon
0.75 =	¾ teaspoon
0.625 =	⅝ teaspoon
0.5 =	½ teaspoon
0.375 =	⅜ teaspoon
0.25 =	¼ teaspoon
0.125 =	⅛ teaspoon

MIXING DYE COLORS

To control color mixing, you need to understand each dye's color, cast, and strength (ability to dye a dark value), as well as whether the color and cast are consistent from a pastel to a dark shade. The earthy palette is easier to mix because the dye powders—Yellow MX-3R, Red MX-5B, and Blue MX-2G 124 or Blue MX-G—have higher solubility levels, similar reactivity rates, and lower substantivity than the dye powders in the jewel palette.

The first rule for mixing dyes is: *visual equilibrium is not necessarily physical equilibrium.* You need three times as much yellow as blue to produce a middle green. Varying the proportion of dye powder changes the color to a blue-green or a yellow-green.

The best way to learn color mixing is to experiment with different proportions. Turquoise MX-G and Yellow MX-8G, bright hues in the jewel palette, have maximum absorption points, and will not dye dark shades no matter how much dye powder you use. Blue MX-G and Red MX-8B, on the other hand, are highly concentrated dye powders that can easily overpower other colors (especially yellow). When mixing colors with Blue MX-G, Red MX-8B, and Red MX-5B, use half the amount listed in the recipes until you are comfortable with the dyes' capabilities and ranges. When mixing colors with Yellow MX-8G, add very small amounts (drops) of a darker color(s) until the mixed color looks right to you.

The second rule for mixing dyes is: *avoid mixing more than three colors to produce one color.* It is always easier to repeat something with fewer variables. Also, the mixed color may dye unevenly. For example, if you want a brown dye, I recommend that you start by mixing just two colors: Orange MX-2R with Blue MX-G.

The illustration on the facing page represents dye colors mixed from Yellow MX-8G, Red MX-8B, and Blue MX-G (the jewel palette). The percentages in the accompanying chart indicate the amount of each dye used to create the numbered color.

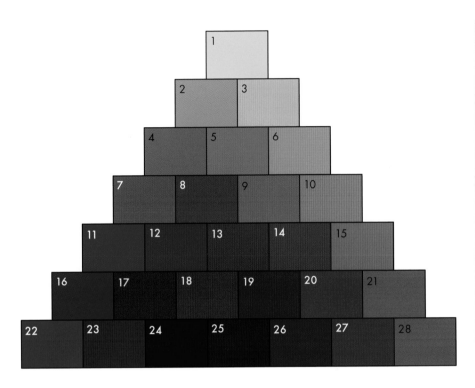

Color Chart
Mixing Percentages

Y = Yellow MX-8G
R = Red MX-8B
B = Blue MX-G

1	Y 100%		15	Y 60%	
	R –			R 40%	
	B –			B –	
2	Y 95%		16	Y 25%	
	R –			R –	
	B 5%			B 75%	
3	Y 98%		17	Y 20%	
	R 2%			R 20%	
	B –			B 60%	
4	Y 80%		18	Y 20%	
	R –			R 40%	
	B 20%			B 40%	
5	Y 85%		19	Y 20%	
	R 8%			R 55%	
	B 7%			B 25%	
6	Y 90%		20	Y 20%	
	R 10%			R 72%	
	B –			B 8%	
7	Y 70%		21	Y 20%	
	R –			R 80%	
	B 30%			B –	
8	Y 75%		22	Y –	
	R 10%			R –	
	B 15%			B 100%	
9	Y 80%		23	Y –	
	R 15%			R 20%	
	B 5%			B 80%	
10	Y 80%		24	Y –	
	R 20%			R 45%	
	B –			B 55%	
11	Y 50%		25	Y –	
	R –			R 60%	
	B 50%			B 40%	
12	Y 50%		26	Y –	
	R 10%			R 80%	
	B 40%			B 20%	
13	Y 50%		27	Y –	
	R 25%			R 95%	
	B 25%			B 5%	
14	Y 50%		28	Y –	
	R 40%			R 100%	
	B 10%			B –	

To determine the amount of dye powder you need to mix a numbered color:

1. Find the percentage mixing amount(s) in the chart at right.
2. Translate the percentage to a decimal by moving the decimal point 2 numbers to the left, for example, 40% = 0.4.
3. Multiply by the number of teaspoons or grams needed for a specific recipe.
4. For English measurements, convert the numbers to teaspoons using the chart on page 44. For metric measurements, use the numbers as is. The decimal numbers are equivalent to grams.

For example, color 12 is 50% Yellow MX-8G, 10% Red MX-8B, and 40% Blue MX-G. If you need 6 teaspoons (15 g), total, of dye powder for an immersion dye bath, you would multiply the color percentages by 6 for English measurements, then convert the decimal amounts to teaspoons.

English	Yellow MX-8G:	6 x 0.5 = 3 (3 tsp)
	Red MX-8B:	6 x 0.1 = 0.6 (⅝ tsp)
	Blue MX-G:	6 x 0.4 = 2.4 (2⅜ tsp)
Metric	Yellow MX-8G:	15 x 0.5 = 7.5 (7.5 g)
	Red MX-8B:	15 x 0.1 = 1.5 (1.5 g)
	Blue MX-G:	15 x 0.4 = 6 (6 g)

Helpful Hint

Understanding Specific Gravity for Dry Measurements

The metric equivalents for dry powders vary based on the specific gravity (the density ratio of substances weighed in air) of each powder. In other words, one teaspoon of soda ash (3 g) may not weigh as much as one teaspoon (7 g) of water softener. For particular weights, see page 155.

Mixing Basics

This section explains how to mix the basic concentrates, solutions, pastes, and mixtures used in immersion dye bath and direct-application recipes. All the fiber-reactive dye recipes in this book refer to this section; read it carefully before you begin working with dyes.

UNDERSTANDING THE VARIABLES

There are a number of variables that can affect your results when you work with fiber-reactive dyes. These variables include measuring techniques, air and water temperature, and reaction time (the reactivity rate) of the ingredients. One of the goals of this book is to provide simple, straightforward directions that help you control these variables—and avoid potential problems—as much as possible.

ACCURATE MEASURING

As you read through the recipes in this book, you will find both English and metric measurements. If you use the metric system and weigh the dye, auxiliary products, and fabric, you will have better control over the results, and it will be easier to repeat them. But do not feel as though you must work in metric. The English volume measurements provided here also work well, although your results may not always be exactly the same.

If you are dyeing fabric for a specific project, increase the recipe and dye more fabric to ensure you have enough from that dye lot. It can be very difficult to exactly match a previously dyed fabric.

Use level measurements for all the recipes in this book.

OPTIMUM WATER TEMPERATURE

Water temperature is one of the variables that can make it difficult to exactly reproduce a dye lot. As a general rule, the closer the temperature is to 105° F (40° C), the more efficient the chemical reaction and the darker your dyed fabric. The dye does not work as well if the water temperature is below 75° F (24° C) or above 105° F (40° C). **Do not** use water warmer than 105° F (40° C) to dissolve dye powder. *Because some dye colors, particularly yellows, are sensitive to water temperature, I recommend using 95° F (35° C) water to mix dye powder and make dye baths.*

Refer to the table below for optimum water temperatures for dissolving dye and auxiliary products.

Product	Water Temperature		Process
	Fahrenheit	Celsius	
Water Softener	75° to 95°	24° to 35°	Add to water
MX Fiber-Reactive Dye	95°	35°	Add water to dye powder
Noniodized table salt	75° to 95°	24° to 35°	Add to water
Soda Ash	110° to 120°	44° to 50°	Add to water
Urea	120°	50°	Add to water
Print Paste Mix SH or F	110° to 120°	44° to 50°	Add to water
Sodium Alginate	110° to 120°	44° to 50°	Add to water

▽ Detail of *Gives Me the Hee Bee Gee Bees* by Laura Wasilowski (see page 131).

Dissolving Dye Powder

Poorly versus Well-Mixed Concentrate

Mixing dye concentrate is a little like mixing gravy; you want it lump-free! Some dye powders take longer to dissolve than others. When the dye powder is fully dissolved, the concentrate appears translucent. If the concentrate appears opaque or cloudy, the powder is not fully dissolved. If necessary, strain the dye concentrate through several layers of nylon stocking, or add about a tablespoon of urea (12 g) to aid solubility, then strain. Dye powder that is not completely dissolved will not dissolve in the salty water of the dye bath and may leave spots of color on your fabric.

Dye Concentrate

The following are general directions for mixing dye concentrate (used in immersion dyeing). See the immersion dye-bath recipes on pages 70–84 and/or "Calculating an Immersion Dye Bath for Different Fabrics" on page 40 to determine the quantities of fiber-reactive dye powder and water needed for a specific recipe.

Read through the directions and assemble all the necessary equipment and supplies before you begin. **1**

Equipment

1-cup (250-ml) measure or graduated cylinder

1-quart (1-L) measure, or larger

1-quart (1-L) plastic or glass container

Cellulose sponge, rags, or paper towels

Dust/mist mask or respirator

Measuring cups and spoons or scale

Mixing box (see page 35)

Newspapers

Plastic drop cloth

Rubber gloves

Scissors

Spray bottle filled with water

Stirring tools

Thermometer

Supplies

MX Fiber-Reactive Dye

1

Procedure

1. Cover your work table with the plastic drop cloth.
2. Set the mixing box on top of the drop cloth. Cut a small stack of newspapers to the inside dimensions of the box. Place the newspapers in the bottom of the mixing box and spray them with water. If you spill any of the powder during the mixing process, it will stick to the damp newspaper.
3. Fill the 1-quart (1-L) container half full with warm water. Use this as a rinse container.
4. Fill the 1-cup (250-ml) measure or graduated cylinder with 95° F (35° C) water.
5. Wear a dust/mist mask or respirator and rubber gloves while working with dye powder. Place the container of dye powder in the mixing box. Before opening the container, tap the lid so the powder settles to the bottom. Carefully open the container. Measure level amounts of the powder into a dry 1-quart (1-L) measure. Recap the container.
6. Slowly add enough water to the dye powder to form a smooth paste (make sure all the powder is wet). Stir as you add the water. Move the dye and water aside; then roll up the top layer of newspaper and discard. Once the powder is dissolved, you can put the mixing box away. **2**
7. Gradually add the remaining water. Stir. Once the powder is fully dissolved, it's ready to use. This is the dye concentrate (the basis for the immersion dye bath).
8. Clean up, using the cellulose sponge, rags, or paper towels.

If needed, you can store the dye concentrate at room temperature up to 5 days. I like to mix new concentrate every few days. If the weather is hot and humid, I mix dye concentrate every day.

2

Dye-Stock Solution

The following are general directions for mixing dye-stock solution (used for direct application of dye). You can prepare more or less dye-stock solution according to the amount and type of fabric that you want to dye. One cup (250 ml) of dye-stock solution will color 1½ to 2 yards (1.46 to 1.82 m) of 100% cotton muslin.

Decide whether you want a light, medium, or dark value of the dye color. See the table that follows to determine the amount of dye powder you need.

To make 1 cup (250 ml) of dye-stock solution:

Value	Light		Medium		Dark*	
	English	Metric	English	Metric	English	Metric
MX Fiber-Reactive Dye	½ tsp	1.25 g	2 tsp	5 g	4 to 6 tsp	10 to 15 g

*For black, use 10 teaspoons (25 g) per cup of urea water.

Read through the directions and assemble all the necessary equipment and supplies before you begin. **1**

Equipment

1-cup (250-ml) measure or graduated cylinder

1-quart (1-L) plastic or glass container

Cellulose sponge, rags, or paper towels

Dust/mist mask or respirator

Measuring cups and spoons or scale

Mixing box (see page 35)

Newspapers

1

Plastic drop cloth

Rubber gloves

Scissors

Spray bottle filled with water

Stirring tools

Thermometer

Supplies

MX Fiber-Reactive Dye (See the table on the facing page for the amount of dye powder needed.)

1 cup (250 ml) urea water (see pages 52–53)

Procedure

1. Cover your work table with the plastic drop cloth.
2. Set the mixing box on top of the drop cloth. Cut a small stack of newspapers to the inside dimensions of the box. Place the newspapers in the bottom of the mixing box and spray them with water. If you spill any of the powder during the mixing process it will stick to the damp newspaper.
3. Fill the 1-quart (1-L) container half full with warm water. Use this as a rinse container.
4. Wear a dust/mist mask or respirator and rubber gloves while working with dye powder. Before opening the container of dye powder, tap the lid so the powder settles to the bottom. Place the dye powder in the mixing box. Carefully open the container. Measure level amounts of the powder into a dry 1-cup (250-ml) measure. Recap the container.
5. Slowly add enough urea water to the dye powder to form a smooth paste (make sure all the powder is wet). Stir as you add the urea water. Move the dye and urea water aside; then roll up the top layer of newspaper and discard.
6. Gradually add the remaining urea water to the 1-cup (250-ml) mark. Stir. Once the powder is fully dissolved (appears translucent), it's ready to use. This is the dye-stock solution. **2**

7. Clean up, using the cellulose sponge, rags, or paper towels.

If needed, you can store the dye-stock solution at room temperature up to 5 days. I like to mix new solution every few days. If the weather is hot and humid, I mix dye-stock solution every day.

Tips

- Dissolve the dye powder in 95° F (35° C) water. If the dye powder floats on the water and does not mix easily, add a drop of Synthrapol.
- If the dye powder does not mix easily and the concentrate or solution appears cloudy, add a tablespoon (12 g) or more of urea.
- To avoid contaminating dye colors, mix the lightest dye color first; then progress to the darkest color.
- As you work, put dirty utensils in a mayonnaise or yogurt container filled with water.
- After mixing each color, clean and dry your utensils.

Urea Water

For direct-application techniques, fiber-reactive dye powder is mixed with urea water. Urea water helps the dye dissolve and prevents the dye from drying completely during the curing process.

This recipe makes 1 quart (1 L) of urea water. For larger quantities, multiply the ingredients as needed. For example, multiply by 4 to make 1 gallon (4 L).

Read through the directions and assemble all the necessary equipment and supplies before you begin. **1**

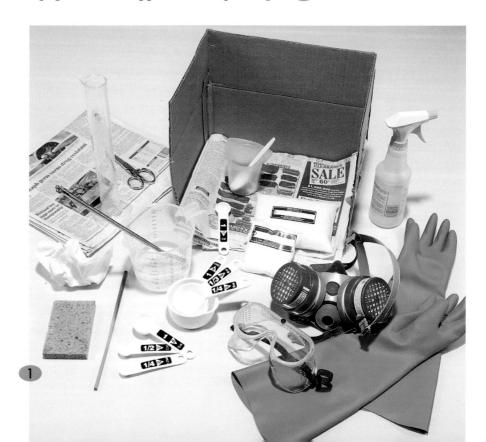

Equipment

Two 1-quart (1-L) measures, or larger
Cellulose sponge, rags, or paper towels
Measuring cup and spoons or scale
Mixing box (see page 35)
Newspapers
Plastic drop cloth
Rubber gloves
Scissors
Spray bottle filled with water
Stirring tools
Thermometer

Supplies

1 teaspoon (7 g) water softener, if you have hard water
1 cup (150 g) urea

Procedure

1. Cover your work table with the plastic drop cloth.
2. Set the mixing box on top of the drop cloth. Cut a small stack of newspapers to the inside dimensions of the box. Place the newspapers in the bottom of the mixing box and spray them with water. If you spill any of the urea during the mixing process it will stick to the damp newspaper.
3. Fill a 1-quart (1-L) measure with 120° F (50° C) water.
4. Pour 3 cups (750 ml) of the water prepared in step 3 into the other 1-quart (1-L) measure.
5. Wear rubber gloves while mixing urea water. Put the container of urea in the mixing box. Carefully open the container. Measure 1 cup (150 g) of urea into the 3 cups (750 ml) of water. Recap the container.
6. Measure 1 teaspoon (7 g) of water softener into the 3 cups (750 ml) of water. Stir until both the urea and water softener are dissolved (the water will look clear). Urea absorbs heat, so the water will also feel cooler.
7. Add water (from step 3) up to the 1-quart (1-L) mark and stir. Cool the urea water to below 95° F (35° C) before using. You can store the urea water in a closed container at room temperature for approximately 6 months. Discard the urea water if you notice a strong, ammonia-like smell.
8. Clean up, using the cellulose sponge, rags, or paper towels.

Making Activated Urea Water

When I'm working and want to lighten the color of a dye-stock solution for a technique such as hand painting, I add mixed alkali to urea water to make "activated urea water." The mixed alkali is a fixative, and it helps ensure that the diluted dye will not wash off during the rinse process.

Add 1 teaspoon (3 g) of mixed alkali (see page 62) to 1 cup (250 ml) of urea water. Label, date, and store urea water in a closed container at room temperature for approximately two months. Discard the activated urea water if you notice a strong, ammonia-like smell.

Print and Dye Pastes

Print paste is made from water, urea, water softener, and seaweed (sodium alginate or Thick SH or F). Purchased print paste has all the ingredients included; you simply add water. Print paste is used to thicken dye-stock solution for direct-application techniques.

Paste consistency is a personal thing; don't be afraid to adjust these recipes. If the dye paste is too thin, thicken it by adding print paste. If the dye paste is too thick, thin it by adding urea water. The consistency that works well for me may not work well for you.

PRINT PASTE FROM A MIX

This recipe makes 1 cup (250 ml) of print paste. Multiply the quantities listed to make larger amounts.

Read through the directions and assemble all the necessary equipment and supplies before you begin. ①

Equipment

2-cup (500-ml) plastic container or jar

Two 1-cup (250-ml) measures

Cellulose sponge, rags, or paper towels

Measuring cups and spoons or scale

Newspapers

Plastic container or jar with tightly fitting lid (for extra print paste)

Plastic drop cloth

Rubber gloves

Stirring tools

Thermometer

Supplies

5½ tablespoons (55 g) PRO Print Paste Mix SH (see "print paste" on page 38)

Procedure

1. Cover your work area with the plastic drop cloth.
2. Wear rubber gloves while mixing print paste. Measure 5½ tablespoons (55 g) of PRO Print Paste Mix SH into a dry 1-cup (250-ml) measure and set aside.
3. Fill the empty 1-cup (250-ml) container with 110° to 120° F (44° to 50° C) water.
4. Pour ¾ cup (190 ml) of the water prepared in step 3 into the 2-cup (500-ml) measure.
5. Gradually add the PRO Print Paste Mix SH measured in step 2 to the ¾ cup (190 ml) of water while stirring rapidly. Continue stirring until you have a smooth paste. This will take approximately 5 minutes.
6. Add water (from step 3) up to the 1-cup (250-ml) mark and stir until thoroughly mixed. Let stand 1 hour, or overnight for smoothest results.
7. Clean up, using the cellulose sponge, rags, or paper towels.

Label, date, and store unused print paste in a closed container for up to 6 months at room temperature. If you live in a hot and humid climate, you should refrigerate the print paste. (Label your container "Print Paste: Do Not Eat Me.") It is important to let print paste return to room temperature—above 75° F (24° C)—before using.

Over time, print paste changes consistency, becoming thinner. You can still use it for thin dye-paste applications, but discard it if you notice a strong ammonia-like smell.

Helpful Hint

Print paste after 24 hours, 15 minutes, and immediately after mixing; note the differences in consistency. For paste that is smooth and lump-free, mix it the day before you plan to use it.

Making Activated Print Paste

When I'm working and want to lighten the color of a dye paste, I add mixed alkali to the print paste to make "activated print paste." Mixed alkali is a fixative that keeps the dye from washing off during the rinse process.

Add 1 teaspoon (3 g) of mixed alkali (see pages 62–63) to 1 cup (250 ml) of prepared print paste. Stir.

Label, date, and store activated print paste in a closed container for up to two months at room temperature. If you live in a hot and humid climate, you should refrigerate the print paste. (Label: "Activated Print Paste: Do Not Eat Me.") It is important to let print paste return to room temperature—above 75° F (24° C)—before using. Discard it if you notice a strong ammonia-like smell.

PRINT PASTE FROM SCRATCH

This recipe makes 1 cup (250 ml) of print paste. For paste that is smooth and lump-free, mix the print paste the day before you plan to use it.

Read through the directions and assemble all the necessary equipment and supplies before you begin. **1**

Equipment

2-cup (500-ml) measure
Two 1-cup (250-ml) measures
Cellulose sponge, rags, or paper towels
Measuring cups and spoons or scale
Mixing box (see page 35)
Newspapers
Plastic container or jar with tightly fitting lid (for extra print paste)
Plastic drop cloth
Rubber gloves
Scissors
Spray bottle filled with water
Stirring tools
Thermometer

Supplies

¼ teaspoon (1.75 g) water softener
1 teaspoon (3 g) sodium alginate, Thick SH (see "print paste" on page 38)
10 teaspoons (40 g) urea

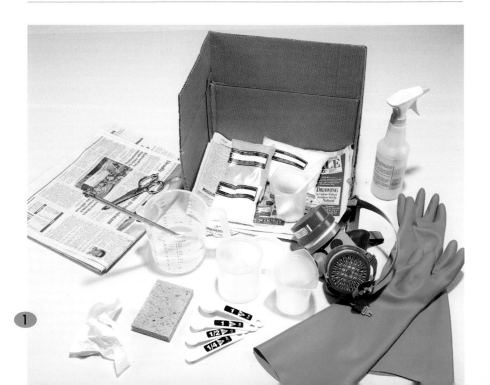

Procedure

1. Cover your work table with the plastic drop cloth.
2. Set the mixing box on top of the drop cloth. Cut a small stack of newspapers to the inside dimensions of the box. Place the newspapers in the bottom of the mixing box and spray them with water. If you spill any of the powder during the mixing process it will stick to the damp newspaper.
3. Wear rubber gloves while mixing print paste. Measure 1 teaspoon (3 g) of sodium alginate, Thick SH into a dry 1-cup (250-ml) measure and set aside.
4. Fill the empty 1-cup (250-ml) container with 110° to 120° F (44° to 50° C) water.
5. Pour ¾ cup (190 ml) of the water prepared in step 4 into the 2-cup (500-ml) measure.
6. Put the container of urea in the mixing box. Carefully open the container. Measure 10 teaspoons (40 g) of urea into the ¾ cup (190 ml) of water. Recap the container.
7. Measure ¼ teaspoon (1.75 g) of water softener into the ¾ cup (190 ml) of water. Stir until both the urea and water softener are dissolved (the water will look clear). Urea absorbs heat, so the water will also feel cooler.
8. Gradually add 1 teaspoon (3 g) of sodium alginate, Thick SH to the ¾ cup (190 ml) of water while stirring rapidly. Continue stirring until you have a smooth paste. This will take approximately 5 minutes.
9. Add water (from step 4) up to the 1-cup (250-ml) mark and stir until thoroughly mixed. Let stand 1 hour or overnight for smoothest results.
10. Clean up, using the cellulose sponge, rags, or paper towels.

You can store unused print paste in a closed container for up to 6 months at room temperature. If you live in a hot and humid climate, you should refrigerate the print paste. (Label it "Print Paste: Do Not Eat Me.") It is important to let print paste return to room temperature—above 75° F (24° C)—before using.

Over time, prepared print paste changes consistency, becoming thinner. You can still use old print paste for thin dye-paste applications, but discard it if you notice a strong ammonia-like smell.

DYE PASTE

Dye paste is a mixture of fiber-reactive dye powder, urea water, and prepared print paste. Thin dye paste flows easily and is ideal for hand painting. Thick dye paste holds a line and stays where you place it, without bleeding around the edges, making it ideal for monoprinting, stenciling, and stamping. Whether your dye paste is thin or thick depends on how much print paste you add.

Print paste is an "antimigrant," meaning it inhibits dye from spreading and penetrating the fabric. Therefore, it is important to use only as much print paste as you need. Make the dye paste as thin as possible for the desired application. Different consistencies work best with different fabrics. Thin dye paste, the consistency of heavy cream, works best on heavy fabric. Thick dye paste, the consistency of honey, works best on lightweight fabric.

If the dye paste is too thin, thicken it by adding print paste. If the dye paste is too thick, thin it by adding urea water.

This recipe makes 1 cup (250 ml) of dye paste. You can prepare more or less dye paste according to the amount of fabric you want to dye. One cup of dye paste will generally color 1½ to 2 yards (1.37 to 1.82 m) of 100% cotton muslin, depending on the recipe.

Read through the directions and assemble all the necessary equipment and supplies before you begin. **1**

Equipment

| 1-quart (1-L) plastic or glass container |
| Two 1-cup (250-ml) measures or graduated cylinders |
| Cellulose sponge, rags, or paper towels |

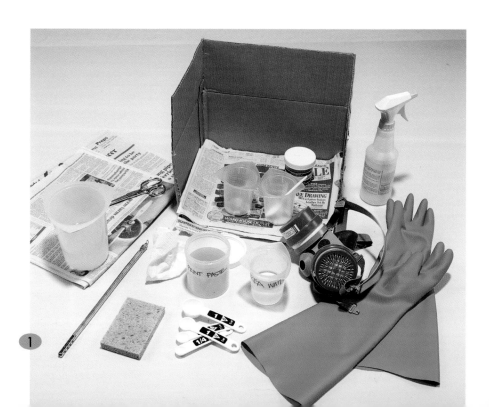

Dust/mist mask or respirator	
Measuring cups and spoons or scale	
Mixing box (see page 35)	
Newspapers	
Plastic container or jar with tightly fitting lid (for extra dye paste)	
Plastic drop cloth	
Rubber gloves	
Scissors	
Spray bottle filled with water	
Stirring tools	
Thermometer	

Supplies

½ to 6 teaspoons (1.25 to 15 g) MX Fiber-Reactive Dye*
1 teaspoon to 1 cup (5 to 250 ml) print paste (see pages 54–57)*
2 tablespoons to 1 cup (30 to 250 ml) urea water (see pages 52–53)*

*Quantity depends on the thickness desired, as explained in the directions that follow.

Procedure

1. Cover your work table with the plastic drop cloth.
2. Set the mixing box on top of the drop cloth. Cut a small stack of newspapers to the inside dimensions of the box. Place the newspapers in the bottom of the mixing box and spray them with water. If you spill any of the powder during the mixing process it will stick to the damp newspaper.
3. Fill the 1-quart (1-L) container half full with warm water. Use this as a rinse container.
4. Decide whether you want to make a light, medium, or dark value of the dye color. See the following table to determine the amount of dye powder you need. Wear a dust/mist mask or respirator and rubber gloves while working with dye powder. Place one of the 1-cup (250-ml) measures in the mixing box. Mix the dye powder with just enough urea water to make a lump-free paste.

To make 1 cup (250 ml) of dye paste:

Value	Light		Medium		Dark*	
	English	Metric	English	Metric	English	Metric
MX Fiber-Reactive Dye	½ tsp	1.25 g	2 tsp	5 g	4 to 6 tsp	10 to 15 g

*For black, use 10 teaspoons (25 g) per cup of dye paste.

5. **To make thin dye paste,** mix 1 to 2 teaspoons (5 to 10 ml) of the prepared print paste with the paste mixed in step 4. Add urea water to make 1 cup (250 ml). Stir until thoroughly mixed. Thin dye paste is ideal for hand painting.

   To make thick dye paste, add prepared print paste to the paste mixed in step 4 to make 1 cup (250 ml). Stir until thoroughly mixed. Thick dye paste is ideal for monoprinting, stenciling, and stamping.

6. Clean up, using the cellulose sponge, rags, or paper towels.

   If needed, you can store the dye paste at room temperature up to 5 days. I like to mix new dye paste every few days. If the weather is hot and humid, I mix dye paste every day.

Soda Ash Soak and Mixed Alkali

There are several ways to fix or "cure" (permanently set) dye when you use a direct-application technique. This book focuses on the two most popular methods: soda ash soak and mixed alkali. In each direct-application recipe, I recommend one curing method or the other based on how easy it is to use, how long the dye needs to react with the fiber, and how easy it is to wash out. However, you can use either of these methods. I encourage you to try both to determine which works best for you. Here are a few helpful guidelines:

- If you need several days to complete a project, it will be easiest to prepare the fabric with soda ash soak. Once you have added fixative (mixed alkali) to the dye paste, you must use it within 4 hours. But, if you have not added fixative, you can use the dye paste for up to 5 days.
- If you plan to apply many layers of dye, you will get the best results using the mixed-alkali method. By mixing the fixative

1

with the dye, you are assured of having enough fixing agent to set the dye. Also, if your design has areas that you don't want to pattern, there is less chance of "back printing," or staining, the light areas during rinsing and washing.

SODA ASH SOAK

Soda ash soak is a mixture of soda ash and water. This mixture pre-fixes the fabric so the dye reacts with the fibers when it is applied. You can soak cotton fabric just prior to dyeing or up to two months in advance. Fabric that is treated just before dyeing seems to yield brighter colors than fabric that has been treated and stored for a long time.

Fabric prepared in advance should be air dried. Use a cool iron to touch up any wrinkles. Do not use a hot iron; fabric treated with soda ash scorches easily. Unfortunately, scorch marks usually do not come out. Treated cotton tends to turn yellow if it is stored for a long time. This color change is usually permanent.

You can also prepare silk in soda ash soak, but you should dye it within 2 weeks. The pH of the soda ash is high, and the silk will begin to deteriorate if the soda ash is not neutralized.

This recipe makes 1 gallon (4 L) of soda ash soak. You can prepare more or less according to the amount of fabric you want to dye. It is important that the fabric be able to move freely while soaking.

Read through the directions and assemble all the necessary equipment and supplies before you begin. **1**

Equipment

1-quart (1-L) measure, or larger

2-gallon (8-L) plastic bucket, or larger, with tightly fitting lid

Cellulose sponge, rags, or paper towels

Dust/mist mask or respirator

Measuring cups and spoons or scale

Mixing box (see page 35)

Newspapers

Plastic drop cloth

Rubber gloves

Scissors

Spray bottle filled with water

Stirring tools

Thermometer

Supplies

9 tablespoons (80 g) soda ash (see "soda ash" on page 38)

Curing Fabric Prepared with Soda Ash Soak or Mixed Alkali

Fabric that has been treated with soda ash soak or mixed alkali, then dyed, should be cured above 70°F (21°C) for four to twenty-four hours. Cure fabric dyed with turquoise or dark colors for a *minimum* of twenty-four hours.

It's important that fabric be kept moist and warm as it cures. If your fabric appears to be drying out, cover it with plastic wrap. There are several ways to maintain a curing temperature of 70° F (21° C). Draw a bathtub full of 120° F (50° C) water; then place the fabric bundle on the edge of the bathtub, or hang open pieces of fabric in the bathroom. Close the door and let the fabric cure. You can also make a tent with an electric blanket and place it over your fabric. Do not lay an electric blanket on the fabric; the dye will cure unevenly.

Procedure

1. Cover your work table with the plastic drop cloth.
2. Set the mixing box on top of the drop cloth. Cut a small stack of newspapers to the inside dimensions of the box. Place the newspapers in the bottom of the mixing box and spray them with water. If you spill any of the powder during the mixing process it will stick to the damp newspaper.
3. Put the bucket in the mixing box.
4. Measure 1 gallon (4 L) of 110° to 120° F (44° to 50° C) water into the bucket. (If you are using a 1-quart measure, 4 quarts makes a gallon.)
5. Wear a dust/mist mask or respirator and rubber gloves while working with soda ash powder. Add 9 tablespoons (80 g) of soda ash powder to the bucket. Stir until dissolved.
6. Clean up, using the cellulose sponge, rags, or paper towels.

Label and date the bucket of soda ash soak. You can store soda ash soak at room temperature, in a bucket with a tightly fitting lid, for 6 to 8 months.

MIXED ALKALI

Mixed alkali is a mixture of soda ash and baking soda. This dry mixture is added directly to the dye-stock solution or paste, which is then applied to fabric. Once you have added mixed alkali to the dye, you must use it within four hours. You may want to write the expiration time on the side of the dye-stock solution or paste container. This way, you'll never labor over a design that will wash out!

Read through the directions and assemble all the necessary equipment and supplies before you begin. **1**

Equipment

4- to 8-ounce (114- to 228-g) wide-mouth container with tightly fitting lid

Cellulose sponge, rags, or paper towels

Dust/mist mask or respirator

Measuring spoons or scale

Mixing box (see page 35)

Newspapers

Plastic drop cloth

Rubber gloves

Scissors

Spray bottle filled with water

Supplies

4 tablespoons (48 g) baking soda

1 tablespoon (9 g) soda ash (see "soda ash" on page 38)

Procedure

1. Cover your work table with the plastic drop cloth.
2. Set the mixing box on top of the drop cloth. Cut a small stack of newspapers to the inside dimensions of the box. Place the newspapers in the bottom of the mixing box and spray them with water. If you spill any of the powder during the mixing process it will stick to the damp newspaper.
3. Wear a dust/mist mask or respirator and rubber gloves while working with soda ash powder. Put the wide-mouth container in the mixing box. Measure 4 tablespoons (48 g) of baking soda and 1 tablespoon (9 g) of soda ash into the wide-mouth container. Cap the container; then shake until well blended.
4. Clean up, using the cellulose sponge, rags, or paper towels.

Label, date, and store the mixed alkali in a cool, dry place. Discard after 6 months. (Label the container "Mixed Alkali: Do Not Eat Me.")

> *The Wind Does Not Require the Grass to Answer*
by Roxana Bartlett, 1994, Boulder, Colorado, 69" x 69". **Method**: Mixed-media quilt. Fiber-reactive dye and textile paint on cotton, rayon, and wool. Machine pieced, hand appliquéd, and hand quilted. Photo by Ken Sanville.

∨ *Soft Stirs the New of Light*
by Roxana Bartlett, 1992, Boulder, Colorado, 69" x 69". **Method**: Mixed-media quilt. Fiber-reactive dye and textile paint on cotton, rayon, and wool. Machine pieced and hand appliquéd and quilted. Photo by Ken Sanville.

▲ *Epiphany*
by Gabrielle Swain, 1995, Watauga,
Texas, 58" x 77". **Method**: Fiber-reactive
dye on cotton. Hand pieced and quilted.
Photo by Brent Kane.

◄ *Life in the Margin #8*
by Caryl Bryer Fallert, 1996, Oswego,
Illinios, 23" x 23". **Method**: Fiber-reactive
dye on cotton. Hand painted. Machine
appliquéd and quilted. Photo by the artist.

Moonstruck
by Melody Johnson, 1997, Cary, Illinois, 60½" x 80".
Method: Fiber-reactive dye on cotton. Hand appliquéd
and machine quilted. Photo by the artist.

⌃ *Drawn to Edges ... Cape Newagen*
by Gayle Fraas and Duncan Slade, 1994, Edgecomb, Maine, 60" x 60". **Method**: Whole-cloth quilt. Fiber-reactive dye on cotton. Hand painted. Machine and hand quilted by the artists. Photo by Dennis Griggs.

⌃ Detail of *Drawn to Edges ... Cape Newagen*

32 Warwick
by Heather Allen, 1997, Asheville, North Carolina, 36" x 75".
Method: Fiber-reactive dye and textile paint on cotton. Machine pieced and quilted and hand beaded.
Photo by Tim Barnwell.

Fire on the Lake
by L. Carlene Raper, 1993, Putney, Vermont, 83" x 102".
Method: Fiber-reactive dye on cotton. Machine pieced and tied.
Photo by Jim Thomas.

Dance in Several Sections
by Astrid Hilger Bennett, 1991, Iowa City, Iowa, 55" x 65".
Method: Fiber-reactive dye on cotton duck. Hand painted. Machine quilted. Photo by the artist.

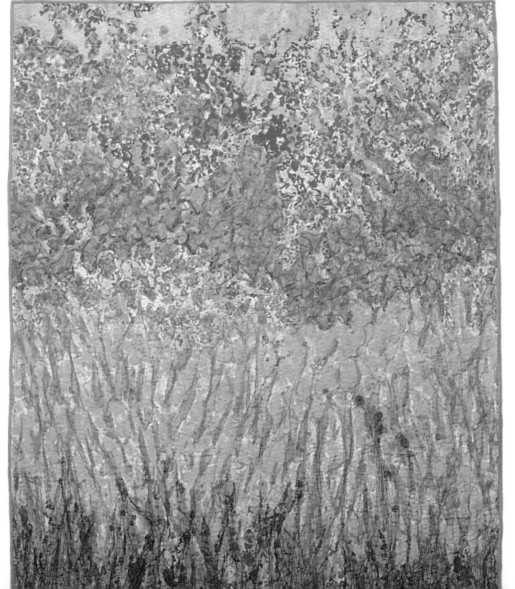

⋀ *Summer Beach I*
by Astrid Hilger Bennett, 1996,
Iowa City, Iowa, 76" x 42".
Method: Fiber-reactive dye on
cotton. Machine pieced and
quilted. Photo by the artist.

⟨ *No Thistles in My
Garden: Hiroshima Series*
by Barbara Moll, 1996,
Muncie, Indiana, 39" x 47".
Method: Whole-cloth quilt.
Fiber-reactive dye on cotton.
Hand printed and painted.
Machine quilted. Photo by
Joan Whitaker.

Immersion Dye Techniques

Immersion dyeing, also called "vat" or "exhaust" dyeing, is the most efficient method for creating a solid-colored fabric. Fabric is submerged in warm water with dye and auxiliary products for sixty to ninety minutes (with periodic stirring for even color). After the fabric has soaked for the allotted time, it is rinsed to remove excess fixative, washed, and dried. There are several tricks to successful immersion dyeing:

- Don't worry if the dye bath changes color during dyeing. Both the dye bath and the fabric may change colors several times as the different dyes "strike" or are absorbed by the fabric.
- If you dye different types of fabric in the same dye bath, the fabrics will dye different colors (or shades of the same color) based on which fabric is more absorbent.
- Be sure to dye your fabric for the full sixty to ninety minutes (refer to the specific recipe). Shortening the dye bath causes "surface dyeing"—the dye does not fully penetrate the fiber. Surface-dyed fabrics are neither lightfast nor washfast. Also, shortening the dye bath prevents mixed colors from being absorbed by fabric and will probably affect your desired color. *Different dye colors strike (are absorbed by and react with) the fiber at different times during the dye bath.*
- Remember that the color of the dried, dyed fabric will be lighter than the color of the wet, dyed fabric. Think about wet versus dry blue jeans. As you gain experience, you will learn to evaluate wet fabric color.
- Be sure to keep a detailed record book (see page 35) of your dyeing, including your disappointments. The more information you gather and experience you gain, the more comfortable you will be mixing colors and predicting results!

This section includes recipes for a basic immersion dye bath, an immersion dye bath in a washing machine, a value gradation, a hue gradation, and resist techniques for immersion dyeing. Review "Protecting Yourself and Your Environment" on pages 16–17 for guidelines on working with dye and auxiliary powders.

USING A BASIC DYE BATH

This recipe will dye 1 yard (91 cm) of 100% cotton muslin a medium value of 1 color. Preparation, dyeing, and cleanup takes approximately 2 hours. (It may take longer if you are not familiar with the immersion dye bath process.) Remember to wear rubber gloves when you work with the fabric in the dye bath.

Read through the directions, and assemble the equipment and supplies before you begin. Wear a dust/mist mask or respirator while working with dye powder and auxiliary products. **1**

Equipment

1-cup (250-ml) measure or graduated cylinder

1-quart (1-L) measure, or larger

2-gallon (8-L) plastic bucket, or larger, for dye bath

Cellulose sponge, rags, or paper towels

Clothesline and clothespins (optional)

Dust/mist mask or respirator

Kitchen timer or watch

Measuring cups and spoons or scale

Mixing box (see page 35)

Newspapers

Plastic drop cloth

Rubber gloves

Spray bottle filled with water

Stirring tools

Thermometer

Immersion-Dyed Fabric

Supplies

⅔ cup (180 g) noniodized table salt

⅜ teaspoon (2.3 g) water softener, if you have hard water

1¾ teaspoons (4.5 g) MX Fiber-Reactive Dye
(see "Color Mixing" on pages 41–45)

5 teaspoons (15 g) soda ash

1 yard (91 cm) scoured, 100% cotton muslin (see pages 22–24)

¼ teaspoon (1.25 ml) Synthrapol (minimum)

Level Dyeing

For "level" dyeing (even color), stir, stir, stir! Rearrange the fabric folds often during the immersion dye-bath process, and make sure the fabric can move freely in the dye bath.

Procedure

1. Cover your work table with the plastic drop cloth. If your scoured fabric is dry, soak it in 1 gallon (4 L) of 110° F (44° C) water with ¼ teaspoon (1.25 ml) of Synthrapol for 10 to 15 minutes.

2. Pour 3 quarts (3 L) of 95° F (35° C) water into the 2-gallon (8-L) plastic bucket. This bucket will contain the dye bath.

3. Add ⅔ cup (180 g) of salt. Stir until dissolved.

4. If you have hard water, add ⅜ teaspoon (2.3 g) of water softener. Stir until dissolved.

5. Following the instructions for mixing dye concentrate on pages 48–50, dissolve 1¾ teaspoons (4.5 g) of dye powder in 1 cup (250 ml) of 95° F (35° C) water. Pour this into the bucket to complete the dye bath.

6. Make sure the fabric is completely wet before adding it to the dye bath. If you are not sure that the fabric is completely wet, add ¼ teaspoon (1.25 ml) of Synthrapol to the dye bath before adding the fabric.

7. Add the wet fabric to the dye bath. Stir to make sure that there are no air bubbles trapped in the fabric. Set the timer for 15 minutes. Stir the fabric intermittently, rearranging the folds. **1**

8. To mix the fixative, dissolve 5 teaspoons (15 g) of soda ash in ½ cup (125 ml) of 110° to 120° F (44° to 50° C) water. Set aside.

9. When the timer rings, remove the fabric from the dye bath and set it aside in the empty bucket. Pour the fixative prepared in step 8 into the dye bath and stir. *Don't worry if the dye bath changes color when you add the fixative; it will not affect the final color of your fabric.* **2**

10. Return the fabric to the dye bath and set the timer for 60 minutes. Stir the fabric continuously for the first 15 minutes, rearranging the folds; then stir every 5 minutes until the timer rings. Stirring at this stage is very important for level dyeing. Make sure to rearrange the folds frequently.

11. When the timer rings, remove the fabric and pour the dye bath down the drain. Dye baths cannot be stored or reused after the fixative has been added.

12. To rinse and wash the fabric by hand, put it in the empty dye bucket and fill the bucket half full with 65° to 75° F (18° to 24° C) water. Swish the fabric around for a minute or so; then pour the rinse water down the drain. Repeat this process, changing the rinse water three or four times. When the fabric feels squeaky clean (not soapy), remove it and empty the rinse bucket. (It's okay for the rinse water to be colored.) Refill the bucket with 140° F (60° C) water. Add ¼ teaspoon (1.25 ml) of Synthrapol and stir. Return the fabric to the rinse bucket and swish it around for 5 minutes. Rinse the fabric in warm (comfortable to the touch) water.

To rinse and wash the fabric by machine, set your washing machine on the small load, warm wash, and warm rinse cycles. After the machine fills and begins to agitate, add the fabric. Close the lid and let the machine continue through the wash, rinse, and spin cycles. After the final spin cycle, reset the machine on the hot wash and warm rinse cycles. After the machine fills with water, add ¼ teaspoon (1.25 ml) of Synthrapol for each yard of fabric and let the machine continue through all the cycles. Check the last rinse cycle. If the rinse water is colored, you may need to repeat this step. For dark colors, 2 short wash treatments may work better than 1 long wash.

13. Dry the fabric in a clothes dryer or on a clothesline. Follow the dryer manufacturer's instructions for the appropriate heat setting.

14. Clean up, using cellulose sponge, rags, or paper towels.

USING A WASHING MACHINE

Washing-machine dyeing is a good technique to use when you want to dye a large amount of fabric a solid color. This technique takes much of the physical work out of the immersion dye bath process. You can dye up to 15 yards (13.6 m) of fabric in an extra-large capacity, top-loading washing machine in 2 to 2½ hours!

For different amounts of fabric, increase or decrease the quantities of dye, auxiliary products, and water. (See "Calculating an Immersion Dye Bath for Different Fabrics" on page 40.) To adjust the amount of water, set your washing machine for small, medium, large, or extra-large loads.

I recommend cutting your fabric into lengths of no more than 4 to 5 yards (3.6 to 4.5 m) each. When working with fabric pieces that are 4 yards or longer, check the fabric frequently during the dye cycle to make sure it is not twisted. Dye cannot evenly penetrate twisted fabric. If the fabric does twist, unwind it during the 5-minute stop cycles (step 6). Remember to wear rubber gloves when you work with the fabric in the dye bath.

Read through the directions, and assemble the equipment and supplies before you begin. Wear a dust/mist mask or respirator while working with dye powder and auxiliary products.

Equipment

2-quart (2-L) measure, or larger
Cellulose sponge, rags, or paper towels
Clothesline and clothespins (optional)
Dust/mist mask or respirator
Kitchen timer or watch
Measuring cups and spoons or scale
Mixing box (see page 35)

Preventing Spotty Dyeing

Always remove your fabric before adding soda ash to the dye bath. Stir well before and after you return the fabric to prevent spotty dyeing.

| Newspapers |
| Nylon stocking or cheesecloth (optional) |
| Plastic drop cloth |
| Rubber gloves |
| Spray bottle filled with water |
| Stirring tools |
| Thermometer |
| Washing machine |

Supplies

The amount of each ingredient needed is based on the weight of the fabric and the value of the dye color. Refer to the table that follows.

| Up to 15 yards (13.6 m) 100% cotton muslin |
| Water softener, if you have hard water |
| MX Fiber-Reactive Dye (see "Color Mixing" on pages 41–45) |
| Noniodized table salt |
| Soda ash |
| Synthrapol |

For 5 pounds (2.3 kg) of dry fabric—approximately 15 yards (14 m) of 100% cotton muslin—use the following amounts. If your fabric weighs more or less than 5 pounds, refer to page 40.

Value	Light		Medium		Dark*	
	English	Metric	English	Metric	English	Metric
Water Softener	5 tsp	35 g	5 tsp	35 g	5 tsp	35 g
MX Fiber-Reactive Dye	5 tsp	13 g	7½ Tbl	68 g	15 Tbl	136 g
Noniodized Table Salt	6 cups	1.8 kg	9 cups	2.72 kg	12 cups	3.6 kg
Soda Ash	¾ cup	115 g	1½ cups	230 g	2¼ cups	345 g

For black, double the amount of dye powder and extend the dyeing time to 90 minutes (after adding soda ash).

Procedure

1. Cover your work area with the plastic drop cloth.
2. Weigh the dry fabric (see page 40). Use the weight of the fabric to determine the exact amount of each ingredient needed.
3. When you use your washing machine to dye large amounts of fabric, it is best to scour (pages 23–24) all the fabric in the machine before preparing the dye bath. Machine wash the fabric on the extra-large load, hot cycle—minimum temperature 140° F (60° C)—with ¼ teaspoon (1 g) of soda ash and ¼ teaspoon

Helpful Hint

Cleaning your Washing Machine

I have not stained any laundry after using my washing machine for dyeing. After dyeing fabric in your washing machine, wipe the outside of your machine with a damp cloth to mop up any spilled dye. The rinse and wash cycles clean the inside of the machine.

(1.25 ml) of Synthrapol per yard (91 cm) of dry fabric. After the rinse cycle, remove the wet fabric and set it aside while you prepare the dye bath.

4. Set your washing machine on the extra-large load, warm wash, and warm rinse cycles. The water temperature should be 95° F (35° C). Remove 2 quarts (2 L) of water from the machine and set aside. After the machine fills and begins to agitate, add the salt and water softener (if needed) indicated in the chart. Let the machine agitate until the salt dissolves; then stop the wash cycle.

5. Refer to the preceding table to determine the amount of dye powder you need. Following the instructions for mixing dye concentrate on pages 48–50, dissolve the dye powder in the water set aside in step 3; then pour it into the washing machine. Let the machine agitate until the dye is thoroughly mixed; then stop the wash cycle.

6. Add the wet fabric, distributing it evenly around the tub. Start the machine and set the timer for 15 minutes. If the wash cycle ends before the 15 minutes are up, stop the machine. Wait 5 to 10 minutes, then restart the wash cycle so the dye bath does not go down the drain. When the timer rings, stop the wash cycle. During the wash cycle, check the fabric frequently to make sure it is not twisted.

7. Refer to the preceding table to determine the amount of soda ash you need. To make the fixative, dissolve the soda ash separately in 2 quarts (2 L) of 110° to 120° F (44° to 50° C) water.

If your washing machine has a spout for liquid bleach, pour 2 cups (500 ml) of the fixative through the spout. Restart the machine and set the timer for 5 minutes. When the timer rings, add another 2 cups (500 ml) of the fixative through the liquid-bleach spout and set the timer for 5 minutes. When the timer rings, add the remaining fixative and set the timer for 5 minutes. Remember to reset the machine so the dye bath does not go down the drain.

If your washing machine does not have a liquid-bleach spout, slowly pour all the fixative into the machine while it is agitating. Do not pour the fixative directly on the fabric; this causes uneven dyeing.

8. When the timer rings, stop the machine and let the fabric sit for 5 minutes. Restart the machine and agitate the fabric for another 5 minutes. Repeat this process for 60 minutes. Adjust your washing machine as necessary (to agitate only) so the dye bath does not go down the drain.

9. At the end of 60 minutes, let the machine continue through the wash, rinse, and spin cycles. After the final spin cycle, reset the machine to the hot wash and warm rinse cycles. Allow the washing machine to fill with water. The water temperature for the hot wash should be 140° F (60° C).

Dealing with Undissolved Dye

If you are not sure that the dye is thoroughly dissolved, strain the dye concentrate through several layers of nylon stocking before pouring it into the washing machine.

After the machine fills with water, add ¼ teaspoon (1.25 ml) of Synthrapol per yard (91 cm) of fabric and let the machine continue through all the cycles. Check the last rinse cycle. If the rinse water is colored, you may need to repeat this step.

10. Dry the fabric in a clothes dryer or on a clothesline. Follow the dryer manufacturer's instructions for the appropriate heat setting.

11. Clean up, using the cellulose sponge, rags, or paper towels.

DYEING A VALUE GRADATION

A value gradation—a progression of values, lightest to darkest, of one color—creates an appealing visual rhythm. Use this recipe to dye a value gradation with 6 even steps—¼ yard (23 cm) of each value. Keep in mind that the more dye baths you use, the longer setup and cleanup will take. Remember to wear rubber gloves when you work with the fabric in the dye bath.

Read through the directions, and assemble the equipment and supplies before you begin. Wear a dust/mist mask or respirator while working with dye powder and auxiliary products.

Equipment

1-quart (1-L) plastic container or jar

6 plastic cups (empty yogurt or margarine tubs)

6 long-handled spoons or assorted stirring tools

Seven 1-gallon (4-L) plastic buckets

Cellulose sponge, rags, or paper towels

Clothesline and clothespins (optional)

Dust/mist mask or respirator

Kitchen timer or watch

Marking pen

Masking tape

Measuring cups and spoons or scale

Mixing box (see page 35)

Newspapers

Plastic drop cloth

Plastic or Styrofoam plates

Rubber gloves

Scissors

Spray bottle filled with water

Thermometer

Six-Step Value Gradation Fabrics

Supplies

1½ teaspoons (10.5 g) water softener, if you have hard water

2 teaspoons (5 g) MX Fiber-Reactive Dye (see "Color Mixing" on pages 41–45)

1½ cups (270 g) noniodized table salt

¼ cup (27 g) soda ash

1½ yards (1.37 m) scoured, 100% cotton muslin (see page 22)

¼ teaspoon (1.25 g) Synthrapol (minimum)

Procedure

1. Cover your work table with the plastic drop cloth.
2. Cut the fabric into 6 fat quarters, 18" x 22" (46 cm x 56 cm), or 6 long quarters, 9" x 44" (23 cm x 112 cm). If your scoured fabric is dry, soak it in 1 gallon (4 L) of 110° F (44° C) water with ¼ teaspoon (1.25 g) of Synthrapol for 10 to 15 minutes.
3. Fill 1 plastic bucket half full with warm water. Use this as a rinse bucket to wash your gloved hands between additions to each dye bath.
4. Label the remaining plastic buckets with masking tape. Number them 1–6. Place the buckets in numerical order, from left to right, on your work table. Place a spoon in each of the 6 buckets.
5. Pour 3½ cups (875 ml) of 95° F (35° C) water into each bucket.
6. Add ¼ cup (45 g) of salt to each bucket. Stir until dissolved.
7. If you have hard water, add ¼ teaspoon (1.2 g) of water softener to each bucket. Stir until dissolved.
8. Following the instructions for mixing dye concentrate on pages 48–50, dissolve 2 teaspoons (5 g) of dye powder in 1 cup (250 ml) of 95° F (35° C) water.

    You may want to experiment with the amount of dye powder. For darker values, use 3 to 4 teaspoons (7.5 to 10 g) of dye powder. For lighter values, use 1 teaspoon (2.5 g) of dye powder.
9. Fill the 1-quart (1-L) container with 95° F (35° C) water.
10. Measure the dye concentrate into the buckets as follows:
    Bucket #1: Pour ½ cup (125 ml) of the dye concentrate into bucket #1 and stir. ①

①

Buckets #2–#5: Using the water from the container you filled in step 9, refill the dye-concentrate cup to the 1-cup (250-ml) mark. Pour ½ cup (125 ml) of the diluted dye concentrate into bucket #2 and stir. Repeat this process for buckets #3, #4, and #5, continuing to dilute the dye concentrate.

Bucket #6: Using the water from the container you filled in step 9, refill the dye-concentrate cup to the 1-cup (250-ml) mark. Pour ½ cup (125 ml) of the diluted dye concentrate into bucket #6 and stir. Discard the remaining ½ cup (125 ml) of dye concentrate.

11. To make the fixative, dissolve ¼ cup (27 g) of soda ash in 1½ cups (375 ml) of 120° F (50° C) water. Use the 1-quart (1-L) container for mixing.

12. Measure ¼ cup (63 ml) of the fixative into each of the 6 plastic cups. Place one plastic cup in front of each dye bath.

13. Make sure all the fabric is completely wet before adding it to the dye baths. If you are not sure that the fabric is completely wet, add ¼ teaspoon (1.25 ml) of Synthrapol to each dye bath before adding the fabric.

14. Add a piece of wet fabric to each dye bath. Set the timer for 15 minutes. Stir the fabric in each dye bath for about 30 seconds, beginning with bucket #1 and ending with bucket #6. Make sure there are no air bubbles trapped in the fabric, and rearrange the folds as you stir. Repeat this process until the timer rings.

    If you use your gloved hands to stir the fabric, make sure to rinse them in the bucket prepared in step 3 before proceeding to the next dye bath.

15. When the timer rings, remove the fabric from bucket #1 and set it aside on a plastic plate. Pour the fixative from the plastic cup into the dye bath and stir. Return the fabric and stir. Repeat this process for all the dye baths, rinsing your gloved hands before proceeding to the next dye bath. **2**

2

16. Set the timer for 60 minutes. Stir the fabric in each dye bath for about 30 seconds, beginning with bucket #1 and ending with bucket #6. Repeat this process for 15 minutes, then once every 5 minutes until the timer rings. Stirring at this stage is very important for level dyeing. Rearrange the folds frequently.

17. When the timer rings, carry each bucket to a sink and remove the fabric. Pour the dye bath down the drain and put the fabric back in the empty bucket.

18. To rinse and wash the fabric by hand, fill each bucket half full with 65° to 75° F (18° to 24° C) water. Swish the fabric around for a minute or so; then pour the rinse water down the drain. Rinse again. Repeat this process for each bucket. After the first 2 rinses, put all the fabric in 1 bucket and repeat the rinse process at least twice. When the fabric feels squeaky clean (not soapy), remove it and empty the rinse bucket. (It's okay for the rinse water to be colored.) Refill the bucket with 140° F (60° C) water. Add ¼ teaspoon (1.25 ml) of Synthrapol per yard of fabric. Return the fabric to the rinse bucket and swish it around for 5 minutes. Rinse the fabric in warm (comfortable to the touch) water.

    To rinse and wash the fabric by machine, set your washing machine on the small load, warm wash, and warm rinse cycles. Wring out each piece of fabric. After the machine fills and begins to agitate, add the fabric. Distribute it evenly around the tub. Close the lid and let the machine continue through the wash, rinse, and spin cycles. After the final spin cycle, reset the machine on the hot wash and warm rinse cycles. After the machine fills with water, add ¼ teaspoon (1.25 ml) of Synthrapol per yard of fabric and let the machine continue through all the cycles. Check the last rinse cycle. If the rinse water is colored, you may need to repeat this step. For dark colors, 2 short wash treatments may work better than 1 long wash.

19. Dry the fabric in a clothes dryer or on a clothesline. Follow the dryer manufacturer's instructions for the appropriate heat setting.

20. Clean up, using a cellulose sponge, rags, or paper towels.

Six-Step Hue Gradation Fabrics

DYEING A HUE GRADATION

A hue gradation is a smooth transition from one color to another. Use this recipe to create striking colors while dyeing a 6-step hue gradation—¼ yard (23 cm) of each hue. Keep in mind that the more dye baths you use, the longer setup and cleanup will take. Remember to wear rubber gloves when you work with the fabric in the dye bath.

Read through the directions, and assemble the equipment and supplies before you begin. Wear a dust/mist mask or respirator while working with dye powder and auxiliary products.

Equipment

1-quart (1-L) plastic container or jar

6 plastic cups (empty yogurt or margarine tubs)

6 long-handled spoons or assorted stirring tools

Seven 1-gallon (4-L) plastic buckets

Cellulose sponge, rags, or paper towels

Clothesline and clothespins (optional)

Dust/mist mask or respirator

Kitchen timer or watch

Marking pen

Masking tape

Measuring cups and spoons or scale

Mixing box (see page 35)

Newspapers

Plastic drop cloth

Plastic or Styrofoam plates

Rubber gloves

Scissors

Spray bottle filled with water

Thermometer

Supplies

1½ teaspoons (10.5 g) water softener, if you have hard water

2 teaspoons (5 g) each of 2 MX Fiber-Reactive Dye colors (see "Color Mixing" on pages 41–45)

1½ cups (270 g) noniodized table salt

¼ cup (27 g) soda ash

1½ yards (1.37 m) scoured, 100% cotton muslin (see pages 22–24)

½ teaspoon (1.25 ml) Synthrapol (minimum)

Procedure

1. Cover your work table with the plastic drop cloth.

2. Cut the fabric into 6 fat quarters, 18" x 22" (46 cm x 56 cm), or 6 long quarters, 9" x 44" (23 cm x 112 cm). If your scoured fabric is dry, soak it in 1 gallon (4 L) of 110° F (44° C) water with ¼ teaspoon (1.25 g) of Synthrapol for 10 to 15 minutes.

3. Fill 1 bucket half full with warm water. Use this as a rinse bucket to wash your gloved hands between additions to each dye bath.

4. Label the remaining buckets with masking tape. Number them 1–6. Place the buckets in numerical order, from left to right, on your work table. Place a spoon in each bucket.

5. Pour 3 cups (750 ml) of 95° F (35° C) water into each bucket.

6. Add ¼ cup (45 g) of salt to each bucket. Stir until dissolved.

7. If you have hard water, add ¼ teaspoon (1.2 g) of water softener to each bucket. Stir until dissolved.

8. Follow the instructions for mixing dye concentrate on pages 48–50. To make the first color, dissolve 2 teaspoons (5 g) of dye powder in 1 cup (250 ml) of 95° F (35° C) water. Repeat this process to make the second color.

9. Fill the 1-quart (1-L) container with 95° F (35° C) water.

10. Measure the dye concentrate for the first color into the buckets as follows:

    Bucket #1: Measure ½ cup (125 ml) of the dye concentrate into the bucket and stir. ①

    Buckets #2–#5: Using the water from the container you filled in step 9, refill the dye-concentrate cup to the 1-cup (250-ml) mark. Measure ½ cup (125 ml) of the diluted dye concentrate into bucket #2 and stir. Repeat this process for buckets #3, #4, and #5, continuing to dilute the dye concentrate. Do not add this concentrate to bucket #6. Discard the remaining ½ cup (125 ml) of dye concentrate.

11. Measure the dye concentrate for the second color into the buckets as follows:

①

Bucket #6: Measure ½ cup (125 ml) of the dye concentrate into the bucket and stir. **2**

Buckets #5–#2: Using the water from the container you filled in step 9, refill the dye-concentrate cup to the 1-cup (250-ml) mark. Measure ½ cup (125 ml) of the diluted dye concentrate into bucket #5 and stir. Repeat this process for buckets #4, #3, and #2, continuing to dilute the dye concentrate. Do not add this concentrate to bucket #1. Discard the remaining ½ cup (125 ml) of dye concentrate.

12. To make the fixative, dissolve ¼ cup (27 g) of soda ash in 1½ cups (375 ml) of 110° to 120°F (44° to 50°C) water; use the 1-quart (1-L) container for mixing.

13. Measure ¼ cup (63 ml) of the fixative into each of the 6 plastic cups. Place one cup in front of each dye bath.

14. Make sure the fabric is completely wet before adding it to the dye baths. If you are not sure that the fabric is completely wet, add ¼ teaspoon (1.25 ml) of Synthrapol to each dye bath before adding the fabric.

15. Add a piece of wet fabric to each dye bath. Set the timer for 15 minutes. Stir the fabric in each dye bath for about 30 seconds, beginning with bucket #1 and ending with bucket #6. Make sure there are no air bubbles trapped in the fabric, and rearrange the folds as you stir. Repeat this process until the timer rings.

    If you use your gloved hands to stir the fabric, make sure to rinse them in the bucket prepared in step 3 before proceeding to the next dye bath.

16. When the timer rings, remove the fabric from bucket #1 and set it aside on a plastic plate. Pour the fixative from the plastic cup into the dye bath and stir. Return the fabric and stir. Repeat this process for all the dye baths, rinsing your gloved hands before proceeding to the next dye bath. **3**

17. Set the timer for 60 minutes. Stir the fabric in each dye bath for about 30 seconds, beginning with bucket #1 and ending with

2

bucket #6. Repeat this process for 15 minutes, then once every 5 minutes until the timer rings.

Stirring at this stage is very important for level dyeing. Make sure to rearrange the folds frequently.

18. When the timer rings, carry each bucket to a sink and remove the fabric. Pour the dye bath down the drain and put the fabric back in the empty bucket.

19. To rinse and wash the fabric by hand, fill each bucket half full with 65° to 75°F (18° to 24°C) water. Swish the fabric around for a minute or so; then pour the rinse water down the drain. Rinse again. Repeat this process for each bucket. After the first 2 rinses, put all the fabric in 1 bucket and repeat the rinse process at least twice. When the fabric feels squeaky clean (not soapy), remove it and empty the rinse bucket. (It's okay for the rinse water to be colored.) Refill the bucket with 140°F (60°C) water. Add ¼ teaspoon (1.25 g) of Synthrapol per yard of fabric. Return the fabric to the rinse bucket and swish it around for 5 minutes. Rinse the fabric in warm (comfortable to the touch) water.

To rinse and wash the fabric by machine, set your washing machine on the small load, warm wash, and warm rinse cycles. Wring out each piece of fabric. After the machine fills and begins to agitate, add the fabric. Distribute it evenly around the tub. Close the lid and let the machine continue through the wash, rinse, and spin cycles. After the final spin cycle, reset the machine on the hot wash and warm rinse cycles. After the machine fills with water, add ¼ teaspoon (1.25 ml) of Synthrapol per yard of fabric and let the machine continue through all the cycles. Check the last rinse cycle. If the rinse water is colored, you may need to repeat this step. For dark colors, 2 short wash treatments may work better than 1 long wash.

20. Dry the fabric in a clothes dryer or on a clothesline. Follow the dryer manufacturer's instructions for the appropriate heat setting.

21. Clean up, using the cellulose sponge, rags, or paper towels.

3

ADAPTING THE GRADATION RECIPES

The gradation recipes in this book are calibrated for ¼ yard (23 cm) pieces of muslin for each value or hue. If you are like me, you'll want to dye larger and larger pieces of fabric (just to make sure you have enough, of course) or extend the number of steps in the gradations. Use the tables below to adapt the gradation recipes.

Gradation Dyeing Calculations

For each dye bath, use the amounts listed below:

	English	Metric	English	Metric	English	Metric
Fabric	½ yd	46 cm	1 yd	91 cm	2 yd	1.82 m
Water Softener	¼ tsp	1.2 g	⅜ tsp	2.3 g	⅝ tsp	4.5 g
Soda Ash	2½ tsp	7.5 g	5 tsp	15 g	10 tsp	30 g
Salt	4 Tbl	90 g	½ cup	180 g	1¼ cups	360 g
Water	6 cups	1.5 L	3 qt	3 L	1½ gal	6 L

Dye Powder

For a single dye bath, use the amounts listed in the table below. For gradation dyeing, double the amount of dye powder. When dyeing more than 6 steps, double the dark value amount and use 2 cups (500 ml) water to mix the dye concentrate and 1 cup (250 ml) of dye concentrate for each dye bath.

	English	Metric	English	Metric	English	Metric
Fabric	½ yd	46 cm	1 yd	91 cm	2 yd	1.82 m
Dye powder for:						
Light value	¼ tsp	0.38 g	⅜ tsp	0.75 g	⅝ tsp	1.5 g
Medium value	⅞ tsp	2.4 g	1¾ tsp	4.5 g	3⅝ tsp	9 g
Dark value*	1¾ tsp	4.5 g	3⅝ tsp	9 g	7¼ tsp	18 g

*For black, double the amount of dye powder and extend the dyeing time to 90 minutes (after adding soda ash).

CREATING PATTERNS WITH RESISTS

A "resist" is anything that prevents dye from penetrating a fabric—creating a pattern based on the undyed and dyed areas. You can create resist patterns by manipulating the fabric, as described in this section, or by using a liquid resist (see pages 120–25). This section describes different ways to fold, pleat, roll, clamp, knot, bunch, bind, and stitch (including overstitching, gathering, pleating, and complex machine stitching) to produce a desired pattern.

Creating patterns with resists is an art form. The photos in this section show just a few patterns you can experiment with in your immersion dye baths; I encourage you to be adventurous. For more ideas, see pages 102–5. Following are some guidelines:

- Bundled fabric takes up less space and uses less water than other immersion dye bath methods. You can decrease the amount of water and salt (in proportion) in the dye bath if desired; just make sure the fabric is completely submerged. Using less water (with the same amount of dye powder) produces darker colors. Keep notes on the changes you make to the dye bath.
- Create complex patterns by overdyeing different colors and patterns. For example, fold a piece of fabric and dye it light blue, then unfold and fold in another direction and dye the fabric yellow. The resulting fabric will have patterned areas that are white, yellow, blue, and various shades of green.

Twisting and Coiling

Twist fabric lengthwise as shown. Hold the two ends together, allowing the fabric to twist together as shown. Wrap a rubber band around the ends.

Twisted and Coiled Fabric

Clamped Fabric

Clamping

Fold the fabric into an accordion shape, alternating folds, then fold the accordion in one direction as shown. Use a clamp to hold the shape during immersion dyeing.

Pole Wrapping

Purchase a segment of polyvinyl chloride (PVC) pipe. To make a sleeve, cut a piece of fabric slightly larger than the pipe, then stitch the long edges as shown. Place the sleeve on the pipe. Twist the sleeve around the pipe, pushing it down ("ruching") as you work. The tighter the ruching, the crisper the pattern. Use masking tape or large rubber bands to hold the ruching during immersion dyeing.

Pole-Wrapped Fabric

Stitching

Running Stitch: Use a double length of heavy thread, such as button-and-carpet thread. Sew lines of running stitches across the fabric, varying the stitch length if desired. Pull the threads very tight as shown, then knot the doubled ends.

Fabrics Prepared with a Running Stitch

Whipstitch: Use a double length of heavy thread, such as button-and-carpet thread. Fold your fabric, then whipstitch the folded edge, varying the stitch depth and length if desired. Pull the threads tight as shown, then knot the doubled ends.

Whipstitched Fabric

Removing Stitching

Let fabric dry before removing thread. Grasp the dyed, dry bundle in one hand and pull the thread ends with the other. Slip a seam ripper under the knot and cut it off. Cut all the knots off before opening the fabric to prevent cutting the fabric by mistake.

Katano stitch: Fold the fabric into an accordion shape. Press. Machine or hand stitch (with a running stitch) as shown.

Katano-Stitched Fabric

Fold and Edge Stitch: Use a double length of heavy thread, such as button-and-carpet thread. Make a small pleat in your fabric. Using a running stitch, sew the pleat in place. Repeat as many times as desired. Pull the threads tight as shown, then knot the doubled ends.

Fold-and-Edge Stitched Fabric

Tuck and Stitch: Make even vertical pleats every few inches, machine basting as shown. Then make even horizontal pleats every few inches, machine basting each pleat.

Fold again and stitch.

Tucked and Stitched Fabric, Both Sides

TROUBLESHOOTING

The color is not as bright as it should be. There are six possible causes. There may not have been enough dye in the dye bath, the water may have been too hot or cold, the water used to dissolve the dye may have been too hot, there may be a finish on the fabric, the fabric may not be 100% cotton, and/or the dye may be too old. **1**

You may have to work through a process of elimination. Use more dye powder, check the temperature of the water (both the dye concentrate and dye bath), do the water-drop test (see page 24), scour the fabric again, use different fabric, or purchase new dye.

The dye washes off in the rinse water. There are three possible causes. There may be a finish on the fabric, the water used to dissolve the dye may have been too hot, and/or you may have forgotten to add the fixative. **2**

Again, work through a process of elimination. Do the water-drop test (see page 24), check the temperature of the water, scour the fabric again, and/or use different fabric.

There are round and spotty cloud-like shapes on the dyed fabric. Either there is a finish or other additive on the fabric (Did you wash or scour the fabric with a commercial detergent containing brightener or softener?), or air bubbles were trapped in the fabric during the dye cycle. Scour the fabric again, referring to the recipe on pages 22–24, or use a different fabric. During dyeing, make sure you squeeze all the air bubbles out of the fabric. **3**

There are icicle-like shapes on the dyed fabric. Folds in the fabric acted as a resist, preventing level dyeing. Stir! Stir! Stir! Start again with undyed fabric and stir more often, making sure to rearrange the folds frequently. **4**

There are pindots of concentrated color on the dyed fabric. The dye was not fully dissolved. Use more water to dissolve the dye powder and strain the dye concentrate through several layers of nylon stocking or cheesecloth before adding it to the dye bath, or add one teaspoon (4 g) to one tablespoon (12 g) of urea to the dye concentrate. Some dyes (particularly yellows, reds, and blacks) dissolve more slowly than others. The urea increases the solubility of the dye, helping the dye dissolve.

Disappointing Fabrics

Fabrics with spots, icicles, clouds, and other problems, as well as fabrics patterned with a resist technique, are great for overdyeing or overprinting with dyes or pigments!

∧ *Sleepless*
by Linda Levin, 1995, Wayland, Massachusetts,
69" x 52". **Method**: Fiber-reactive dye on cotton. Machine pieced and quilted. Photo by Joe
Ofria at The Image Inn.

❯ *Composition III*
by Linda Levin, 1993, Wayland, Massachusetts,
30" x 40". **Method**: Fiber-reactive dye on cotton.
Machine pieced and quilted. Photo by Joe
Ofria at The Image Inn.

◄ *Pikadon: Hiroshima Series*
by Barbara Moll, 1996, Muncie, Indiana, 41" x 64". **Method**: Whole-cloth quilt. Fiber-reactive dye on cotton. Hand painted. Machine quilted with laminated fabric details. Photo by Joan Whitaker.

▼ *Pallone: Lowtano da Siena*
by Linda Levin, 1987, Wayland, Massachusetts, 53" x 49".
Method: Fiber-reactive dye on cotton. Machine pieced and quilted. Photo by Joe Ofria at The Image Inn.

> *Flow*
by Natasha Kempers-Cullen, 1992, Topsham, Maine, 85" x 69". **Method**: Whole-cloth quilt. Fiber-reactive dye and textile paint on cotton. Hand painted and stamped. Machine pieced and machine and hand quilted. Hand embroidered and embellished with glass beads, fetishes, and shells. Photo by Dennis Griggs.

< *Mira, the Wonderful Star*
by Diana Dabinett, 1995, Torbay, Newfoundland, Canada, 40" x 67½". **Method**: Fiber-reactive dye on silk. Hand painted using resist. Photo by the artist.

∨ *Atrium*
by Elizabeth Owen, 1994, Baton Rouge, Louisiana, 60" x 71". **Method**: Fiber-reactive dye on cotton. Machine pieced and hand embroidered and quilted. Photo by Ron E. Dobbs.

❯ *Bear at Crossroads*
by Mia Rozmyn, 1996, Seattle, Washington, 44" x 33". **Method**: Hand-dyed silk. Machine pieced and quilted. Photo by the artist.

3rd page proofs

Sweet Aquarian
by Kathleen O'Connor, 1997, Putney,
Vermont, 75" x 47". **Method**: Fiber-
reactive dye and textile paint on cotton.
Machine pieced and quilted. Photo by
Mark Corliss.

Mountain Aspens
by Lenore Davis, 1994, Newport,
Kentucky, 60" x 60". This is the last quilt
Lenore made before her untimely death in
1995. **Method**: Whole-cloth quilt. Fiber-
reactive dye and textile paint on cotton
velveteen. Monoprinted. Hand quilted.

⋀ *Sails*
by Mickey Lawler, 1992, West Hartford, Connecticut, 58" x 47". **Method**: Textile paint on cotton. Hand painted. Machine pieced and hand quilted. Photo by Jack McConnell.

⟨ *Faces II*
by Elizabeth Hendricks, 1995, Seattle, Washington, 40" x 54". **Method**: Hand-dyed and commercially dyed fabrics. Machine pieced and quilted. Photo by Roger Schreiber.

Direct-Application Dye Techniques

Using direct-application techniques, you can create fabric with many different colors (including all three primary colors). There are many distinctive and inspirational direct-application techniques; this section covers fold-and-dip dyeing, tie dyeing, color washing, hand painting, monoprinting, and stamping. Also included are silk-painting techniques for cotton fabric and using a prepared resist.

For all these techniques, you apply a concentrated dye-stock solution and auxiliary products to the fabric. This concentrated solution can be thick (like jelly), thin (like water), or any consistency in between. After the dye is applied, the fabric is left to cure for a specific amount of time. The excess dye is rinsed and washed out, then the fabric is dried.

There are many ways to fix dye when using a direct-application technique. This book focuses on the two most popular methods: soda ash soak and mixed alkali. Each direct-application recipe includes a fixing-method recommendation based on my experiences with dye fixing prematurely, ease of washout, and length of time needed to create a pattern. I encourage you to try both methods. See "Soda Ash Soak and Mixed Alkali" on pages 60–63 for guidelines.

Treat yourself to mercerized cotton for your first attempts. Your time and energy will be rewarded with fabric that is rich in color and visual texture. Review "Protecting Yourself and Your Environment" on pages 16–17 for guidelines on working with dye and auxiliary powders.

FOLD-AND-DIP DYE

For fold-and-dip dyeing, you fold fabric into an accordion shape, then dip it in dye-stock solution. The resulting fabric has a delicate geometric pattern; the size of the folds and the fabric weight determine the pattern scale. The thinner the fabric, the easier it is to fold and the more manageable. It is difficult to dye large pieces and heavy-weight fabrics, but not impossible. You do not need to dye the entire bundle; some areas can be left white as part of the design.

Use this recipe to fold-and-dip dye 2 to 3 yards (1.82 to 2.74 m) of 100% cotton muslin. I recommend adding mixed alkali to the dye-stock solution. Mark the time on the container of dye-stock solution; you have 4 hours to use it.

Read through the directions and assemble all the necessary equipment and supplies before you begin. Wear a dust/mist mask or respirator while working with dye powder and auxiliary products, and remember to wear rubber gloves when you work with the fabric and liquid dye.

Fold-and-Dip Dyed Fabrics

Equipment

Two 2-gallon (8-L) plastic buckets (1 bucket is optional)
Cellulose sponge, rags, or paper towels
Clothesline and clothespins (optional)
Measuring cups and spoons or scale
Mixing box (see page 35)
Newspapers
Plastic drop cloth
Plastic or Styrofoam plates
Rubber gloves
Stirring tools
Thermometer
Watch or clock
Wide-mouth plastic containers (one for each color you want to use)

Supplies

2 to 3 yards (1.82 to 2.74 m) scoured, 100% cotton muslin (see pages 22–24)*
½ cup (125 ml) each of at least 3 colors of dye-stock solution (see pages 50–52)
½ teaspoon (2 g) mixed alkali per ½ cup (125 ml) of dye-stock solution (see pages 62–63)
¼ teaspoon (1.25 ml) Synthrapol (minimum)

*Begin with small pieces of fabric, ¼ yard (23 cm) or smaller. As you become comfortable with fold-and-dip dyeing, increase the size of your pieces.

Procedure

1. Cover your work table with the plastic drop cloth.
2. Fill a bucket half full with warm (comfortable to the touch) water. Use this as a rinse bucket for washing your gloved hands.
3. Accordion-fold the fabric into a narrow strip. Fold again into a triangle or square, repeating to complete an accordion fold as shown. For sharp folds, press the fabric before dyeing.

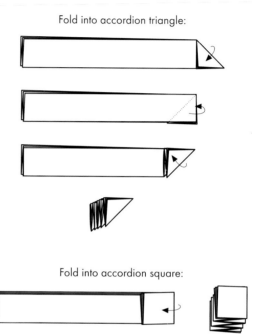

Fold into accordion triangle:

Fold into accordion square:

4. Prepare ½ cup (125 ml) dye-stock solution for each color you want to use. When the dye is completely dissolved, pour each solution into a wide-mouth container.
5. Prepare the mixed alkali: add ½ teaspoon (2 g) of the mixed alkali powder to each ½ cup (125 ml) of dye-stock solution. Stir until the powder dissolves. Note the time; discard the dye-stock solution after 4 hours.
6. Dip a corner of the folded fabric into one of the dye-stock solutions. Squeeze excess solution back into the container. Turn the fabric and dip another corner into a different color. Repeat this process for the third and fourth corners. Place the fabric on a plastic or Styrofoam plate and check the folds to be sure the fabric is completely saturated. **1 2 3**
7. Allow the fabric to cure at a temperature **above 70° F (21° C)** for a minimum of 24 hours. See page 62 for ways to maintain the curing temperature.
8. After curing, rinse and wash the fabric by hand or machine. To rinse and wash by hand, fill a bucket half full with 65° to 75° F (18° to 24° C) water. Carefully unfold the fabric and open it completely. **4**

Carefully and quickly immerse the fabric in the bucket of rinse water. It is important to keep the fabric moving during the entire rinse process so that the dye colors do not stain another part of the fabric. Swish the fabric around the bucket for 1 to 2 minutes. Remove the fabric and change the rinse water. Repeat this rinse 3 to 4 times. You may want to use 2 rinse buckets; the second bucket will be ready and waiting when it is time to change water. When the fabric feels squeaky clean (not soapy), remove it and empty the rinse bucket. (It's okay if you still see color in the rinse water, so long as the fabric feels squeaky clean.) Refill the bucket with 140° F (60° C) water. Add ¼ teaspoon (1.25 ml) of Synthrapol per yard of fabric. Return the fabric to the bucket and swish it around for 5 minutes. Rinse the fabric in warm (comfortable to the touch) water.

To rinse and wash the fabric by machine, set your washing machine on the small load, warm wash, and warm rinse cycles. After the machine fills and begins to agitate, carefully unfold the fabric and open it completely. Add the fabric, distributing it evenly around the tub. Close the lid and let the machine continue through the wash, rinse, and spin cycles. After the final spin cycle, reset the machine on the hot wash and warm rinse cycles. After the machine fills with water, add ¼ teaspoon (1.25 ml) of Synthrapol per yard of fabric and let the machine continue through all the cycles. Check the last rinse cycle. If the rinse water is colored, you may need to repeat this step. For dark colors, 2 short wash treatments may work better than 1 long wash.

9. Dry the fabric in a clothes dryer or on a clothesline. Follow the dryer manufacturer's instructions for the appropriate heat setting.

10. Clean up, using the cellulose sponge, rags, or paper towels.

TIE DYE

Tie dye is a technique that can produce simple or sophisticated patterns. Use this easy recipe to tie-dye 2 to 3 yards (1.82 to 2.74 m) of 100% cotton muslin.

I recommend that you prepare the fabric in soda ash soak, fold as described on pages 102–5, then apply the dye-stock solution while the fabric is still wet or damp. Experiment by soaking fabric in the soda ash and drying it before dyeing. Keep notes on your experiments so you can repeat those "happy accidents."

Read through the directions and assemble all the necessary equipment and supplies before you begin. Wear a dust/mist mask or respirator while working with dye powder and auxiliary products, and remember to wear rubber gloves when you work with the fabric and liquid dye.

Experimenting with Fold-and-Dip Dyeing

Try dampening the fabric bundle before dyeing. Dampening the fabric decreases its absorbency, and the resulting color is lighter. Or, for lighter values, dilute the dye-stock solution with activated urea water.

Tie-Dyed Fabrics

Equipment

Two 2-gallon (8-L) plastic buckets (1 bucket is optional)

Cellulose sponge, rags, or paper towels

Clothesline and clothespins (optional)

Funnel (optional)

Kitchen timer or watch

Measuring cups and spoons or scale

Plastic drop cloth

Plastic or Styrofoam plates

Rubber bands, string, or clothespins

Rubber gloves

Scissors

Sponge brushes and/or syringes (optional)

Squeeze bottles (1 bottle for each dye-stock solution and additional bottles if you want to mix colors)

Stirring tools

Thermometer

Supplies

2 to 3 yards (1.82 to 2.74 m) scoured, 100% cotton muslin*
(see pages 22–24)

1 gallon (4 L) soda ash soak (see pages 60–62)

½ cup (125 ml) each of at least 4 colors of dye-stock solution
(see pages 50–52)

¼ teaspoon (1.25 ml) Synthrapol (minimum)

Urea water (optional)

*Begin with small pieces of fabric, ¼ yard (23 cm) or smaller. As you become comfortable with tie dyeing, increase the size of your pieces.

Procedure

1. Cover your work table with the plastic drop cloth.
2. Fill a plastic bucket half full with warm (comfortable to the touch) water. Use this as a rinse bucket for your gloved hands.
3. Prepare the soda ash soak. Place the scoured fabric in the soda ash soak and set the timer for 15 minutes. Stir periodically. Make sure the fabric is completely submerged and can move freely.
4. When the timer rings, remove the fabric and wring it out. **Do not rinse!** Fold the fabric into the shape you want and secure it with rubber bands, string, or clothespins (see pages 102–5).
5. Prepare ½ cup (125 ml) of dye-stock solution for each color you want to use. When the dye is completely dissolved, pour each solution into a squeeze bottle. (You may want to use a funnel.)

6. Place the folded, damp fabric on a plastic or Styrofoam plate. Apply the dye-stock solution to the fabric with squeeze bottles, sponge brushes, or syringes. Check the folds of the fabric to make sure the dye has soaked through. Avoid overlaying more than 2 colors. Overlaying 3 primary colors produces brown. **1** **2**

    Gently massage the fabric between your gloved fingers to ensure that the colors blend. Carefully turn the fabric over and apply the dye to the other side.

    Take care not to apply so much dye that it runs into a pool on the plate. If this happens, gently squeeze out the excess dye and carefully move the dyed fabric to a clean plate. **3**

    For lighter values, dilute the dye-stock solution with activated urea water.

    Don't be alarmed by the murky black appearance of your fabric; the rinse and wash process will remove any unfixed dye. The finished colors will be clear and several shades lighter.

7. Allow the fabric to cure at a temperature **above 70° F (21° C)** for a minimum of 4 hours. For dark colors and turquoise, allow the fabric to cure for a minimum of 24 hours. See page 62 for ways to maintain the curing temperature.

8. After curing, rinse and wash the fabric by hand or machine. To rinse and wash by hand, fill a bucket half full with 65° to 75° F (18° to 24° C) water. Carefully unfold the fabric and open it completely. Carefully and quickly immerse the fabric in the bucket of rinse water. It is important to keep the fabric moving during the entire rinse process so that the dye colors do not stain another part of the fabric. Swish the fabric around the bucket for 1 to 2 minutes. Remove the fabric and change the rinse water. Repeat this rinse 3 to 4 times. You may want to use 2 rinse buckets; the second bucket will be ready and waiting when it is time to change water. **4**

   When the fabric feels squeaky clean (not soapy), remove it and empty the rinse bucket. (It's okay if you still see color in the rinse water, so long as the fabric feels squeaky clean.) Refill the bucket with 140° F (60° C) water. Add ¼ teaspoon (1.25 ml) of Synthrapol per yard of fabric. Return the fabric to the bucket and swish it around for 5 minutes. Rinse the fabric in warm (comfortable to the touch) water.

   To rinse and wash the fabric by machine, set your washing machine on the small load, warm wash, and warm rinse cycles. After the machine fills and begins to agitate, carefully unfold the fabric and open it completely. Add the fabric, distributing it evenly around the tub. Close the lid and let the machine continue through the wash, rinse, and spin cycles. After the final spin cycle, reset the machine on the hot wash and warm rinse cycles. After the machine fills with water, add ¼ teaspoon (1.25 ml) of Synthrapol per yard of fabric and let the machine continue through all the cycles. Check the last rinse cycle. If the rinse water is colored, you may need to repeat this step. For dark colors, 2 short wash treatments may work better than 1 long wash.

9. Dry the fabric in a clothes dryer or on a clothesline. Follow the dryer manufacturer's instructions for the appropriate heat setting.

10. Clean up, using the cellulose sponge, rags, or paper towels.

CREATING PATTERNS WITH RESISTS

As explained on page 85, you can fold, pleat, roll, clamp, knot, bunch, bind, and/or stitch your fabric, working neatly or loosely, to produce original and elegant visual textures. The following are more examples showing the range of pattern you can create. Remember, there are no wrong ways to fold, bind, or tie your fabric, only variations! Experiment to find your favorites.

Lumpy Pancake

Working with your gloved fingertips, pinch wet fabric into a lumpy pancake. Place the fabric pancake on a leak-proof tray or plate before applying dye-stock solution.

Lumpy-Pancake Fabrics

Accordion

Fold the fabric into an accordion shape. Use clothespins or bulldog clips to hold the shape.

Accordion Fabrics

Bias Accordion

Working on the bias, fold the fabric into an accordion shape. Use clothespins or bulldog clips to hold the shape.

Bias-Accordion Fabrics

Double Chevron

Fold the fabric into an accordion shape. Press the folds. Fold again on the bias (diagonally).

Double-Chevron Fabric

Uneven Accordion Fold and Zigzag Stitch

Fold the fabric into an uneven accordion shape. Using a machine zigzag stitch, stitch each fold.

Uneven-Accordion-Fold
and-Zigzag-Stitched Fabric

Accordion Circle

Fold the fabric in half, then make triangle-shaped accordion folds from the center. Use rubber bands or string to hold the shape.

Accordion-Circle Fabric

Spiral-Folded Chevron

Fold the fabric into an accordion shape. Press the folds. Fold triangles, working back and forth as shown. Use clothespins to hold the triangles.

Spiral-Folded-Chevron Fabric

Machine Zigzag Stitch

Fold the fabric into knife pleats and press the folds. Using a machine zigzag stitch, sew each pleat in place.

Machine-Zigzag-Stitched Fabric

Color-Wash Fabric

HAND PAINTING A COLOR WASH

A color wash can transition gently from one value or color to another or blend in complex layers. As you paint, move your arm from the elbow rather than just moving your hand at the wrist. Practice will give your work a looseness and fluency.

This recipe is for painting a hue gradation using thin dye paste. I recommend that you prepare the fabric with soda ash soak as described below, then apply thin dye paste to wet or damp fabric. (It is easier to blend and create subtle shading on damp or wet fabric.)

Use this recipe to hand paint 1 to 2 yards (91 cm to 1.82 m) of 100% cotton muslin. Read through the directions and assemble all the necessary equipment and supplies before you begin. Wear a dust/mist mask or respirator while working with dye powder and auxiliary products, and remember to wear rubber gloves when you work with the fabric and liquid dye.

Equipment

2-gallon (8-L) plastic bucket (optional)

Artists' stretcher frame or embroidery hoop
(or pin the fabric between 2 sawhorses)

Assortment of wide-mouth containers with lids (one for each color you want to use and one for rinsing the brushes)

Cellulose sponge, rags, or paper towels

Clothesline and clothespins (optional)

Masking tape or T-pins

Measuring cups and spoons or scale

Plastic drop cloth

Rubber gloves

Sponge brushes, ½" to 2½" (1.27 cm to 6.3 cm) wide

Stirring tools

Thermometer

Watch or clock

Supplies

1 to 2 yards (91 cm to 1.82 m) scoured, 100% cotton muslin
(see pages 22–23)*

1 gallon (4 L) soda ash soak (see pages 60–62)

½ cup (125 ml) each of at least 2 colors of thin dye paste (see pages 58–60)

¼ teaspoon (1.25 ml) Synthrapol (minimum)

Activated print paste (optional)

Activated urea water (optional)

*Begin with small pieces of fabric, ¼ yard (23 cm) or smaller. As you become comfortable with hand painting, increase the size of your pieces.

Procedure

1. Cover your work table with the plastic drop cloth.
2. Stretch the fabric on the artists' stretcher frame or embroidery hoop and secure it with masking tape or T-pins.
3. Fill a wide-mouth container half full with warm (comfortable to the touch) water. Use this to rinse your brushes between colors, or use different brushes for each color. This helps ensure a clean transition between colors or values.
4. Prepare the soda ash soak. Using a sponge brush, apply the soda ash soak to the fabric. Make sure the fabric is completely wet. Re-pin the fabric so it is held taut. If the fabric sags during the painting process, the dye will migrate to the sagging area, making it darker. **1**
5. Prepare ½ cup (125 ml) of thin dye paste for each color you want to use. Pour each color of thin dye paste into a wide-mouth container.
6. Using a clean sponge brush and long, even horizontal strokes, apply one color of thin dye paste to the bottom third of the fabric (from the bottom edge). Using a clean sponge brush, apply the second color to the upper third of the fabric (from the top edge). Apply only a small amount of color with each stroke; it is much easier to add color than to remove it!

   Blend the colors together in the middle, blending the edges of each stroke for the smoothest transition. **2**
7. Allow the fabric to cure at a temperature **above 70° F (21° C)** for a minimum of 4 hours. For dark colors and turquoise, allow the fabric to cure for a minimum of 24 hours. See page 62 for ways to maintain the curing temperature. If the fabric appears to be drying out, cover it with plastic wrap.

Experimenting with a Color Wash

Try one of the following.

- Paint very wet, just damp, and dry fabric. Each produces different results. The wetter the fabric, the more migration of color and the lighter the final color. It's easier to blend colors on wet fabric.

- Allow the fabric to dry slightly after you paint it. Remove it from your work table and hang it from a clothesline so the dye will migrate. Place newspaper underneath the damp fabric to catch drips.

- Use T-pins to secure lengths of fabric between two sawhorses. When the fabric gets wet and stretches, there will be no need to unpin. Just move the sawhorses to take the sag out of the fabric.

Hand-Painted Fabric

8. After curing, rinse and wash the fabric by hand or machine. To rinse and wash by hand, fill the bucket half full with 65° to 75° F (18° to 24° C) water. Carefully remove the fabric from the artists' stretcher frame or embroidery hoop. Immerse the fabric in the bucket of rinse water. It is important to keep the fabric moving during the entire rinse process so that the dye colors do not stain another part of the fabric. Swish the fabric around the bucket for 1 to 2 minutes. Remove the fabric and change the rinse water. Repeat this rinse 3 to 4 times. You may want to use 2 rinse buckets; the second bucket will be ready and waiting when it is time to change water. When the fabric feels squeaky clean (not soapy), remove it and empty the rinse bucket. (It's okay if you still see color in the rinse water, so long as the fabric feels squeaky clean.) Refill the bucket with 140° F (60° C) water. Add ¼ teaspoon (1.25 ml) of Synthrapol per yard of fabric. Return the fabric to the bucket and swish it around for 5 minutes. Rinse the fabric in warm (comfortable to the touch) water.

To rinse and wash the fabric by machine, set your washing machine on the small load, warm wash, and warm rinse cycles. After the machine fills and begins to agitate, carefully remove the fabric from the artists' stretcher frame or embroidery hoop and add it to the machine. Close the lid and let the machine continue through the wash, rinse, and spin cycles. After the final spin cycle, reset the machine on the hot wash and warm rinse cycles. After the machine fills with water, add ¼ teaspoon (1.25 ml) of Synthrapol per yard of fabric and let the machine continue through all the cycles. Check the last rinse cycle. If the rinse water is colored, you may need to repeat this step. For dark colors, 2 short wash treatments may work better than 1 long wash.

9. Dry the fabric in a clothes dryer or on a clothesline. Follow the dryer manufacturer's instructions for the appropriate heat setting.

10. Clean up, using the cellulose sponge, rags, or paper towels.

HAND PAINTING A DESIGN

Hand painting is a versatile technique and easier than you may think. Draw or transfer a design to fabric using a soft pencil, then fill in the design with thin or thick dye paste. Fabric responds well to traditional watercolor techniques such as watermarks, dry brush, wet on wet, and dry on dry.

You can apply thick dye paste with a sponge brush, artists' brush, syringe, or squeeze bottle. Your brush strokes can be bold, loose, or tightly controlled. Using a 12" × 12" (30 cm × 30 cm) square of muslin, experiment with brushes to see how many different marks you can make. Pull, push, twist, roll, and dab the brushes to create interesting textures and patterns. **1** *Note*: these marks will look different on different-weight and -weave fabrics.

Use this recipe to paint 1 to 2 yards (91 cm to 1.82 m) of 100% cotton muslin. I recommend adding mixed alkali to the thin dye paste. You can paint up to 3 colors on top of one another; additional colors will probably not be able to penetrate to the fabric. For lighter values, dilute the thin dye paste with activated print paste.

Read through the directions and assemble all the necessary equipment and supplies before you begin. Wear a dust/mist mask or respirator while working with dye powder and auxiliary products, and remember to wear rubber gloves when you work with the fabric and liquid dye.

Equipment

2-gallon (8-L) plastic bucket (optional)

Artists' stretcher frame, embroidery hoop, or canvas-covered padded table

Assortment of artists' brushes, sponge brushes, and syringes

Assortment of wide-mouth plastic containers

Cellulose sponge, rags, or paper towels

Clothesline and clothespins (optional)

Masking tape or T-pins

Measuring cups and spoons or scale

Mixing box (see page 35)

Newspapers

Plastic drop cloth

Rubber gloves

Soft drawing pencil (5b)

Stirring tools

Thermometer

Watch or clock

Supplies

1 to 2 yards (91 cm to 1.82 m) scoured, 100% cotton muslin (see pages 22–24)*

½ cup (125 ml) each of at least 3 colors of thin dye paste (see pages 58–60)

½ tsp (2 g) mixed alkali per ½ cup (125 ml) of thin dye paste (see pages 62–63)

¼ tsp (1.25 ml) Synthrapol (minimum)

Activated print paste (optional)

Activated urea water (optional)

*Begin with small pieces of fabric, ¼ yard (23 cm) or smaller. As you become comfortable with hand painting, increase the size of your pieces.

Making a Light Table at Home

Helpful Hint

Creating Dark Patterns

If you plan to hand paint a pattern with very little white or light area, prepare the fabric in soda ash soak, allow the fabric to dry before using, and add mixed alkali to the dye-stock solution or dye paste.

Procedure

1. Cover your work table with the plastic drop cloth.

2. Using the soft pencil, draw or transfer a design to your fabric. You may want to make a light table to help you transfer the design. Lay a piece of glass or translucent plastic between 2 tables (or on a table with the leaf removed) and place a lamp underneath.

   You can also use a window or sliding glass door. Tape the pattern to the glass surface; then center the fabric over the pattern. Pull the fabric taut—not taut enough to stretch the fabric—and tape it to the glass.

3. Stretch the fabric on an artists' stretcher frame or embroidery hoop and secure it with masking tape or T-pins, or secure the fabric to a canvas-covered padded table.

4. Fill a wide-mouth container half full with warm (comfortable to the touch) water. Use this to rinse your brushes.

5. Prepare ½ cup (125 ml) thin dye paste for each color you want to use. Pour ½ cup of each color of thin dye paste into a wide-mouth container.

6. Prepare the mixed alkali. Add ½ teaspoon (2 g) of the mixed alkali powder to each ½ cup (125 ml) of thin dye paste. Stir until the powder dissolves. Note the time; discard the dye paste after 4 hours.

7. Apply the dye pastes with artists' brushes, sponge brushes, syringes, or squeeze bottles. Continue painting until the design is complete. Remember, dye paste prepared with mixed alkali is only good for 4 hours. **2**

8. Allow the fabric to cure at a temperature **above 70° F (21° C)** for a minimum of 24 hours. See page 62 for ways to maintain the curing temperature.

9. After curing, rinse and wash the fabric by hand or machine. To rinse and wash by hand, fill the plastic bucket half full with 65° to 75° F (18° to 24° C) water. Carefully remove the fabric from the

artists' stretcher, embroidery hoop, or canvas. Immerse the fabric in the bucket of rinse water. It is important to keep the fabric moving during the entire rinse process so that the dye colors do not stain another part of the fabric. Swish the fabric around the bucket for 1 to 2 minutes. Remove the fabric and change the rinse water. Repeat this rinse 3 to 4 times. You may want to use 2 rinse buckets; the second bucket will be ready and waiting when it is time to change water. When the fabric feels squeaky clean (not soapy), remove it and empty the rinse bucket. (It's okay if you still see color in the rinse water, so long as the fabric feels squeaky clean.) Refill the bucket with 140° F (60° C) water. Add ¼ teaspoon (1.25 ml) of Synthrapol per yard of fabric. Return the fabric to the bucket and swish it around for 5 minutes. Rinse the fabric in warm (comfortable to the touch) water.

To rinse and wash the fabric by machine, set your washing machine on the small load, warm wash, and warm rinse cycles. After the machine fills and begins to agitate, carefully remove the fabric from the artists' stretcher, embroidery hoop, or tabletop and add it to the machine. Close the lid and let the machine continue through the wash, rinse, and spin cycles. After the final spin cycle, reset the machine on the hot wash and warm rinse cycles. After the machine fills with water, add ¼ teaspoon (1.25 ml) of Synthrapol per yard of fabric and let the machine continue through all the cycles. Check the last rinse cycle. If the rinse water is colored, you may need to repeat this step. For dark colors, 2 short wash treatments may work better than 1 long wash.

10. Dry the fabric in a clothes dryer or on a clothesline. Follow the dryer manufacturer's instructions for the appropriate heat setting.
11. Clean up, using the cellulose sponge, rags, or paper towels.

MONOPRINTING

Monoprinting is a transfer printing process that literally means "one print." You begin by painting a design, using your fingers or artist's brushes, on a printing plate: a hard, nonporous surface such as glass, Formica, or clear acrylic. Different surfaces produce different textures. I like to use clear acrylic, lightly brushed with steel wool or fine sandpaper. This surface has enough "tooth" to hold a smooth layer of dye paste.

Use this recipe to print 2 yards (1.82 m) of 100% cotton muslin. I recommend adding mixed alkali to the dye paste. Remember to take notes on the sequence of dye colors. The process can be difficult to reinvent.

Read through the directions and assemble all the necessary equipment and supplies before you begin. Wear a dust/mist mask or respirator while working with dye powder and auxiliary products, and remember to wear rubber gloves when you work with the fabric and liquid dye.

Monoprinted Fabric

Helpful Hint

Monoprinting Tips

I like to use one, or occasionally two, colors for a print. Limiting colors helps prevent your print from becoming muddy.

Put the lightest colors down first, building to the darkest. Do not layer more than three colors.

You need to paint quickly in warm, dry weather. The dye paste doesn't take long to dry.

If you don't like your design, simply wipe it off and start again. When you're satisfied with the design, transfer it to fabric.

Equipment

1 square, 12" x 12" (30 cm x 30 cm), of clear acrylic, lightly brushed with steel wool or sanded on one side
2-gallon (8-L) plastic bucket (optional)
Assortment of artists' brushes, sponge brushes and/or rollers, and syringes
Assortment of wide-mouth plastic containers with lids (one for each color you want to use and one for rinsing the brushes)
Canvas drop cloth
Cellulose sponge, rags, or paper towels
Clothesline and clothespins (optional)
Masking tape or T-pins
Measuring cups and spoons or scale
Mixing box (see page 35)
Newspapers
Padded table
Rubber gloves
Stirring tools
Thermometer
Watch or clock

Supplies

2 yards (1.82 m) scoured, 100% cotton muslin (see pages 22–24)*
½ cup (125 ml) each of 3 or more colors of thick dye paste (see pages 58–60)
½ tsp (2 g) mixed alkali per ½ cup (125 ml) of thick dye paste (see pages 62–63)
¼ teaspoon (1.25 ml) Synthrapol (minimum)
Activated print paste (optional)

*Begin with small pieces of fabric, ¼ yard (23 cm) or smaller. As you become comfortable with monoprinting, increase the size of your pieces.

Procedure

1. Cover your padded table with the canvas drop cloth.
2. Stretch the fabric on top of the canvas covering your work area. Secure with masking tape or T-pins. **1**
3. Fill a wide-mouth container half full with warm (comfortable to the touch) water. Use this to rinse your brushes between color changes.
4. Prepare ½ cup (125 ml) of thick dye paste for each color. Pour each color of thick dye paste into a wide-mouth container. The dye paste should be the consistency of honey. For lighter values, dilute the dye paste with activated print paste.

5. Prepare the mixed alkali. Add ½ teaspoon (2 g) of the mixed alkali powder to each ½ cup (125 ml) of thick dye paste. Stir until the powder dissolves. Note the time; discard the dye paste after 4 hours.

6. Using artists' brushes or a wide sponge brush or sponge roller, apply a thin layer of dye paste onto the acrylic square, your printing plate. Saturate the brush or roller evenly, using strokes that cross each other to ensure a uniform surface. If you are too generous with the dye paste, the image will smudge and blur when you transfer the design. Using your fingers and/or other tools, draw on the painted surface. Reverse letters and numbers. **2**

7. Carefully place the printing plate, dye side down, on the fabric. Walk the palms of your hands over the back of the square to transfer the design. **3**

8. Without sliding the printing plate, carefully peel up one edge and lift the plate off the fabric. This is the first layer of your print. **4** **5**

Experimenting with Monoprinting

Try one of the following.

- For different textures, apply dye paste with rumpled fabric, a paper towel, a cake-decorating edge tool, a tool for laying tile cement, a plastic comb, a teasing comb, or a sponge. Use your imagination.

- Place the printing plate on the fabric, paint side down, then flip the two over so the fabric is on top. Using a blunt-tipped tool, draw on the fabric. Remember to reverse letters and numbers.

- For a veinlike pattern, paint a thin layer of dye paste onto the printing plate. Lay the fabric on top of the plate, and lightly pat the two. Peel the fabric off the printing plate and set it aside to cure.

- For a feathery pattern, lightly sponge dye paste onto the printing plate.

- For a subtle variation, place leaves or paper shapes onto the painted printing plate before placing it on the fabric, then print. For the second print, brush more dye paste over the leaves or paper.

- Print on dry, damp, or wet fabric.

9. Wipe excess dye paste off the surface of the square. Repeat steps 6–8 with a different color of dye paste. You can print over the first design or on a clean area of the fabric. Do not allow the first print to dry before you print again. The thickener in the dye paste may act as a resist if it dries.

10. Allow the fabric to cure at a temperature **above 70° F (21° C)** for a minimum of 24 hours. See page 62 for ways to maintain the curing temperature.

11. After curing, rinse and wash the fabric by hand or machine. To rinse and wash by hand, fill the plastic bucket half full with 65° to 75° F (18° to 24° C) water. Untape or unpin the fabric and immerse it in the bucket of rinse water. Swish the fabric around the bucket for 1 to 2 minutes. Remove the fabric and change the rinse water. Repeat this rinse 3 to 4 times. You may want to use 2 rinse buckets; the second bucket will be ready and waiting when it is time to change water. When the fabric feels squeaky clean (not soapy), remove it and empty the rinse bucket. (It's okay if you still see color in the rinse water, so long as the fabric feels squeaky clean.) Refill the bucket with 140° F (60° C) water. Add ¼ teaspoon (1.25 ml) of Synthrapol per yard of fabric. Return the fabric to the bucket and swish it around for 5 minutes. Rinse the fabric in warm (comfortable to the touch) water.

To rinse and wash the fabric by machine, set your washing machine on the small load, warm wash, and warm rinse cycles. After the machine fills and begins to agitate, carefully untape or unpin the fabric and add it to the machine. Close the lid and let the machine continue through the wash, rinse, and spin cycles. After the final spin cycle, reset the machine on the hot wash and warm rinse cycles. After the machine fills with water, add ¼ teaspoon (1.25 ml) of Synthrapol per yard of fabric and let the machine continue through all the cycles. Check the last rinse cycle. If the rinse water is colored, you may need to repeat this step. For dark colors, 2 short wash treatments may work better than 1 long wash.

12. Dry the fabric in a clothes dryer or on a clothesline. Follow the dryer manufacturer's instructions for the appropriate heat setting.

13. Clean up, using the cellulose sponge, rags, or paper towels.

STAMPING

Stamping is an easy introduction to creating a repeat pattern. Stamped patterns can be simple or complex, made with common household items or purchased stamps.

Basically, a stamp is any object that you can paint and apply to fabric. Look around your house—inside and outside—for ideas. You can stamp with or make stamps from corks, empty thread spools, kitchen utensils, string, screw heads, erasers, carved or cut vegetables such as potatoes or green peppers, leaves, cellulose sponges, and bunched-up paper towels. I like to create stamp designs with foam weather stripping and small acrylic squares (see page 118). Be sure to take careful notes so you can re-create or expand on your work later.

Use this recipe to stamp 1 yard (91 cm) of 100% cotton muslin. I recommend adding mixed alkali to the dye paste. Stamping generally creates patterns with a fairly open, light background. The mixed-alkali method leaves less alkali residue than the activator soak, so the dye is easier to rinse out and less likely to stain the light areas.

Read through the directions and assemble all the necessary equipment and supplies before you begin. Wear a dust/mist mask or respirator while working with dye powder and auxiliary products, and remember to wear rubber gloves when you work with the fabric and liquid dye.

Stamped Fabric

Equipment

2-gallon (8-L) plastic bucket (optional)
Artists' brushes (brights)
Assortment of wide-mouth plastic containers with lids (one for each color you want to use and one for rinsing the brushes)
Canvas drop cloth
Cellulose sponge, rags, or paper towels
Clothesline and clothespins (optional)
Masking tape or T-pins
Measuring cups and spoons or scale
Mixing box (see page 35)
Newspapers
Padded table
Rubber gloves
Soap and old toothbrush for cleaning the stamp(s)
Stamp(s) (see page 118)
Stirring tools
Thermometer
Watch or clock

Helpful Hint

Stamping Variations

Experiment with stamping designs, referring to the examples below and at right. Use different colors and different stamps. Build up layers of color and pattern to create a complex, textured look. Stamp 2 or 3 prints before repainting. The change in value is more interesting than a perfect print.

Supplies

1 yard (91 cm) scoured, 100% cotton muslin (see pages 22–24)*

½ cup (125 ml) each of at least 2 colors of thick dye paste (see pages 58–60)

½ teaspoon (2 g) mixed alkali per ½ cup (125 ml) of thick dye paste (see pages 62–63)

¼ teaspoon (1.25 ml) Synthrapol (minimum)

*Begin with small pieces of fabric, ¼ yard (23 cm) or smaller. As you become comfortable with stamping, increase the size of your pieces.

Procedure

1. Cover your padded table with the canvas drop cloth.
2. Stretch the fabric on top of the canvas covering your work area. Secure with masking tape or T-pins.
3. Fill a wide-mouth container half full with warm (comfortable to the touch) water. Use this to rinse your brush.
4. Prepare ½ cup (125 ml) of thick dye paste for each color you want to use. Pour each color into a wide-mouth container.
5. Prepare the mixed alkali. Add ½ teaspoon (2 g) of the mixed alkali powder to each ½ cup (125 ml) of dye paste. Stir until the powder dissolves. Note the time; discard the dye paste after 4 hours.
6. Using an artists' bright (flat brush), spread a thin layer (1 or 2 colors) of prepared dye paste on the stamp surface. Test the stamp on a piece of paper or scrap of fabric. The amount of dye paste that transfers from the stamp to the fabric depends on how much dye paste is on the stamp and the amount of pressure you use. **1**
7. Stamp your fabric with an all-over, spot, random, or border pattern, as desired. See the illustrations for ideas.

   Allow the fabric to cure at a temperature **above 70° F (21° C)** for a minimum of 24 hours. See page 62 for ways to maintain the proper temperature.

1

8. Clean all stamps with warm water and soap. Use an old toothbrush to coax dye out of crevices.

9. After curing, rinse and wash the fabric by hand or machine. To rinse and wash by hand, fill the plastic bucket half full with 65° to 75°F (18° to 24°C) water. Untape or unpin the fabric and immerse it in the bucket of rinse water. Swish the fabric around the bucket for 1 to 2 minutes. Remove the fabric and change the rinse water. Repeat this rinse 3 to 4 times. You may want to use 2 rinse buckets; the second bucket will be ready and waiting when it is time to change water. When the fabric feels squeaky clean (not soapy), remove it and empty the rinse bucket. (It's okay if you still see color in the rinse water, so long as the fabric feels squeaky clean.) Refill the bucket with 140°F (60°C) water. Add ¼ teaspoon (1.25 ml) of Synthrapol per yard of fabric. Return the fabric to the bucket and swish it around for 5 minutes. Rinse the fabric in warm (comfortable to the touch) water.

To rinse and wash the fabric by machine, set your washing machine on the small load, warm wash, and warm rinse cycles. After the machine fills and begins to agitate, carefully untape the fabric and add it to the machine. Close the lid and let the machine continue through the wash, rinse, and spin cycles. After the final spin cycle, reset the machine on the hot wash and warm rinse cycles. After the machine fills with water, add ¼ teaspoon (1.25 ml) of Synthrapol per yard of fabric and let the machine continue through all the cycles. Check the last rinse cycle. If the rinse water is colored, you may need to repeat this step. For dark colors, 2 short wash treatments may work better than 1 long wash.

10. Dry the fabric in a clothes dryer or on a clothesline. Follow the dryer manufacturer's instructions for the appropriate heat setting.

11. Clean up, using the cellulose sponge, rags, or paper towels.

Experimenting with Stamping

The following methods for loading stamps with dye paste are good for stamps with large, bold surfaces. (Detailed surfaces easily fill with paste, and you lose the design.)

- With an acrylic or sponge brush, spread a thin layer of prepared dye paste on a plastic or Styrofoam plate. Dip the stamp in the paste, then stamp the fabric.

- On a plastic or Styrofoam plate, saturate a piece of thin (¼" thick) foam, sponge, or felt with dye paste. Stamp on the saturated material, then stamp the fabric.

- With a foam brush, paint a thin layer of dye paste directly on the stamp surface. Stamp the fabric.

- Try Karen Perrine's method: use a small foam roller to paint stamps with a large surface area. Be careful not to load the roller too full.

MAKING STAMPS

I like to make stamps by attaching pieces of foam weather stripping to a piece of clear acrylic. These stamps take the guesswork out of patterning fabric because you can see the design as you work.

Equipment and Supplies

Several 2" x 2" (5 cm x 5 cm) or slightly larger squares of clear acrylic or Plexiglas

Scissors

Foam weather stripping with adhesive back (You can also use camper mounting tape, Super Glue, foot and shoe padding, or a hot glue gun and an absorbent material, such as ⅛"-thick (3 mm) foam pad or shoe padding.)

Procedure

1. Cut out pieces of foam weather stripping with scissors. **1**
2. Create stamp designs by peeling the adhesive backing off the pieces of foam and attaching them to the acrylic squares. **2**
3. To make a handle, cut a 3" (7.6 cm) -long piece of masking tape and fold it in half; then attach it to the back side of the acrylic square with 2 smaller pieces of masking tape.

Using Liquid Resists

In addition to the folding and binding techniques on pages 85–88 and 102–5, you can use *liquid* resists to prevent dye from penetrating and coloring fabric. Liquid resists are based on water, solvent, or wax. This book focuses on water-based resists, which are the safest and most convenient for the home dyer. Solvent- and wax-based resists are associated with potential health concerns, and are not addressed in this book.

Water-based resists work best with direct-application techniques that use dye-stock solution and mixed-alkali fixative. You apply the resist to fabric, allow it to dry, paint or stamp dye up to the resist, allow the dye to cure, then rinse the fabric. The area protected by the resist remains the undyed color.

Water-based resists include Sabra Silk, Presist, Silkpaint Brand Water-Soluble Resist, and gutta. (See "Resources" on page 158.) Many water-based resists are clear, but pigment gutta is available in a range of glossy and pearlescent colors that are easy to see. (*Note*: Pigment gutta will change the hand of the fabric.)

You cannot use water-based resists in an immersion dye bath; they will dissolve. Also, if you are working in high humidity or in a damp area, the resist may not completely dry. This will diminish its effectiveness.

There are many ways to apply liquid resist, including painting, stamping, and screen printing. Different resists work better with different techniques. The following recipes use two resists—Sabra Silk for traditional silk-painting techniques and Presist for stamping an image.

The best way to apply a liquid resist to fabric is to stretch the fabric taut and elevate it above the table surface. Use an artists' stretcher frame, silk-painting frame, or embroidery hoop to elevate the fabric. Use T-pins to secure lengths of fabric between two sawhorses. When the fabric gets wet and stretches, there will be no need to unpin. Just move the sawhorses to take the sag out of the fabric.

Fabric Hand Painted with a Resist
and Dye-Stock Solution

HAND PAINTING WITH A RESIST

This recipe applies traditional silk-painting techniques to cotton. Before you begin, plan your design. Then, use the resist to trace or draw your design on fabric. The resist line does not have to be thick, but it must penetrate the fabric to prevent dye from flowing into other areas. Be sure to check the back of the fabric as described below. For more information on silk painting, refer to "Further Reading" on pages 159–60. If you don't want to create an original design, Dover publishes great books of copyright-free images.

You can use any fabric with this recipe, but lightweight fabrics, such as silk and light cotton, tend to be most successful. You may want to experiment on fabric scraps.

Use this recipe to hand paint 1 yard (91 cm) of 100% cotton muslin. I recommend adding mixed alkali to the dye-stock solution.

Read through the directions and assemble all the necessary equipment and supplies before you begin. Wear a dust/mist mask or respirator while working with dye powder and auxiliary products, and remember to wear rubber gloves when you work with the fabric and liquid dye.

Equipment

2-gallon (8-L) plastic bucket (optional)

Artists' brushes: Rounds (#0, #2, #6, and #8) for small areas; Brights (#6 and #8) for large areas

Artists' stretcher frame, embroidery hoop, or silk-painting frame

Assortment of wide-mouth plastic containers with lids (one for each color you want to use and one for rinsing the brushes)

Cellulose sponge, rags, or paper towels

Clothesline and clothespins (optional)

Cotton swabs

Fine-line applicator bottles or squeeze bottles (optional: most water-based resists are sold in these types of bottles)

Masking tape or T-pins

Measuring cups and spoons or scale

Mixing box (see page 35)

Newspapers

Original designs and/or copyright-free images

Plastic drop cloth

Rubber gloves

Soft drawing pencil

Stirring tools

Thermometer

Watch or clock

Supplies

1 yard (91 cm) scoured, 100% cotton muslin (see pages 22–24)*

1/2 cup (125 ml) each of at least 3 colors of dye-stock solution (see pages 50–52)

½ teaspoon (2 g) mixed alkali per ½ cup (125 ml) of dye-stock solution (see pages 62–63)

¼ teaspoon (1.25 ml) Synthrapol (minimum)

Water soluable resist (Sabra Silk resist or Silkpaint Brand resist)

*Begin with small pieces of fabric, ¼ yard (23 cm) or smaller. As you become comfortable with hand painting, increase the size of your pieces.

Procedure

1. Cover your work table with the plastic drop cloth.
2. Using the soft pencil, draw or transfer a design to your fabric. You may want to make a light table to help you transfer the design. Lay a piece of glass or translucent plastic between 2 tables (or on a table with the leaf removed) and place a lamp underneath.

   You can also use a window or a sliding glass door. Tape the pattern to the glass surface; then center the fabric over the pattern. Pull the fabric taut (but not taut enough to stretch the fabric) and tape it to the glass.
3. Stretch the fabric on an artists' stretcher frame, embroidery hoop, or silk-painting frame and secure it with masking tape or T-pins.
4. Place the tip or nozzle of the applicator bottle on one of your pencil lines, pressing the tip firmly against the fabric. Squeeze the bottle gently to force the resist along the line. It is important to maintain an even flow and a continuous line as you trace the design. The dye-stock solution will flow through gaps in the line. **1**

   Check the back of the fabric to make sure the resist penetrated the fabric. The resist should be visible from the back. If you see any gaps in the design, fill them in from the front. You may need to apply the resist to both the front and back of heavy fabric.

   Allow the resist to dry. Hold the fabric up to the light and check again to make sure there are no gaps in the resist before you begin painting. **2**

Working with Resists and Dye-Stock Solution

If the dye-stock solution does not flow to the resist line, add a drop of Synthrapol or rubbing alcohol. The Synthrapol or rubbing alcohol helps the solution flow and prevents halos from forming at the edge of the resist line. You can also dampen the fabric slightly, using a sponge dipped in water, but this will dilute the dye color. For lighter values, dilute the dye-stock solution with activated urea water.

3

Experimenting with an Applied Resist

Try one of the following.

- Blend the colors while the dye-stock solutions are wet.

- Make a colored resist line by adding about ³/₈ teaspoon (1g) of dye powder per ½ cup (125 ml) of liquid resist. Color the resist at least one day before using to make sure the dye powder dissolves.

- Sprinkle salt crystals on the design while the dye-stock solution is wet. The salt crystal absorbs the dye, creating darker spots with light-colored halos. Different kinds of salt and different sizes of salt crystal produce different effects. In general, the larger the crystal, the more dramatic the effect.

- Use T-pins to secure lengths of fabric between two sawhorses. When the fabric gets wet and stretches there will be no need to unpin. Just move the sawhorses to take the sag out of the fabric.

5. Prepare ½ cup (125 ml) of dye-stock solution for each color you want to use. When the dye is completely dissolved, pour each solution into a wide-mouth container.

6. Prepare the mixed alkali. Add ½ teaspoon (2 g) of the mixed alkali powder to each ½ cup (125 ml) of dye-stock solution. Stir until the powder dissolves. Note the time; discard the dye-stock solution after 4 hours.

7. Fill a wide-mouth container half full with warm (comfortable to the touch) water. Use this to rinse your brushes.

8. To paint the design, fill an artists' brush with one of the dye-stock solutions prepared in steps 5–6. Touch the brush to the center of an enclosed area. Allow the dye-stock solution to flow to the resist line. Add dye-stock solution as needed to fill the enclosed area. Repeat this process to complete the design. **3**

Work quickly to prevent the dye from drying before you have all your color applied to an area. Do not paint up to the edges or paint on top of the resist line. If you apply too much dye-stock solution, it will pool and may flow into other areas or soak through the resist line. Use a dry brush or cotton swab to mop up dye pools. Remember to rinse your brushes before you use a new color.

9. Allow the fabric to cure at a temperature **above 70° F (21° C)** for a minimum of 24 hours. See page 62 for ways to maintain the curing temperature.

10. After curing, rinse and wash the fabric by hand or machine. To rinse and wash by hand, fill the plastic bucket half full with 65° to 75° F (18° to 24° C) water. Remove the fabric from the artists' stretcher frame and immerse it in the bucket of rinse water. Swish the fabric around the bucket for 1 to 2 minutes. Remove the fabric and change the rinse water. Repeat this rinse 3 to 4 times. You may want to use 2 rinse buckets; the second bucket will be ready and waiting when it is time to change water. When the fabric feels squeaky clean (not soapy), remove it and empty the rinse bucket. (It's okay if you still see color in the rinse water, so long as the fabric feels squeaky clean.) Refill the bucket with 140° F (60° C) water. Add ¼ teaspoon (1.25 ml) of Synthrapol per yard of fabric. Return the fabric to the bucket and swish it around for 5 minutes. Rinse the fabric in warm (comfortable to the touch) water.

To rinse and wash the fabric by machine, set your washing machine on the small load, warm wash, and warm rinse cycles. After the machine fills and begins to agitate, remove the fabric from the artists' stretcher frame and add it to the machine. Close the lid and let the machine continue through the wash, rinse, and spin cycles. After the final spin cycle, reset the machine on the hot wash and warm rinse cycles. After the machine fills with water, add ¼ teaspoon (1.25 ml) of Synthrapol per yard of fabric and let the machine continue through all the cycles. Check the last rinse cycle. If the rinse water is colored, you may need to repeat this step. For dark colors, 2 short wash treatments may work better than 1 long wash.

11. Dry the fabric in a clothes dryer or on a clothesline. Follow the dryer manufacturer's instructions for the appropriate heat setting.

12. Clean up, using the cellulose sponge, rags, or paper towels.

STAMPING WITH PRESIST

Use this technique to explore the principles of positive/negative space on 1 yard (91 cm) of 100% cotton muslin. Use Presist to pattern your fabric, then paint the fabric with thick dye paste. I recommend adding mixed alkali to the thickened dye paste.

Read through the directions and assemble all the necessary equipment and supplies before you begin. Wear a dust/mist mask or respirator while working with dye powder and auxiliary products, and remember to wear rubber gloves when you work with the fabric and liquid dye.

Equipment

2-gallon (8-L) plastic bucket (optional)
Artists' (#12) or sponge brush
Artists' stretcher frame or embroidery hoop
Assortment of wide-mouth plastic containers with lids (one for each color you want to use and one for rinsing the brushes)
Cellulose sponge, rags, or paper towels
Clothesline and clothespins (optional)
Masking tape or T-pins
Measuring cups and spoons or scale
Mixing box (see page 35)
Newspapers
Plastic drop cloth
Plastic or Styrofoam plates
Rubber gloves
Scissors
Spatula
Stamp(s)
Stirring tools
Thermometer
Watch or clock

Fabric Stamped with Presist and Painted with Dye Paste

Making Sponge Stamps

Use a sponge stamp for large images. With a felt-tip marker, draw a design on a dry sponge. Cut out the design with an X-Acto knife or scissors. Attach the cut-out to clear acrylic with a hot glue gun. Look for sponges with different textures for added visual interest.

Experimenting with Presist

Try one of the following.

- Substitute thinned textile paints for dye. Heat set, using a pressing cloth, before rinsing out the Presist.

- Hand paint designs with Presist, then apply dye or textile paints.

Supplies

1 yard (91 cm) scoured, 100% cotton muslin (see pages 22–24)*
Presist
½ cup (125 ml) each of at least 2 colors of thick dye paste (see pages 58–60)
½ teaspoon (2 g) mixed alkali per ½ cup (125 ml) of dye-stock solution (see pages 62–63)
¼ teaspoon (1.25 ml) Synthrapol (minimum)

*Begin with small pieces of fabric, ¼ yard (23 cm) or smaller. As you become comfortable with stamping, increase the size of your pieces.

Procedure

1. Cover your work table with the plastic drop cloth.
2. Stretch the fabric on the artists' stretcher frame or embroidery hoop and secure.
3. Using the spatula, spread a thin layer of Presist on a plastic or Styrofoam plate and dip your stamp in it, or use a sponge brush to apply a layer of Presist to the stamp. (If you are using a sponge stamp, dampen the stamp and wring out excess water before using.) Reload the stamp after each print as you pattern the fabric. When you have completed your design, allow the Presist to air dry. **1**
4. Prepare ½ cup (125 ml) of thick dye paste for each color you want to use. Pour each color of paste into a wide-mouth container.
5. Prepare the mixed alkali. Add ½ teaspoon (2 g) of the mixed alkali powder to each ½ cup (125 ml) of dye paste. Stir until the powder dissolves. Note the time; discard the prepared paste after 4 hours.
6. Fill a wide-mouth container half full with warm (comfortable to the touch) water. Use this to rinse your brushes.
7. Using an artists' or sponge brush and long strokes, apply 1 color to the stretched fabric. Apply additional colors, blending as

1

desired. Wipe excess dye paste off patterned Presist areas. If you don't wipe off the dye paste, the Presist will dissolve and the dye will penetrate to the fabric. **2**

8. Allow the fabric to cure at a temperature **above 70° F (21° C)** for a minimum of 24 hours. See page 62 for ways to maintain the curing temperature.

9. After curing, rinse and wash the fabric by hand or machine. To rinse and wash by hand, fill the plastic bucket half full with 65° to 75° F (18° to 24° C) water. Remove the fabric from the artists' stretcher frame and immerse it in the bucket of rinse water. Swish the fabric around the bucket for 1 to 2 minutes. Remove the fabric and change the rinse water. Repeat this rinse 3 to 4 times. You may want to use 2 rinse buckets; the second bucket will be ready and waiting when it is time to change water. When the fabric feels squeaky clean (not soapy), remove it and empty the rinse bucket. (It's okay if you still see color in the rinse water, so long as the fabric feels squeaky clean.) Refill the bucket with 140° F (60° C) water. Add ¼ teaspoon (1.25 ml) of Synthrapol per yard of fabric. Return the fabric to the bucket and swish it around for 5 minutes. Rinse the fabric in warm (comfortable to the touch) water.

To rinse and wash the fabric by machine, set your washing machine on the small load, warm wash, and warm rinse cycles. After the machine fills and begins to agitate, remove the fabric from the artists' stretcher frame and add it to the machine. Close the lid and let the machine continue through the wash, rinse, and spin cycles. After the final spin cycle, reset the machine on the hot wash and warm rinse cycles. After the machine fills with water, add ¼ teaspoon (1.25 ml) of Synthrapol per yard of fabric and let the machine continue through all the cycles. Check the last rinse cycle. If there is still Presist on the fabric or if the rinse water is colored, you may need to repeat this step. For dark colors, 2 short wash treatments may work better than 1 long wash.

Alternative Curing Methods for Dyes

The direct-application dyeing recipes include fixing-agent and curing instructions, but you may want to try one of the following alternatives as you become more experienced.

Baking Soda Fixative: I do not recommend this method for silk. Add 1 teaspoon (4 g) baking soda per cup (250 ml) of dye-stock solution or dye paste. To cure, choose one of the following: air dry fabric then steam set for 15 minutes, dry fabric in a clothes dryer for 45 minutes on the hottest setting, or preheat your oven to 275° F (135° C), then bake fabric for 2 to 5 minutes. Rinse and wash as directed in the direct-application dyeing recipes.

Citric Acid Crystals: This method is for curing silk only. Add 1 teaspoon (5.8 g) citric acid crystals per cup (250 ml) of dye-stock solution or dye paste. To cure, cover fabric with plastic for 24 hours in a 70°F (21°C) room (minimum temperature), or steam set fabric for 15 minutes. Rinse and wash as instructed in the direct-application dyeing recipes.

2

10. Dry the fabric in a clothes dryer or on a clothesline. Follow the dryer manufacturer's instructions for the appropriate heat setting.
11. Clean up, using the cellulose sponge, rags, or paper towels.

TROUBLESHOOTING

Light or white areas in the pattern are stained.

The fabric was not properly rinsed. Use 65° to 75° F (18° to 24° C) rinse water only and agitate continuously for the first two rinses. You may be able to remove stains by washing the fabric again in 140° to 160° F (60° to 71° C) water with ¼ teaspoon (1.25 ml) of Synthrapol per yard of fabric.

The color is not as bright as it should be and the dye washes off in the rinse water. 2

There are six possible causes: there may not have been enough dye, the water used to dissolve the dye may have been too hot, there may be a finish on the fabric, the curing temperature may have been too low, the dye-stock solution was too old, and/or you forgot to add fixative.

You may have to work through a process of elimination: use more dye; check the temperature of the water used to dissolve the dye powder; check the curing temperature; or do the water-drop test (see page 24), scour the fabric again, use different fabric, or mix fresh dye-stock solution.

The fabric did not dye evenly. 3

The fabric was not correctly scoured or the activator soak was not evenly applied. Scour the fabric again or use another fabric that has been scoured. When you place the fabric in the soda ash soak, it should be completely submerged and able to move freely.

▲ *Remember the Chalice*
by Natasha Kempers-Cullen, 1993,
Topsham, Maine, 81" x 102". **Method**:
Fiber-reactive dye and textile paint on cotton.
Hand painted and stamped. Machine
pieced and hand quilted. Hand embroidered
and embellished with beads, semiprecious
stones, and fetishes. Photo by Dennis Griggs.

❯ *Saints and Sinners: Revelations*
by Natasha Kempers-Cullen, 1996,
Topsham, Maine, 48" x 48". **Method**:
Fiber-reactive dye and textile paint on cotton.
Hand painted and printed. Machine pieced
and hand quilted and beaded. Photo by
Dennis Griggs.

▲ *Caterpillar Hill*
by Elizabeth A. Busch, 1991,
Glenburn, Maine, 32" x 33".
Method: Fiber-reactive dye and textile
paint on cotton. Hand painted and
monoprinted. Machine pieced and
quilted. Photo by Dennis Griggs.

❯ *Coping IV*
by Erika Carter, 1997, Bellevue,
Washington, 23½" x 23½".
Method: Textile paint on cotton.
Hand painted. Machine pieced,
appliquéd, and quilted. Photo by
Howard Carter.

Parameters: Window
by Erika Carter, 1994, Bellevue,
Washington, 58" x 58". **Method**:
Textile paint on cotton. Hand painted.
Machine pieced and quilted. Photo
by Howard Carter.

Persephone's Dream
by Elizabeth A. Busch, 1993,
Glenburn, Maine, 34" x 27½".
Method: Fiber-reactive dye and
textile paint on cotton. Hand painted.
Machine pieced and hand quilted
and embroidered. Photo by Dennis
Griggs.

▲ *Medicine Lodge*
by Gayle Fraas and Duncan Slade, 1994, Edgecomb, Maine, 60" x 60". **Method**: Whole-cloth quilt. Fiber-reactive dye on cotton. Hand painted and printed. Machine and hand quilted by the artists. Embellished with foil. Photo by Dennis Griggs.

➤ *Leaves 2*
by Ann Johnston, 1995, Lake Oswego, Oregon, 48" x 48". **Method**: Fiber-reactive dye on cotton. Patterned with resist. Machine pieced and quilted. Photo by Bill Bachhuber.

‹ *Nude Blue Chair Reclining*
by Laura Wasilowski, 1996, Elgin, Illinois,
42" x 50". **Method**: Fiber-reactive dye on cotton.
Hand dyed and stamped. Machine pieced,
appliquéd, and quilted. Photo by Melody
Johnson.

⌄ *Gives Me the Hee Bee Gee Bees*
by Laura Wasilowski, 1994, Elgin, Illinois,
50½" x 49". **Method**: Fiber-reactive dye on
cotton. Hand dyed, stamped, screen printed, and
painted. Machine pieced and quilted. Photo by
Melody Johnson.

Part III: Paints

Textile paints are fun to use because they are easy to apply and they produce immediate results. Like fiber-reactive dyes, paints can be thick (like jelly), thin (like water), or any consistency in between. You can thin textile paints to paint washes of color and to produce elaborate marbled patterns.

The different types of textile paints include transparent, opaque, and pearlescent. Some transparent paints behave like dyes; you can blend colors, and the value becomes darker as you apply more layers. Opaque paints, in most cases, do not change in value as you apply layers. You can use opaque paints to obscure the color or pattern already on the fabric and to apply color or pattern to dark fabric. Pearlescent paints add both color and sparkle. For a hint of shimmer, mix a small amount of pearlescent paint with another color. You can also dilute pearlescent paint to paint a color wash (see pages 106–8).

All textile paints contain finely ground particles of color that are not soluble in water. They are, in essence, glued to fabric with binders or adhesives. The binders adhere to almost any kind of fabric, including synthetic blends.

Common brands of textile paint include Setacolor, PROfab Textile Paint, Versatex, Lumiere, Neopaque, and Deka. (See "Resources" on page 158.) You can mix the colors and types of paint within each brand. Different manufacturers use different binders or adhesives. These adhesives can alter the hand and drape of fabric. Test several brands before investing in large quantities of any one. (I like using Setacolor transparent textile paints for white or light-colored fabric and Setacolor opaque textile paints for dark fabric. This brand offers a wide range of colors and does not leave a heavy residue on the fabric.)

Fabric colored with textile paints is resistant to fading from exposure to light and dry cleaning. However, these paints are known for their tendency to crock (rub off) with repeated or harsh wash and wear. To extend the life of an image on a garment, turn the garment inside out when laundering.

Textile paints are nontoxic, but they do have an odor that some people find objectionable. Always work in a well-ventilated area.

> **❝**
> We must always remember that a *method* is neither creative nor uncreative: it is the artist's *mind* that creates.
> Susan Bosence
> **❞**

Equipment

The following is a general overview of the equipment needed for working with textile-paint techniques. Some of this equipment is the same as that needed for working with fiber-reactive dyes. Browse yard sales, hardware stores, dye suppliers, art suppliers, and craft stores for equipment you do not have at home. A list of what is absolutely necessary is included at the beginning of each recipe.

Containers: Use assorted sizes of wide-mouth plastic or glass containers with tightly fitting lids for mixing, rinsing brushes, and storing textile paints. You will also need one-quart (1-L), two-gallon (8-L), and five-gallon (20-L) containers or buckets. Refer to the recipes for specific requirements.

Measuring cup: Both plastic cups and Pyrex glassware are suitable. Some suppliers offer plastic safety beakers with markings. You need a one-cup (250 ml) measure.

Measuring spoons: You need a set of plastic or stainless steel measuring spoons.

Mixing box: See the directions for making a mixing box on page 35. Use a mixing box when measuring the activator for scouring.

Newspaper and/or plastic drop cloth: You'll want to cover your workspace with something to protect it from stains.

Using Fiber-Reactive Dyes in the Textile-Paint Recipes

With the exceptions of sun printing and marbling, you can use fiber-reactive dyes instead of textile paints with any of the techniques in this section. Prepare scoured, 100% cotton muslin in soda ash soak or add mixed alkali to the dye-stock solution or paste. Mix dye-stock solution, adding print paste if you want to thicken the consistency. Pattern the fabric as described in the textile-paint recipe; then cure and wash as described in the direct-application recipes.

Textile Painting Equipment

Rubber gloves: You can use disposable latex or reusable rubber gloves. Make sure they fit well so you will be comfortable.

Scale: There are many different types of scales available (for example, kitchen, digital, counterbalance, and triple-beam). Choose a scale that you find easy to use. Make sure that it is accurate. A scale that measures from 1 gram to 2 pounds is handy. Use a bathroom scale to weigh large amounts of fabric. (Weigh yourself while holding the dry fabric; then weigh yourself without the fabric. The difference is the weight of the fabric.)

Shallow tray: For marbling, I recommend a white, 2" to 3" (5 to 7.6 cm) deep tray that is slightly longer and wider than the fabric you plan to marble. A good size to begin with is 10" x 10" (25 cm x 25 cm). It's important that the tray be white or another light color so you can clearly see the marbling colors on the surface of the prepared size.

You can make a simple tray by cutting down a cardboard box and covering it with a white plastic garbage bag.

Stirring tools: You need several small spoons, swizzle sticks, or wooden tongue depressors. You may find a wire whisk and rubber scraper or spatula helpful.

Thermometer: You can use any kind of thermometer, as long as it measures to 140° F (60° C).

Timer: You need a kitchen timer, watch, or clock.

Tools that are useful for specific techniques include: pushpins and/or masking tape; Styrofoam plates or plastic trays; foam pad; artists' stretcher frame or embroidery hoop; assorted artists', sponge, and stencil brushes; assorted sizes of squeeze bottles and/or syringes; rubber or acrylic stamps; cellulose sponges; index cards or precut stencils; an X-Acto or other sharp knife; a marbling rake, hair stylus, teasing comb, or cardboard and toothpicks; a clothesline and plastic clothespins; and rags, old towels, or paper towels.

Supplies

Alum (potassium aluminum sulfate): This chemical acts like a magnet, picking up the marbling colors that float on the size. If fabric is not prepared with alum, the colors will not adhere to the fabric. You can purchase alum that is appropriate for marbling through mail-order companies that specialize in dye supplies (see page 158). Follow the mixing instructions provided by the manufacturer.

Store alum in a cool, dry place. Keep it in a container with a tightly fitting lid. You can continue using the alum as long as you are able to dissolve it.

Clear household ammonia: Thicken methyl cellulose size with clear household ammonia that contains clear ammonia or ammonium hydroxide solution. Avoid products that contain alcohol, nonionic surfactant, perfume, detergent, or color. These will disrupt the surface tension of the size, and the marbling colors will not float. If the ammonia is old, the size will not thicken.

Distilled water: If you have hard water, use only distilled water to mix your size.

Methyl cellulose: There are many different thickeners used for size: methyl cellulose, carrageenan or Irish moss tea (seaweed), wallpaper paste, liquid starch, gelatin, and marbling medium. I recommend methyl cellulose because it produces a very smooth surface, is easy to prepare, has a long shelf life (once prepared), and is less expensive than other types of size. Also, methyl cellulose is biodegradable and can be poured down the drain into any septic or city disposal system.

Prepared methyl cellulose lasts longer if made with distilled water. I have stored it in a plastic bucket with a tightly fitting lid for more than six months. As methyl cellulose degrades, the consistency becomes thinner.

Marbling colors: Although you can thin many water-based textile paints for marbling, I recommend purchasing paints that have been prepared for marbling. Preparing marbling colors from textile paints can be a time-consuming process. Fabric marbling kits are available from art and craft stores and mail-order suppliers.

Store marbling colors in a cool, dry place. Secure lids tightly. You can use marbling colors as long as they have not dried out or been frozen.

Marbling surfactant: This is the surface active agent responsible for changing the surface tension of marbling colors. Marbling surfactant is added to the marbling colors to facilitate spreading or floating of the colors. Surfactants include Synthrapol, dish washing liquid, rubbing alcohol, and products made specifically for marbling. For best results, I recommend marbling surfactants that are designed for marbling.

Store marbling surfactant with your marbling colors in a cool, dry place. You can use marbling surfactant as long as it has not dried out or been frozen.

Textile paints: There are transparent, opaque, and pearlescent paints. Common brands include Setacolor, PROfab Textile Paint, Versatex, Lumiere, Neopaque, and Deka.

I like using Setacolor transparent paints for white and light-colored fabric and Setacolor opaque paints for dark fabric. For more information, refer to "Assembling a Palette" on page 136.

Consult the manufacturer for shelf life information. In general, you can use paints as long as they have not dried out or been frozen. If the paint and base separate, stir thoroughly before using (so it is lump-free).

PRO Chem Colorless Extender: This is a marbling color without the color. If you want the fabric color to be part of the design, use colorless extender to create the design.

Textile Paints

Heat Setting Textile Paints

Although some textile paints will cure over time, heat setting ensures the colors are permanent. It is important to follow the manufacturer's instructions. Most paints will cure with one of the following methods. Always air dry before heat setting, preferably for twenty-four hours.

- If you are using a cellulose fabric (cotton, linen, viscose rayon, jute, ramie, or any combination of these fibers), you can heat-set the textile paints with an iron. Iron the fabric on a hot setting (cotton/linen) from the back side for five minutes. You can also place a clean, dry cloth—a "pressing cloth"—over the front of the fabric and iron it for five minutes. Do not use steam. Keep the iron moving to prevent scorching. *Silk is easily scorched, so be sure to use a pressing cloth.*

- Put the painted, air-dried fabric in a commercial clothes dryer for thirty to sixty minutes or in a home clothes dryer for sixty to ninety minutes. Use the hottest setting on the dryer.

- Coil the fabric in a loose roll and place it in an oven for 2 to 3 minutes at 300°F (148°C). Be careful not to scorch the fabric. Remove the fabric from the oven, turn it inside out, and roll it in the opposite direction. Place the fabric in the oven for another 2 to 3 minutes. This method is not recommended for silk, rayon, or other delicate fabrics.

- An old-fashioned mangle—a large press that uses dry heat and pressure—works well. Make sure there is a protective cloth between the hot rollers and the painted fabric.

Store colorless extender in a cool, dry place. You can use colorless extender as long as it has not dried out or been frozen.

Vinegar: Distilled white vinegar is an optional marbling supply. It is necessary only if your water source is very alkaline.

Assembling a Palette

Color mixing with textile paints is much simpler than color mixing with dyes; what you see is what you get. Try mixing small amounts of different-color paints to gain experience. For light colors and values, add a very small amount of the darker color then mix well before adding more. It takes very little paint to darken a light color, but a lot of paint to lighten a dark color.

The textile paint user's palette includes Setacolor Lemon Yellow 17, Setacolor Buttercup 13, Setacolor Vermilion 26, Setacolor Fuchsia 49, Setacolor Ultramarine Blue 12, Setacolor Cobalt Blue 11, Setacolor Black Lake 19, and Setacolor Titanium White 10. If you like adding sparkle to your fabrics, you also need Setacolor Pearl 44. The following colors are referred to by the manufacturer's name and number. The colors shown below are approximate; the actual color may vary slightly.

Textile Paint Palette

Textile Paint Techniques

As you can imagine, there are a multitude of ways to apply textile paints to fabric. This book covers just a few: printing with found objects, stenciling, sun printing, and marbling. For more information, see "Further Reading" on pages 159–60.

STAMPING WITH FOUND OBJECTS

You can use many things to stamp textile paint on fabric: common household items, shaped sponges, purchased stamps, and so on. This easy recipe produces sumptuous natural patterns using the backs of shells and the undersides of leaves.

If you can go to the beach (or have a friend go), pick up shells and pieces of shells. Look for leaves with intriguing shapes and textures. Try to select leaves that are supple, fuzzy, or thick. Avoid young or tender leaves; new growth becomes limp and tears easily, which makes stamping frustrating and messy.

Use this recipe to pattern ½ yard (46 cm) of 100% cotton muslin. Read through the directions and assemble all the necessary equipment and supplies before you begin.

Fabrics Stamped with Found Objects

Equipment

Artists' brushes: Brights (#6 and #12) for large areas
Assortment of shells and/or fresh leaves
Canvas drop cloth (optional)
Cellulose sponge, rags, or paper towels
Foam pad, 1" (2.5 cm) thick for shell printing (It's easiest when the pad is the same width and length as your fabric.)
Glass cleaner and/or liquid dish soap (optional)
Masking tape
Plastic drop cloth
Rubber gloves (optional)
Wide-mouth plastic container
Resealable plastic sandwich bags (optional)

Supplies

½ yard (46 cm) scoured, 100% cotton muslin (see pages 22–24)
Setacolor transparent or textile paints, at least 4 colors*

*Use opaque textile paints for dark fabrics.

Helpful Hint

Layering Textile Paint

To mix and layer textile paints on fabric, you must work while the paints are wet. New layers will not adhere to dry paint.

Procedure

1. Cover your work table with the plastic drop cloth. If working with shells, lay a piece of foam pad on the drop cloth, then lay your fabric on the pad. If working with leaves, cover your work table with a plastic or canvas drop cloth, then lay your fabric on top. Secure the fabric with masking tape.

2. The shells and leaves must be clean—test by painting them with water. If the water beads up, dry the shell or leaf and spray it with glass cleaner. Pat it dry and test again. You may need to wash slick leaves. Use a drop of liquid dish detergent, then rinse and pat dry.

3. Fill the wide-mouth container half full with warm (comfortable to the touch) water. Use this to rinse your brushes.

4. Using a brush, apply a thin layer of 1 color of textile paint to the round side of a shell or the underside of a leaf. When painting a leaf, start at the center of the leaf and work out to the edges. Make sure the shell or leaf is completely covered with paint. Be careful not to apply too thick a layer of paint; if you use too much, the image will smudge when you press the shell or leaf on the fabric. **1**

5. If you are working with a shell, carefully roll the painted side on the fabric to transfer the image. **2**

   If you are working with a leaf, carefully place the painted side on the fabric. Holding the leaf in place with a finger, cover it with a paper towel. (Don't forget to remove your finger.) Gently walk your fingers over the paper towel to transfer the image. Carefully peel back the paper towel and remove the leaf. **3**

6. Wipe or pat the excess paint off the shell, leaf, or plastic drop cloth. Repeat steps 4 and 5 until the fabric is completely patterned.

   If you change colors, wipe or pat the excess paint off the shell or leaf, then apply the new color.

   Store firm leaves in a resealable plastic bag in your refrigerator. They will remain usable for several days.

7. Allow the fabric to air dry before heat setting it, preferably for 24 hours.

8. See the manufacturer's directions for heat setting. For more information on heat setting, see "Heat Setting Textile Paints" on page 136.

9. Clean up, using the cellulose sponge, rags, or paper towels.

STENCILING

Used to embellish fabric for hundreds of years, stenciling is an easy, versatile technique that lends itself to large patterns. The imagery can be bold and sharp or soft with painstakingly blended colors. Stenciling is a great technique for patterning the border of a garment or a length of fabric. Try using the same design element but gradually varying the colors for interest.

You can purchase or make stencils (see page 140). I prefer to begin with uncomplicated shapes, neither too small nor tightly curved. For more control over the painted image, apply textile paint with a stencil brush, a round brush with stiff, even bristles. For a mottled effect, apply paint with a sponge or sponge roller (for large areas).

Use this recipe to stencil ½ yard (46 cm) of 100% cotton muslin. Read through the directions and assemble all the necessary equipment and supplies before you begin.

Stenciled Fabric

Equipment

Cellulose sponge or rags
Masking tape
Paper towels
Paper or Styrofoam plates
Plastic drop cloth
Rubber gloves (optional)
Stencil(s)
Stencil brushes, ¼" or ½" (0.5 or 1.25 cm), or small natural sponges
Wide-mouth plastic container

Supplies

½ yard (46 cm) scoured, 100% cotton muslin (see pages 22–24)
Setacolor transparent paints, at least 4 colors*

*Use opaque textile paints for dark fabrics.

Procedure

1. Cover your work table with the plastic drop cloth, then lay your fabric on top. Secure the fabric with masking tape.
2. Place a stencil on the fabric and secure with masking tape.
3. Fill the wide-mouth container half full with warm (comfortable to the touch) water. Use this to rinse your brushes.
4. Dip the tip of a brush in paint. Do not overload your brush! Place a paper towel on a paper or Styrofoam plate. Dab the brush on the towel to remove excess paint. The brush should be nearly dry, but moist enough to produce a light stipple effect when you pull it across a sheet of paper. If you use too much paint, it may creep under the edge of the stencil and blur the design.

Making Stencils

You can purchase ready-made stencils at art- and craft-supply stores, or you can design your own. To make a stencil, draw a design on an index card, file folder, or a piece of heavy-gauge plastic. Translating a design to a stencil can be tricky; enclosed shapes must be connected to other shapes with "bridges." Some images may need to be simplified or stylized. Use an X-Acto or other sharp knife to cut out the design. Be sure to cut on a self-healing cutting mat.

To prevent stencils made from paper from degrading, spray them with clear varnish. For more information on making stencils, refer to "Further Reading" on pages 159–60.

5. Hold the brush so the tip is pointed straight down, rather than at an angle. Use a dabbing (or pouncing) motion to color the open areas of the stencil. Work from the outside edges toward the inside. Gradually build up color(s) by applying several layers of paint and/or by blending colors. Allowing the brush to run out of paint as you work gives the design shading and texture. **1**

6. When you have completely filled in the design, remove the masking tape from the edges of the stencil and carefully peel off the stencil. (Be careful not to smudge the paint.) Check the underside of the stencil for paint; remove any excess with a cellulose sponge, rag, or paper towel.

If you want to pattern the entire fabric, tape the stencil to another area and repeat steps 4–6. Before you place the stencil on top of a patterned area, make sure the paint is dry.

7. Allow the fabric to air dry before heat setting, preferably for 24 hours.

8. See the manufacturer's directions for heat setting. For more information, see "Heat Setting Textile Paints" on page 136.)

9. Clean up, using the cellulose sponge, rags, or paper towels. Place stencils on a flat surface to clean. Try to avoid catching and tearing the edges.

1

SUN PRINTING

Use stencils, salt, sunshine, and Setacolor transparent textile paints to create luminous colors and patterns on fabric. Setacolor paints are sensitive to sunlight. If the sun isn't cooperative, you can use a halogen lamp, sun lamp with ultraviolet light, or an infrared heat lamp. Sun printing can be tricky in arid regions because the fabric dries too quickly. For best results, work with small pieces of fabric and work as quickly as possible.

Thin Setacolor paints with water so you can apply a color wash, or dip the fabric in a container of diluted paint, then wring the paint out. Lay the fabric in the sun, then cover it with stencils or other objects.

This recipe is for printing ½ yard (46 cm) of 100% cotton muslin. Read through the directions and assemble all the necessary equipment and supplies before you begin.

Sun-Printed Fabric and Baseball Cap

Equipment

Cellulose sponge, rags, or paper towels
Artists' stretcher frame or embroidery hoop
Masking tape or T-pins
Measuring cups and spoons or scale
Plastic drop cloth
Rubber gloves
Stirring tools
Sponge brush, 2" (5 cm) wide
Stencils, leaves, lace, or index-card cutouts (any opaque item)
Wide-mouth containers with lids (one for each color you want to use and one for rinsing the brush)

Supplies

½ yard (46 cm) scoured, 100% cotton muslin (see pages 22–24)
Setacolor transparent or textile paints, at least 2 colors*
Coarse table, kosher, or sea salt

*Begin with small pieces of fabric, 12" x 12" (30 cm x 30 cm), or smaller. As you become comfortable with sun printing, increase the size of your pieces.

Procedure

1. Cover your work table with the plastic drop cloth.
2. Stretch the fabric on an artists' stretcher frame or embroidery hoop and secure it with masking tape or T-pins.
3. Fill a wide-mouth container half full with warm (comfortable to the touch) water. Use this to rinse your brush and moisten your fabric.

4. Dilute the textile paints with water, using the wide-mouth containers for mixing. Begin with 1 part Setacolor paint and 2 parts water. Experiment to determine how much you want to dilute the paint.

5. Paint your fabric, working rapidly. Blend colors as desired.

6. Place the stencils, leaves, lace, or cutouts on the fabric. **1**

7. Sprinkle the fabric with coarse table, kosher, or sea salt. The salt reacts with the paint and sunlight to create halos of color.

8. Place the fabric (still on the artists' stretcher frame or in an embroidery hoop) in sunlight or under a lamp. Leave the fabric in sunlight or under the lamp until it is completely dry; then remove the opaque objects and brush off the salt. **2**

9. See the manufacturer's directions for heat setting. For more information on heat setting, see "Heat Setting Textile Paints" on page 136.)

10. Clean up, using the cellulose sponge, rags, or paper towels.

MARBLING

The graceful lines and intricate patterns of marbling are mesmerizing, and the moment you transfer the pattern is magical. Although the technique requires planning and preparation, the finished result is well worth it. You must prepare the alum soak, fabric, and size (steps 1–6) in advance. Because the fabric must air dry, you may want to split this recipe into 2 days, doing steps 1–6 on the first day, then proceeding through the remaining steps another day.

There are few limits to marbling. Experimenting is essential! You can use white, colored, or patterned fabric for background. In fact, marbling is an excellent way to pattern dyed fabrics that are not up to par. You can even marble a previously marbled image. This is referred to as shadow marbling.

This recipe is based on colors made by PRO Chem specifically for marbling. Although you can thin many water-based textile paints for marbling, I recommend that you purchase colors prepared for marbling. Preparing marbling colors from paints can be a time-consuming process. Fabric-marbling kits are available from art and craft stores and through mail-order suppliers (see page 158).

You can marble any surface that absorbs alum, including fabric, paper, tennis shoes, egg shells, and even wood! For additional information on marbling, refer to "Further Reading" on pages 159–60.

Use this recipe to marble 4 to 5 yards (3.65 to 4.57 m) of 100% cotton fabric. Read through the directions and assemble all the necessary equipment and supplies before you begin. **1**

Marbled Fabric (Nonpareil Pattern)

Making a Marbling Rake and Comb

For traditional marbling patterns, you need special rakes and combs that extend the width and length of your marbling tray. To make a marbling rake, cut a piece of cardboard, foam core, or balsa wood 1" (2.5 cm) shorter than the width of your tray. Tape toothpicks or plastic hairpins at 1" (2.5 cm) intervals. To make a marbling comb, cut a piece of cardboard, foam core, or balsa wood 1" (2.5 cm) shorter than the width of your tray. Tape or push long sewing pins through the material at ¼" (6.3 mm) intervals.

Marbled Vest by Judy Simmons, 1997, Marietta, Georgia. Marbled silk lining.

Equipment

1-quart (1-L) plastic measure
5-gallon (20-L) plastic bucket
Two 2-gallon (8-L) plastic buckets with lids
Cellulose sponge, rags, or paper towels
Clothesline and clothespins
Kitchen timer or watch
Measuring cups and spoons or scale
Newspaper (cut to ¼ page)
Plastic drop cloth
Plastic-lined garbage can or plastic trash bag
Rubber gloves (optional)
Scissors
Shallow tray
Stirring tools
Teasing comb, marbling rake, toothpicks, and/or plastic hairpins
Thermometer

Supplies

4 tablespoons (60 g) alum
4 to 5 yards (3.6 to 4.5 m) scoured, 100% cotton muslin (see pages 22–24)
3½ tablespoons (25 g) methyl cellulose M112 powder (for size)
1 teaspoon (5 ml) clear household ammonia
1 gallon (4 L) distilled water, if your water is hard or heavily chlorinated
1 teaspoon (5 ml) distilled white vinegar, if your water is very alkaline
PRO Chem Colorless Extender (optional)
Marbling colors, at least 4
Marbling surfactant

Procedure

Part 1

1. Hang the clothesline and place clothespins nearby. Cover your work area with the plastic drop cloth. Position your shallow tray near the edge of the work table. Place a plastic-lined garbage can or plastic trash bag under the edge of the table to catch drips.
2. To make the alum soak, dissolve 4 tablespoons (60 g) of alum in 1 gallon (4 L) of 120° F (50° C) water. Stir until dissolved.
3. Add scoured fabric (wet or dry) to the alum soak. Soak the fabric for 10 to 15 minutes, stirring intermittently. Make sure the fabric is completely submerged and can move freely in the bucket.

4. Remove the fabric from the bucket. Holding the fabric over the bucket, wring out the excess solution. Do not rinse the fabric!

5. Hang the fabric on a clothesline to dry. Make sure the fabric is not folded or overlapping. Do not use a clothes dryer to dry alum-soaked fabrics; heat tenderizes cotton.

    If necessary, press the line-dried fabric with a cool iron to remove creases. Do not press with a hot iron. When the fabric is dry, cut it to the inside dimensions of your tray.

6. To make the size, measure 1 gallon (4 L) of 75° to 95° F (24° to 35° C) water into the other 2-gallon (8-L) bucket. Add 3½ table-spoons (25 g) of methyl cellulose M112 powder to the bucket. Stir until the methyl cellulose dissolves. While stirring, add 1 teaspoon (5 ml) of clear household ammonia. Continue stirring until the solution begins to look clear (2 to 3 minutes). Stir intermittently for 30 minutes.

    If you have hard or heavily chlorinated water, use distilled water to make the size. The impurities in the water can disrupt the surface tension of the size.

    If you have very alkaline water, add 1 teaspoon (5 ml) of distilled white vinegar to each gallon (4 L) of size.

    The size is ready for marbling. For best results, allow the size to sit for 12 hours or overnight before using. Store the size and marbling colors in the same room at 60° to 80° F (16° to 27° C) before using.

Part 2

1. Fill the 5-gallon (20-L) plastic bucket half full with warm (comfortable to the touch) water.

2. Fill the shallow tray with 1" to 2" (2.5 to 5 cm) of the size.

3. To skim the size, drag a strip of newspaper across the surface of the size, then discard the paper. This evens out the surface tension and clears the bubbles. Do not worry about the bubbles remaining along the edges of the marbling tray. These will not disrupt the pattern. **2**

Tips for Using Alum

You can keep the alum soak in a plastic bucket with a tight-fitting lid for 2 to 3 months. Store at room temperature. Alum crystallizes when it is too cold or old. If new alum solution crystallizes, reheat it to dissolve the crystals. Discard old solution. Do not store alum-treated cotton fabric for longer than 2 to 3 weeks before marbling; alum causes cotton fibers to disintegrate.

4. Shake the marbling colors and Colorless Extender (if using) well before each use and periodically during the marbling session. Using a pushpin, make a fine hole in the nozzle of the applicator bottle.

   Test each of the marbling colors. Hold the applicator bottle close to the size and squeeze 1 drop of color onto the surface. The marbling color should float and spread out in a circle measuring from ½" to 2" (1.5 to 5 cm) in diameter. If the drop does not spread, add marbling surfactant to the marbling color in the applicator bottle, 2 to 3 drops at a time, and test again. Be careful; you cannot remove the surfactant if you add too much.

   Test the colors to make sure they all float together, then skim the surface. **3**

5. To make the marble pattern, carefully squeeze drops of your first color on the size. (Use as many drops as you like.) Using your other marbling colors, repeat this process until you have completely covered the surface. *Note:* The fabric shows through areas not completely covered with marbling color. You can place drops side by side or on top of previous color(s). The more drops, the deeper the color. **4** **5**

3

4

5

6. Using a teasing comb, marbling rake, toothpick, or plastic hairpin, pattern the marbling colors. See the illustrations on page 148 for ideas. **6**

7. Trim all loose threads from the edges of the fabric.

8. Hold 2 opposite corners of the piece of fabric. In one fluid movement, gently lay the middle of the fabric on top of the marbling colors and drop the edges. **7** **8**

9. Remove the fabric from the tray, then immerse it several times in the rinse bucket. Do not rub the fabric. Gently squeeze excess water from the fabric and hang it on the clothesline to dry. **9**

10. Clean up, using the cellulose sponge, rags, or paper towels.

11. Allow the fabric to air dry and cure for 3 days before washing. Some paints need to be heat set. Follow the manufacturer's directions (remember to use a cool iron).

After the fabric has cured, you can wash it by hand or in a washing machine. Set the machine for the gentlest cycle. Use cool water and mild soap. Rinse the fabric in 75° to 95° F (24° to 35° C) water and hang to dry.

Helpful Hint

Cleaning Equipment

Do not clean your equipment with soap; use water and a stiff brush. Soap residue interferes with surface tension and can cause some of the problems listed in "Troubleshooting" on page 149.

MARBLING PATTERNS

Freestyle Pattern

Apply drops of different colors.

Pattern with stylus.

Spiral Pattern

Apply drops of different colors.

Pattern with stylus.

Waved Get-Gel Pattern

Apply drop of different colors.

Pattern with 1" rake.

Pattern with 2" rake.

Nonpareil Pattern

Apply drops of different colors.

Pattern with 1" rake.

Pattern with ¼" comb.

TROUBLESHOOTING

The marbling colors sink into the size.

There are three possible causes: a skin may have formed on the size, the size may be too thick, and/or the marbling color(s) may need surfactant.

Try skimming the surface of the size with newspaper just before you apply drops of marbling color, adding water to the size and/or adding surfactant to the marbling color. Skim the size before each test drop and test between additions of surfactant. The more surfactant you add to the marbling color, the better it will float, the wider it will spread, and the lighter the color will be.

The marbling colors are spreading too fast.

There are two possible causes: the size may be too thin, and/or you may have added too much surfactant to the marbling colors.

To thicken the size, use 7 tablespoons (50 g) of methyl cellulose powder per gallon of water. If you think you have added too much surfactant, place drops of PRO Chem Colorless Extender on the surface of the size before testing marbling colors. The Extender changes the surface tension and slows the spread of the marbling colors.

The marbling colors floating on the size appear grainy.

The paint in the marbling color has settled. Shake the bottles of marbling color well before each use.

The drops of marbling color have jagged edges.

A skin has formed on the size. Skim the surface of the size and reapply the marbling colors.

The colors wash off the fabric in the rinse bucket and the remaining colors are pale, uneven, and streaked.

There are three possible causes: there may be a finish on the fabric, the alum soak may be too weak, and/or the alum soak may be too strong.

If you think you may not have adequately washed the fabric, scour it again (see pages 22–24). If the alum soak is too weak, it cannot hold the colors on the fabric. If the alum soak is too strong, the colors will adhere to the alum and will flake off in the rinse. If you think the solution is too weak or strong, make a new alum soak.

This fabric is a good candidate for shadow marbling.

4

5

There are white or dark fold marks in the marbled areas.

Either the fabric did not uniformly absorb the alum while it was in the soak or it was not laid down properly on the marbling colors. Soak smaller pieces of fabric and stir frequently. You may also need to practice laying the fabric down smoothly.

The fabric is fragile and rips after marbling.

Did you use a hot iron? Line dry the fabric after the alum soak. Use only a cool iron on fabric treated with alum. If the fabric was soaked in alum more than three weeks earlier, the alum may have caused the fabric to disintegrate.

There are white fractures in the marbled pattern. 5

There was a thread on the surface of the fabric. Trim all excess threads from the fabric before marbling.

> **Marbled Shirt**
by Robin Golinski for Robin Boston, 1994, Boston, Massachusetts. **Method**: Textile paints on cotton. Hand marbled.

Appendixes

Appendix A: Helpful Terms

Auxiliary products: The term for products used to assist the dye process. These products help the dye penetrate the fabric (for even color, lightfastness, and washfastness.

Cellulose: Fiber that is of plant origin, such as cotton, linen, ramie, flax, jute, or viscose rayon (regenerated cellulose). Although silk is classified as a protein (animal) rather than as a cellulose fiber, you can still dye it using the processes outlined in this book.

Cure: The process of permanently fixing dyes or paints to fabric.

Dye concentrate: A concentrated mixture of water and dye that is added to immersion dye baths.

Dye lot: Fabric dyed at the same time with the same color.

Dye paste: A mixture of urea, water softener, sodium alginate, dye powder, and water used for stamping and other direct-application techniques.

Dye site: Location on the fiber where the reaction takes place.

Dye-stock solution: A solution of water, dye, and urea that is used for tie dye and other direct-application techniques.

Fiber-reactive dyes: Manufactured dyes that reacts chemically with cellulose fibers. I recommend Procion MX fiber-reactive dyes because they are easy to use and provide brilliant colors. These dyes are considered nontoxic.

Fiber-reactive dyes can be permanently applied to protein (animal) fibers with additional auxiliary products.

Fixative: A chemical that permanently fixes MX Fiber-Reactive Dyes to fabric.

Gutta: A type of resist (the word "gutta" actually means resist). This is a liquid with the consistency of syrup. When applied to fabric, it creates a barrier that keeps the dye solution within defined areas. Gutta is available in both water- and solvent-based forms.

Hand: The way fabric feels to the touch. Some textile paints and liquid resists can change the hand of the fabric, making it stiffer.

Hue: A synonym for "color," hue is the pure state of a color.

Intensity: The purity, or saturation, of a color.

Level dyeing: Even dyeing, without spotting or irregular color.

Marbling colors: Although you can thin many water-based textile paints for marbling, I recommend that you purchase paints that have been prepared for marbling. Preparing marbling colors from paints can be a time-consuming process. Fabric-marbling kits are available from art and craft stores and through mail-order suppliers.

Marbling surfactant: This is the surface active agent that changes the surface tension of the marbling color. Marbling surfactant is added to the marbling colors to facilitate spreading or floating of the colors. Surfactants include Synthrapol, dish washing liquid, rubbing alcohol, and substances made specifically for marbling.

Each surfactant has a different capacity for altering the surface tension of the marbling color. Some, such as Synthrapol and rubbing alcohol, are very strong and should be used sparingly. For best results, I recommend marbling surfactants designed for marbling.

Maximum absorption point: The point of full saturation of a color. The maximum absorption point depends on the dye molecule's attainable depth of shade (which depends on its manufacturing) and the number of dye sites available on the fabric. Dye and fabric have independent maximum absorption points.

Mercerized cotton: Cotton is a single, elongated cell that, when dry, becomes flat and twists. The mercerization process produces microscopic changes in the appearance of the cell. The cotton is treated with caustic soda (sodium hydroxide) during the finishing process in manufacturing. The cotton cells swell and gradually untwist to produce a single tube—a fatter fiber. Because more light can reflect off the fatter fiber, the dyed, mercerized fabric appears, to our eyes, about 25% darker than unmercerized cotton treated with the same amount of dye. The mercerization treatment also improves the strength and increases the luster of the cotton fibers.

Overdye: To add color on top of a colored or patterned fabric.

Primary color: A color that cannot be made by mixing other colors: red, yellow, and blue.

Print paste: An inert mixture containing urea, water softener, sodium alginate (Thick SH or F), and water. Print Paste controls the flow of the dye paste for direct-application dyeing techniques.

Procion: The trade name for the fiber-reactive dyes originally manufactured by ICI. The MX series is the most popular for home dyeing.

Reactivity rate: The rate at which dye molecules bond with fiber molecules. Some dyes, such as Procion Red MX-8B and Yellow MX-8G, react faster than others, which can effect the color of the dyed fabric.

Room temperature: The ideal temperature, 75° to 95° F (24° to 35° C), for MX Fiber-Reactive Dyes to permanently fix to fiber.

Scour: The first step in the dye process. This procedure removes excess wax, oil, dirt, and surface finishes.

Secondary color: A color that can be made by mixing two primary colors. Purple, orange, and green are secondary colors.

Shadow marbling: The process of marbling over another marbled design. (Marbled fabric must be treated again with alum before it can be shadow marbled.)

Shelf life: The length of time a product is useable. This can refer to the powdered state and/or the liquid state.

Size: Water that has been thickened so that marbling colors can float on top. There are many different thickeners used for marbling sizes, including methyl cellulose, carrageenan or Irish moss tea (seaweed), wallpaper paste, liquid starch, gelatin, and marbling medium.

I recommend methyl cellulose because it produces a smoother surface, is easier to prepare, has a longer shelf life, and is less expensive than other types of thickeners. Methyl cellulose is biodegradable and can be poured down the drain into any septic or disposal system.

Solubility level: The ability of a dye to dissolve. Low solubility means it will be more difficult to dissolve than a dye with high solubility. Some dyes, such as Yellow MX-8G, Red MX-8B, and Blue MX-R dissolve slowly and take up more space in water. These dyes benefit from the addition of water or urea to the dye-stock solution or concentrate.

Substantivity: A dye's affinity for fiber. This relates to the ability of excess (unbonded) dye to rinse off fabric. Unbonded dye that is not properly removed in the final rinse and hot wash will come off in subsequent laundering, with the appearance of bleeding. Low substantivity means dye will wash off more easily than dye with high substantivity.

Textile paints: Insoluble organic or inorganic particles of color (pigment) that can be attached to fiber with a binder or adhesive.

Value: The lightness or darkness of a hue.

Appendix B: Helpful Products and Recipes

The following products are available at quilt shops, art and craft supply stores, and through mail-order suppliers.

Anti-chlor (sodium bisulfite): Chlorine is a strong oxidizing agent frequently used for stripping color in discharging processes. It has a strong affinity for fabric and does not completely wash out. An Anti-chlor bath is the safest way to remove traces of free chlorine, which, if left in fabric, will weaken it over time.

When using Anti-chlor, make sure there is ample ventilation, and wear safety goggles, a respirator, and gloves. Rinse each yard (91 cm) of fabric well in 95°F (35°C) water. While wearing a respirator and gloves, mix ¾ teaspoon (2 g) Anti-chlor in 1 gallon (4 L) of 110°F (44°C) water. Swish the fabric around for 15 minutes, then rinse well in room-temperature water. You can dry or redye the fabric without tenderizing it.

PROsoft: Fabric, in particular knits, can have a harsh hand or feel once they have been dyed. PROsoft is an industrial-strength liquid textile softener. It imparts a very soft hand without fragrances and is semipermanent. It can be applied in your washing machine and does not discolor fabric over time.

Wearing rubber gloves and safety goggles, mix 1 teaspoon (5 ml) per yard (91 cm) of fabric in 1 gallon (4 L) of 105° to 120°F (40° to 50°C) water. Swish the fabric around for 20 minutes or add PROsoft to the washing machine during the last rinse cycle. Do not rinse. Wring and dry fabric. Do not apply PROsoft if you plan to overdye your fabric; it will inhibit dye penetration.

Retayne: Retayne improves the colorfastness of *commercially* dyed fabrics that have a tendency to bleed when washed. It is especially useful for deep red and maroon shades. You can use Retayne in the washing machine or while hand washing.

Fill your washing machine with hot—140°F (60°C)—water. Heat water on the stove and add it to the machine if necessary. Add 1 teaspoon (5 ml) Retayne per yard (91 cm) of fabric. Add fabric and set the washing machine for a 20 minute wash. (Reset the washing machine, if necessary, so the Retayne does not go down the drain.) Rinse on warm cycle and dry at once. For subsequent laundering, wash the fabric in cool water.

Snowy Bleach (sodium perborate): If your fabric is not adequately rinsed and washed, the dye may bleed or "back stain"—leave a halo of color. Back staining is difficult to remove. Wash your fabric with Snowy Bleach (from the grocery store) according to the directions on the box. This frequently removes or lightens redeposited dye. If you notice staining while the fabric is wet, wash the fabric again in hot —140°F (60°C)—water with Synthrapol to remove excess dye.

Testing Commercial Fabric for Colorfastness

Dampen a 2" x 2" piece of white, 100% cotton muslin. Place this 2" square on the fabric to be tested. Iron the fabrics with a hot iron until dry. Inspect the muslin for color. If there has been some color transfer, treat the fabric with Retayne before washing.

Synthrapol: This is a surfactant (surface active agent) that interacts with the surface of the fiber, functioning as a lubricant. In essence, Synthrapol makes water wetter. Add Synthrapol to the dye bath to increase your fabric's absorbency, add a couple drops to dye concentrate to help dye powder dissolve, and use it to wash hand-dyed fabrics. Always wear gloves when using Synthrapol; it does a good job of cleaning the natural oils from your hands.

Appendix C: Weights of Auxiliary Products

The following weights were measured in a temperature- and humidity-controlled room and are approximate, because humidity affects weight. Some products compact when they are measured in large quantities. This accounts for the variations in weight between teaspoon, tablespoon, and cup measurements.

Product	Weight		
	Teaspoon	Tablespoon	Cup
Activator	3 g	9 g	153 g
Alum	4.4 g	14.4 g	
Anti-chlor	2.2 g	6.6 g	
Bicarbonate of soda	4.1 g	12 g	
Citric acid	5.8 g	17.5 g	
Ludigol	2.3g	7.5g	
Metaphos (water softener)	7 g	21 g	
Methyl cellulose	2.6 g	8 g	
Mixed alkali	3.1 g	10.8 g	
MX fiber-reactive dye	2.5g	9 g	
Print Paste Mix F	3.1 g	10.1 g	
Print Paste Mix SH	3.2 g	9.8 g	
Salt, common table	5.6 g	14.8 g	299 g
Salt, glauber	6.6 g	20 g	
Soda ash	3 g	9 g	153 g
Thick F	3.2 g	9.9 g	
Thick SH	2.6 g	8.7 g	
Urea	4 g	12 g	

Appendix D: English and Metric Abbreviations, Measurements, and Conversion Charts

ENGLISH AND METRIC ABBREVIATIONS

" = inch

cm = centimeter

g = gram

gal = gallon

kg = kilogram

L = liter

lb = pound

m = meter

ml = milliliter

oz = ounce

qt = quart

Tbl = tablespoon

tsp = teaspoon

yd = yard

ENGLISH AND METRIC EQUIVALENCIES

Length

English

12 inches = 1 foot

3 feet = 1 yard

Metric

100 centimeters = 1 meter

English and Metric

1 inch = 2.54 centimeters

0.39 inch = 1 centimeter

39 inches = 1 meter

1 yard = 0.91 meter

Volume (Liquid Measure)

English

3 teaspoons = 1 tablespoon

16 tablespoons = 8 ounces (1 cup)

1 cup = 8 ounces

1 pint = 16 ounces (2 cups)

1 quart = 32 ounces (4 cups or 2 pints)

1 gallon = 128 ounces (16 cups or 4 quarts)

Metric

1 milliliter = 1 cubic centimeter

1,000 milliliters = 1 liter

English and Metric

1 teaspoon = 5 milliliters

1 tablespoon = 15 milliliters

1 ounce = 29.5 milliliters

1 cup = 236 milliliters (approximately 250 milliliters)

1 pint = 453 milliliters (approximately 500 milliliters)

1 quart = 946 milliliters (approximately 1 liter)

1 gallon = 3,784 milliliters (approximately 4 liters)

Weight (Dry Measure)

English

3 teaspoons = 1 tablespoon

2 tablespoons = 1 ounce

16 tablespoons = 1 cup (8 ounces)

2 cups = 1 pound (16 ounces)

Metric

1,000 grams = 1 kilogram

English and Metric

1 ounce = 28.5 grams

1 pound = 454 grams

2.2 pounds = 1 kilogram

English and Metric Conversion Charts

English to Metric Standards

To convert	into	multiply by
Lengths		
inches	mm	25.4
inches	cm	2.54
inches	meters	0.0254
feet	meters	0.3048
yards	meters	0.9144
Volumes		
cubic inches	cm^3	16.387
cubic inches	liters	0.016387
cubic feet	m^3	0.028317
cubic feet	liters	28.317
cubic yards	m^3	0.7646
liquid ounces	cm^3	29.57
gallons U.S.	m^3	0.003785
gallons U.S.	liters	3.785
Weights		
ounces	grams	28.35
ounces	kg	0.02835
pounds	kg	0.4536

Metric to English Standards

To convert	into	multiply by
Lengths		
mm	inches	0.03937
cm	inches	0.3937
meters	inches	39.37
meters	feet	3.281
meters	yards	1.0936
Volumes		
cm^3	liquid ounces	0.03381
m^3	gallons U.S.	264.2
liters	gallons U.S.	0.2642
Weights		
grams	grains	15.432
grams	ounces	0.03527
kg	ounces	35.27
kg	pounds	2.2046

THERMOMETER COMPARISON

°F*	392	302	284	266	248	230	212	194	176	158	140	122	104	86	68	50	41	32
°C*	200	150	140	130	120	110	100	90	80	70	60	50	40	30	20	10	5	0

Here is a handy formula for converting Fahrenheit to Celsius (formerly Centigrade). Subtract 32 from the Fahrenheit temperature, then divide by 1.8. For example, 95°F - 32 = 63; 63 ÷ 1.8 = 35°C.

To change Celsius to Fahrenheit, multiply the Celsius figure by 1.8, then add 32. For example, 60°C x 1.8 = 108; 108 + 32 = 140°F.

Resources

United States

Aljo Manufacturing Co.
81-83 Franklin Street
New York, NY 10013
Phone: 212-966-4046
Fax: 212-274-9616
(dyes, paints, tools, supplies)

Dharma Trading Co.
PO Box 150916
San Rafael, CA 94915
Phone: 800-542-5227, 415-456-7657
Fax: 415-456-8747
www.dharmatrading.com
(dyes, paints, tools, supplies, books, fabric)

Earth Guild
33 Haywood Street
Asheville, NC 28801
Phone: 800-327-8448
Fax: 828-255-8593
www.earthguild.com
(dyes, paints, tools, supplies, books, fabric)

Exotic Silks
1959 B Leghorn
Mountain View, CA 94043
Phone: 800-854-7455, CA: 800-345-7455
Fax: 650-965-0712
www.exoticsilks.com
(silk)

Lunn Fabrics, Ltd.
317 East Main Street
Lancaster, OH 43130
USA & Canada Toll Free 800-880-1738
Phone: 740-654-2202
Fax: 740-654-3949
www.lunnfabrics.com
(fabric)

PRO Chemical & Dye
PO Box 14
Somerset, MA 02726
Phone: 800-993-2828, 508-676-3838
Fax 508-676-3980
www.prochemical.com
(dyes, paints, tools, supplies, books, fabric)

Qualin International
PO Box 31145
San Francisco, CA 94131
Phone: 415-970-8888
Fax: 415-282-8789
qualinint@aol.com
(silk)

Rupert, Gibbon & Spider
PO Box 425
Healdsburg, CA 95448
Phone: 800-442-0455, 707-433-9577
Fax: 707-433-4906
www.jacquardproducts.com
(dyes, paints, tools, supplies, books, fabric)

Silkpaint Corporation
18220 Waldron Drive
Waldron, MO 64092
Phone: 800-563-0074
Fax: 816-891-7775
www.silkpaint.com
(Silkpaint! Brand Resist, the AirPen, tools, supplies)

Testfabrics, Inc.
415 Delaware Avenue
PO Box 26
West Pittston, PA 18643
Phone: 570-603-0432
Fax: 570-603-0433
www.testfabrics.com
(fabric)

Wildfiber
1453-e 14th Street
Santa Monica, CA 90404
Phone: 800-382-7067, 310-458-2748
Fax: 310-458-9000
www.wildfiber.com
(dyes, paints, tools, supplies, books, fabric)

International Suppliers

Australia

Batik Oetoro Pty. Ltd.
203 Avoca Street
Randwick 2031
Phone: 61-2-9398-6201
Fax: 61-2-9398-1173
www.dyeman.com
(dyes, paints, tools, supplies, books, fabric)

Kraftkolour
242 High Street
Northcote, Victoria 3070
Phone: 03-9482-9234
Fax: 03-9482-9279
www.kraftkolour.com.au
(dyes, paints, tools, supplies)

Canada

G&S Dye Ltd.
250 Dundas Street West, Unit #8
Toronto, Ontario M5T 2Z5
Phone: 800-596-0550
Fax: 905-415-8560
www.gsdye.com
(dyes, paints, tools, supplies)

Maiwa Handprints, Ltd.
#6 - 1666 Johnston Street
Vancouver, BC V6H 3S2
Phone/fax: 604-669-3939
www.maiwa.com
(dyes, paints, tools, supplies, books)

Denmark

Karen Noe Design
Søndergade 23
7171 Uldum
Phone: 45-7567-9733
www.karen-noe.dk
(dyes, paints, tools, supplies)

Germany

Galerie Smend
Mainzer Strasse 31
50678 Koln
Phone: 49-221-31-20-47
Fax: 49-221-932-0718
www.smend.de
(dyes, paints, tools, supplies, books, fabric)

Quilt und Art
Postfach 1254
63152 Muhlheum/Main
Phone: 49-610-87-30-60
Fax: 49-610-870-9949
www.quiltundart.de
(dyes, paints, tools, supplies, books, fabric)

Holland

Zijdelings
Kapelstraat 93A
5046 CL Tilburg
Phone: 31-13-5453456
Fax: 31-13-5800345
www.zijdelings.com
(dyes, paints, tools, supplies, fabric)

New Zealand

Craft Supplies
31 Gurney Road
Belmont, Lower Hutt
Phone/fax: 04-565-0544
www.dianaparkes.co.nz
(dyes, paints, tools, supplies, books, fabric)

United Kingdom

George Weil
Old Portsmouth Road
Peasmarsh
Guildford, Surrey GU3 1LZ
Phone: 01-483-565800
Fax: 01-483-565807
www.fibrecrafts.com
(dyes, paints, tools, supplies, books)

Whaleys (Bradford) Ltd.
Harris Court, Great Horton
Bradford, West Yorkshire BD7 4EQ
Phone: 44-1274-576718
Fax: 44- 274-521309
www.whaleys.co.uk
(fabric)

Bibliography

Albers, Josef. *Interaction of Color*. New Haven, Conn.: Yale University Press, 1975.

———. *An Outline of the Chemistry and Technology of the Dyestuffs Industry*. Manchester, England: ICI Colours & Fine Chemicals, 1968.

Blumenthal, Betsy and Kathryn Kreider. *Hands-on Dyeing*. Loveland, Colo.: Interweave Press, 1988.

Ingamells, Wilfred. *Colour for Textiles: A User's Handbook*. West Yorkshire, England: Society of Dyers and Colourists, 1993.

Johnson, Meda Parker and Glen Kaufman. *Design on Fabrics*. 2nd ed. New York: Van Nostrand Reinhold Company, 1981.

Klapper, Marvin. *Fabric Almanac*. New York: Fairchild Publications, Inc., 1966.

Maile, Anne. *Tie and Dye as a Present-Day Craft*. New York: Ballantine Books, 1963.

Nea, Sara. *Tie-dye: Designs, Materials, Technique*. New York: Van Nostrand Reinhold Company, 1971.

ICI Limited, Organics Division. *Procion Dyes: A Rational Basis of Dye Selection for Cotton, Pattern Leaflet 125*. Manchester, England, 1976.

Proctor, Richard and Jennifer Lew. *Surface Design for Fabric*. 2nd ed. Seattle: University of Washington Press, 1995.

Rivlin, Joseph. *The Dyeing of Textile Fibers, Theory and Practice*. Philadelphia: Philadelphia College of Textiles and Science, 1992.

Storey, Joyce. *The Thames and Hudson Manual of Dyes and Fabrics*. New York: Thames and Hudson, Inc., 1985.

Taylor, Carol. *Marbling Paper & Fabric*. New York: Sterling Publishing Co., Inc., 1991.

Trotman, E. R. *Dyeing and Chemical Technology of Textile Fibres*. London: Charles Griffin & Company Limited, 1975.

Wada, Rice, and Barton. *Shibori: The Inventive Art of Shaped Resist Dyeing*. Tokyo: Kodansha International, Ltd., 1983.

Wilcox, Michael. *Blue and Yellow Don't Make Green*. Cincinnati: Northlight Books, 1987.

Further Reading

BOOKS

Chambers, Anne. *Suminagashi: The Japanese Art of Marbling, A Practical Guide*. London: Thames and Hudson, Ltd., 1991.

Clark, Nancy, M.A.; Thomas Cutter, P.E.; Jean-Ann McGrane, M.S. *Ventilation: a Practical Guide for Artists, Craftspeople, and Others in the Arts*. New York: Center for Occupational Hazards, Inc., 1984.

Dunnewold, Jane. *Complex Cloth*. Bothell, Wash.: Fiber Studio Press, 1996.

Johnston, Ann. *Dye Painting!* Paducah, Ky.: American Quilter's Society, 1992.

Knutson, Linda. *Synthetic Dyes for Natural Fibers*. Seattle: Madrona Publishers, 1982.

Maurer, Diane Vogel and Paul Maurer. *Marbling: A Complete Guide to Creating Beautiful Patterned Papers and Fabrics*. New York: Friedman/Fairfax Publishers, 1994.

McCann, Michael, Ph.D., C.I.H. *Artist Beware*. New York: Lyons & Burford, 1992.

Moyer, Susan. *Silk Painting: The Artist's Guide to Gutta and Wax Resist Techniques*. New York: Watson-Guptill Publications, 1991.

Murashima, Kumiko. *Katazome: Japanese Paste-Resist Dyeing for Contemporary Use*. Asheville, N.C.: Lark Books, 1993.

Porcella, Yvonne. *Colors Changing Hue*. Lafayette, Calif.: C&T Publishing, 1994.

Rossol, Monona. *The Artist's Complete Health and Safety Guide*. New York: Allworth Press, 1990.

Laury, Jean Ray. *Imagery on Fabric*. Lafayette, Calif.: C&T Publishing, 1992.

Schleicher, Patty and Mimi Schleicher. *Marbled Designs: A Complete Guide to Fifty-Five Elegant Patterns*. Asheville, N.C.: Lark Books, 1993.

Wiener, Donald. *The Best of Q&A*. Surface Design Association, 1991.

Widger, Katy. *Color Wheel Fabric Dyeing*. Edgewood, N. Mex.: self-published, 1991.

Wolfrom, Joen. *The Magical Effects of Color*. Lafayette, Calif.: C&T Publishing, 1992.

Index

Biography

Photo by John Robson

Describing herself as "fascinated and intrigued by the link between observation and visual design," Elin Noble is a fiber artist whose talents include papermaking, bookbinding, and dyeing cloth. She began working with dyes in the summer of 1977 while attending the University of Washington. Elin's work has been exhibited nationwide, and she has taught papermaking and dyeing classes throughout North America.

Elin lives and dyes in East Freetown, Massachusetts, with her husband and two dogs.

"... I highly recommend this book to anyone who is committed to working with MX dyes and/or fabric paints. It demystifies the chemistry and offers an array of alternative methods for accurately and creatively getting color into cloth. Elin Noble's writing is warm and straight-forward and helps us to understand easily an unusually complex subject."
–**Jason Pollen**, Kansas City Art Institute, Kansas City, MO

"... an excellent hands-on reference manual that should be in a the collection of anyone working with fabric dyes."
–*Library Journal*

"Although your dye book shelf is probably bulging, add this book for its excellent instruction and as a reference you will use over and over."
–**Lynn Lewis Young**, *Art/Quilt Magazine*

"... a thoughtful and well researched book that will clarify conflicting information which has been accumulating over the years."
–**Joyce Hayes**, *Shuttle Spindle & Dyepot*

"I've been using *Dyes & Paints* for three years now in all of my Surface Design Classes. I quickly found that it not only meets those basic needs but more specifically has excellent instructions for expanding the students color abilities with dye."
–**Laura Strand Mills**, Southern Illinois University, Edwardsville

"At last a textbook for Intro to Surface Design! *Dyes & Paints* covers all the basics, provides detailed answers to student queries and then becomes a reliable studio reference book for further exploration."
–**Barbara Goldberg**, University of Massachusetts at Dartmouth, *retired*

"This is the book that we recommend most often to both new and experienced dyers. *Dyes & Paints* is clearly written and illustrated by one of the surface design industry's foremost dye experts. When we have technical questions about dyeing and painting on fabric, Elin is the first person we ask."
–**Debra Lunn & Michael Mrowka**, Lunn Fabrics, Lancaster, OH

To order books and for information
on workshops and lectures contact:

Elin Noble
PO Box 161
East Freetown, MA 02717
USA
http://www.elinnoble.com